0 1341 1319211 5

MW01121550

Adapt or Die
Plays New and Used

Adapt or Die
Plays New and Used
by Jason Sherman

THE BROTHERS KARAMAZOV
from the novel by Fyodor Dostoevsky
(Constance Garnett translation)

THE BEAR
a new version of the vaudeville by Anton Chekhov

ENEMIES
an adaptation of the play by Maxim Gorky

AFTER THE ORCHARD
a new play inspired by Anton Chekhov's
The Cherry Orchard

Playwrights Canada Press
Toronto • Canada

Playwrights Canada Press
The Canadian Drama Publisher
215 Spadina Avenue, Suite 230, Toronto, Ontario CANADA M5T 2C7
416-703-0013   fax 416-408-3402
orders@playwrightscanada.com • www.playwrightscanada.com

Financial support provided by the taxpayers of Canada and Ontario through the Canada Council for the Arts and the Department of Canadian Heritage through the Book Publishing Industry Development Programme, and the Ontario Arts Council.

Cover image by Luke Painter. Cover design by JLArt and Jason Sherman.
Production editor: JLArt

Library and Archives Canada Cataloguing in Publication

Sherman, Jason, 1962-
    Adapt or die : plays new and used / Jason Sherman.

Contents: The Brothers Karamazov -- The bear -- After the orchard -- Enemies.
ISBN 978-0-88754-896-3

    I. Title.
PS8587.H3858A19 2006   C812'.54   C2006-904114-8

Printed in 2007.
Printed and bound by Canadian Printco at Scarborough, Canada.

Acknowledgements

"Big Yellow Taxi"
Words and Music by JONI MITCHELL
© 1970 (Renewed) CRAZY CROW MUSIC.
All Rights Administered by SONY/ATV MUSIC PUBLISHING
8 Music Square West, Nashville, TN 37203
All Rights Reserved   Used by Permission

"Four Strong Winds" by Ian Tyson
with permission of Ian Tyson

Table of Contents

ADAPT OR DIE
PLAYS NEWS AND USED

A Brief Introduction
by Prof. Harold "Bud" Miller-Harrelson,
Prof. Emeritus, Yorkton University, Sheffield

It gives me great delight to introduce this iridescent collection of plays by Jason Sherman, who has been for nearly two decades—to borrow a Rumsfeldian pleonasm—one of the best-known unknown writers in western theatre. To "adapt" is to render a thing fit for new use. It may be said that many of the characters in Mr Sherman's plays fit this particular bill. One thinks of the grieving widow Popova (a pun, no doubt, on the slangy phrase "I'll just pop over") in *The Bear*, which was of course first penned by the man famously called by Prof. Shemp "The Answer," Anton Chekhov, whose early demise may have been a way to avoid the vicissitudes of revolution.

But I digress. To adapt, as I started to explain, is to make that which is old new again, as the lyricist said. And that is what Mr Sherman is doing with these four plays, each of them written via commission, taken on by economic imperative by a playwright who ought by rights to have made his living from his own works but didn't, and who therefore undertook dramas more palatable to the workings of the modern Canadian theatre sensibility, where brand names are more acceptable than the untried. It is easier to sell a Chekhov, a Dostoevsky, a Gorky than it is to sell a Sherman; easier a Nike shoe than an unadvertised boot. Be that as it may, these four plays allowed Mr Sherman to bring his own sensibility to the four (forgive the pun), dusting them off, making them new, adapting them in the truest sense. *After the Orchard* is more than an adaptation and yet less than one; a new play made from an old one. The Gorky, it should be said, is now a tight little two act where once it was an unwieldy three. *The Brothers Karamazov* was reduced (nothing pejorative meant) from a thousand-page Penguin to some three hours' traffic.

Now, to "adapt or die," if I may comment on Mr Sherman's cheeky title, is quite possibly a comment not only on the act of adapting, but on the need for playwrights to take on, if you will, drudge work in order to survive *as* playwrights. For the new play, especially in such dire times as these, such conservative times as these, has little chance to succed, to earn the playwright much in the way of wage. But an old play may find itself in favour at any number of classical repertory theatres. Does one go so far as to agree with the Scottish playwright who, working on an adaptation of *Madame Bovary*, was heard to remark that adaptations are a form of censorship? Hardly. And yet the man may have had a point. If only I could remember his name. But his point is well taken, that by refusing to stage new plays, the larger of our theatres essentially make voiceless the very voices they hire to give voice to old works. Well. It's a long argument, and this is a short introduction.

I was also going to mention some of the other characters of whom it may be said "they must adapt or die." One thinks of Dmitry in *The Brothers Karamazov*, who must try to become "the new man," the old one being buried by rationalism; of Alyosha in the same piece, struggling to adapt in a world without faith; of the many characters in *After the Orchard*, failing to adapt to the changing social and economic realities of life in North America, circa the end of the 20th century. In *Enemies*, too, things are changing, and only those who "see it coming," and adapt, will survive. So there it is. The title fits. And, as Julius Marx noted in his famous essay, "On Titles," better to save the best for first. And so he has.

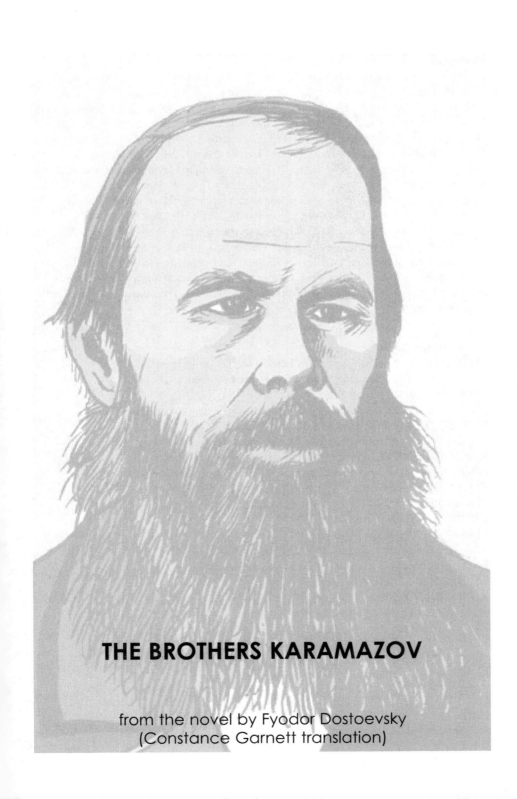

THE BROTHERS KARAMAZOV

from the novel by Fyodor Dostoevsky
(Constance Garnett translation)

Production

The Brothers Karamazov was first produced by the Stratford Festival, Ontario, in May 2005. In the cast were Brendan Averett (Polish Officer), Maggie Blake (Lise Hohlakov), Don Carrier (Kirillovitch), Shane Carty (Ivan Karamazov), David Francis (Grigory), Stephen Gartner (Monk), Michelle Giroux (Katerina), Jonathan Goad (Dmitry Karamazov), Dana Green (Grushenka), Paul Hopkins (Police Captain), Kate Hurman (Fenya), Haysam Kadri (Trifon), Ron Kennell (Pavel Smerdyakov), Andrew Massingham (President), Jennifer Mawhinney (Peasant Woman), Sarah McVie (Weeping Woman), Adam O'Byrne (Monk), Parnelli Parnes (Monk), Jeffrey Renn (Vrublevsky), Dixie Seatle (Mrs Hohlakov), Joseph Shaw (Father Zossima), Evan Stillwater (Father Paissy), Peter van Gestel (Alyosha Karamazov), Scott Wentworth (Fyodor Karamazov), Jeffrey Wetsch (Clerk). Richard Rose was the director, with design by Graeme S. Thomson (set and lighting), Charlotte Dean (costume) and Todd Charlton (sound). Don Horsburgh was the composer, Michael Waller was assistant director. Louise Currie was the stage manager with Jenny Sinclair and Tamerrah Volkovskis as assistants and Laura Nanni as apprentice.

Characters

FYODOR KARAMAZOV, a wealthy landowner.
DMITRY (MITYA), his eldest son, a former army captain.
IVAN, the middle son, a writer.
ALYOSHA (ALEXEI), the youngest, a novice in the nearby monastery.
SMERDYAKOV, the bastard.
GRIGORY, servant in the house of Karamazov.
KATERINA (KATYA), Dmitry's fiancee; Ivan's object of affection.
GRUSHENKA, Dmitry's lover; Karamazov's object of affection.
FENYA, Grushenka's maid.
THE POLISH OFFICER, Grushenka's former lover.
VRUBLEVSKY, his friend.
MRS HOHLAKOV, the town gossip.
LISE, her daughter; Alyosha's object of affection.
FATHER ZOSSIMA, Alyosha's elder at the monastery.
FATHER PAISSY, a monk.
KIRILLOVITCH, the prosecutor.
POLICE CAPTAIN.
TRIFON, an innkeeper.
PRESIDENT OF THE COURT, the presiding judge.
PEASANT WOMAN, seeking solace from Zossima.
Peasant women, novitiates, policemen.

Note

Scenes between asterisks are flashbacks.

THE BROTHERS KARAMAZOV

ACT 1

Scene 1. Karamazov house.

KARAMAZOV, IVAN, GRIGORY and—addressing us—SMERDYAKOV, who remains on stage throughout the play.

SMERDYAKOV Ladies and gentlemen, I am a bastard. In the old-fashioned sense…. I don't say it to elicit your sympathy. It's merely a fact, and I'm a great believer in facts. My name is Smerdyakov. I don't fancy myself a hero, having ever amounted to nothing more than soupmaker in the house of Karamazov. Fyodor Karamazov: wealthy landowner, a drunkard and a brute. His recent violent murder made our little town the talk of all Russia. He was father to three sons—four, if you include me, but don't, for he didn't. From the first marriage came Dmitry, a real scoundrel, if I may use a word that's fallen out of fashion. Ex-captain of the guard, ladies man; he also liked to drink. From the second marriage came Ivan, a scholar, an atheist—a bit withdrawn. Then came the youngest, Alyosha, a monk-in-training. A sweet lad, really. If you're looking for a hero, he's your man. Alyosha Karamazov, who believes in good. In doing good.

ALYOSHA enters.

KARAMAZOV Alyosha! You're here! Come in, my boy, join us, have a seat. Smerdyakov, liqueur, from the cupboard, take the keys, chop chop.

ALYOSHA I really shouldn't.

KARAMAZOV Okay, fine. But *we* will. Did you eat? Some nice cabbage soup? At the monastery? Uh? Ha ha ha!

ALYOSHA I did eat. But I wouldn't mind some coffee.

KARAMAZOV He wouldn't mind some coffee. Fine, anything you want, my boy. It's excellent coffee, really it is. Smerdyakov made it. He's a terrific cook; his soup is the talk of the kitchen. But wait a second, wait a second: I told you to bring your mattress and pillow, didn't I? Uh? Didja bring 'em?

ALYOSHA *(grinning)* No, I didn't.

KARAMAZOV Ha ha ha! I love this boy, the way he looks at a person and smiles. See, he knows his old man. He knows I'm just a clown. Hey, lookit me, I'm Father Zossima, I'm Father Zossima. Ha ha ha! *(gets to his knees and bows)* What was that supposed to mean? *(beat)* You haven't seen Dmitry, have you? No? *Good.* I hope I never see that ingrate again. Come here, Alyosha. Let me give you my blessing—a father's blessing.

ALYOSHA rises.

Never mind, let me just make the sign of the cross over you. Now, listen, Alexei, we need your opinion on a question of, what, morality. It seems that Ivan was overheard the other day saying in the presence of certain *laaaa*dies that if man didn't believe in God and the afterlife, anything would be possible.

SMERDYAKOV Anything?

KARAMAZOV Anything! Theft, murder, even cannibalism! Hee hee hee!

SMERDYAKOV That's something worth thinking about.

GRIGORY No one asked for your opinion.

IVAN No, let's hear what he has to say.

KARAMAZOV Yes, dammit, Smerdyakov, speak up! Quit smirking and start sperking.

GRIGORY He shouldn't be allowed to speak.

KARAMAZOV Oh leave him alone, Grigory.

GRIGORY When he was a boy—do you know something?—he used to torture cats! He'd string them up, then pretend to be a priest, and give them last rites! I found him doing it one time, and believe you me I gave him a beating he never forgot.

SMERDYAKOV You did?

GRIGORY Infidel! You've been a misery from the day you were born.

SMERDYAKOV Then you should have put me out of my misery *on* that day.

GRIGORY Heretic! You weren't even born, you grew from the mould in the bathroom tub!

SMERDYAKOV You should have cleaned it better.

KARAMAZOV Alright, that's enough! Out!

GRIGORY *(as he leaves with SMERDYAKOV)* Soup-maker.

KARAMAZOV This is all your doing, Ivan. The only reason that smirker hangs around after dinner is because he looks up to you. What have you done to fascinate him?

IVAN Not a thing. He's a lackey, that's all. He'll be good material come the revolution.

KARAMAZOV You're right about that. He thinks too damn much. And he can't stand the lot of us—especially you, Alyosha, he despises you. Still, he's honest as they come—you know he found some money of mine in a tree one time and gave it back to me, every last kopeck.

ALYOSHA Ivan, did you really say these things about God and immortality?

IVAN   I did.

KARAMAZOV   Hold it, hold it, hold it, are we really gonna talk about this? Cause if we're really gonna talk about this: hand me that bottle.

IVAN   That's enough brandy, don't you think?

KARAMAZOV   One more. And one more after that, then I'll stop. Now, let's be serious. Is there a God? Ivan?

IVAN   No, there's no God.

KARAMAZOV   Alyosha? Is there a God?

ALYOSHA   Yes, there is.

KARAMAZOV   Mm hm. A tie. Ivan: is there immortality—of some kind? Not even a lot of immortality, just a little, just a teensy weensy, *(pinching his fingers)* just that much?

IVAN   No, there's no immortality.

KARAMAZOV   None?

IVAN   None at all.

KARAMAZOV   So there's nothing, nothing at all, just nothing… ness. But dammit there must be *something*. I mean, *something* is better than *nothing*. Right?

IVAN   There is absolutely nothing.

KARAMAZOV   Alyosha: is there immortality?

ALYOSHA   There is.

KARAMAZOV   God and immortality?

ALYOSHA   In God is immortality.

KARAMAZOV   *(beat)* Well I think Ivan wins that one. And to think, to think how much energy, how much—what man has wasted on that dream, that—and for so long, for so long. Do you hear that? Laughter. Someone's laughing at us, at mankind. Ivan, for the last time now, for the last time, let's settle this, once and for all: is there or is there not a God?

IVAN   For the last time: there is not.

KARAMAZOV   Then who's laughing at us?

IVAN   Must be the devil.

KARAMAZOV   Ah. So there's a devil?

IVAN   No. There's no devil, either.

KARAMAZOV   That's too bad. Dammit, what I wouldn't give to meet the man who invented God. I'd— *(mimes strangling the man who invented God)* I mean I'd— *(twisting his head off)*

IVAN   But without God there'd be no civilization. And without civilization there'd be no brandy.

KARAMAZOV   Now, now, I never said I didn't believe in God, did I?... I'll just have one more little glass. *(beat)* Alyosha. Did I hurt your feelings? Back there at the monastery? You're not mad at me, are you?

ALYOSHA   No.

KARAMAZOV   I'm always saying the wrong thing, but what can I do, I'm a clown, a buffoon.

ALYOSHA   I know you mean well.

KARAMAZOV   I do. I mean well. This boy. This *boy*. Ivan: do you love your brother?

IVAN   Of course I do.

KARAMAZOV   Yes. Love him. You must love him.

IVAN   Yes. Only now I'm going. You've had too much to drink.

KARAMAZOV   Wait. Have you decided? About Chermashnya? For Christ's sake, I've been begging you to go, just for a day or two, just to take care of some business for me.

IVAN   If you want me to go, I'll go.

KARAMAZOV   Oh, you won't, though. Youuuuuuuuuu... *won't*. You're keeping an eye on me, aren't you? That's why you won't go. Well what are you looking at? I know what you're thinking: I can see it in your eyes, your suspicious little eyes: "Stinking drunk!" Look at him, Alyosha, look how he looks at me, with con*tempt*. Alyosha, never love your brother, you mustn't love him.

ALYOSHA   Leave him alone, father. Why are you angry with him?

Pause.

KARAMAZOV   Take the brandy away. How many times do I have to say it? You mustn't be angry with a feeble old man, Ivan. There's no reason you should love me. Go to Chermashnya. I'll meet you there. I'll bring you a present. There's a beautiful little whore there. I've had my eye on her for some time. Still barefoot, you know. Those barefoot little whores, don't look down on them, they're pearls— *(kisses the tips of his fingers with a smack)* —Pearls! You know, my children, my little suckling pigs, the way I see it, there's not an ugly woman in the world. That's been my rule! Do you understand? How could you? You've got milk in your veins. My rule has been you can always find something in one woman that you can't find in another. But you have to know how to extract it. That's the trick. It's a talent! And if you can do it, you'll see: there are no ugly women. You see, an unattractive woman will be amazed, shocked, delighted, that a gentleman should fall in love with a little slut. Masters and slaves, that's what it's all about. Alyosha, wait a minute, listen to me, I'll tell you something.

Your mother, your mother, I always used to surprise her. See, I'd—I'd pay her no attention, for weeks at a time, then, all of a sudden, I'd get on my knees to her, kiss her feet, and I always, always—I remember like it was yesterday— I always managed to get her to laugh like a little girl. She had the quietest little laugh, a very peculiar laugh. Sometimes she'd laugh like that but not from joy, no, no not from joy, because pretty soon she'd be screaming, hysterically, and yelling at me, all kinds of things, "don't touch me," she'd scream, "don't come near me again!" So finally I had to take her to the monastery, you know, so the Holy Fathers could pray for her, bring her back to her senses. But I swear to you, Alyosha, I never did anything unkind toward that woman. Except, well maybe once, when she suddenly got religion. Oh, how she got it—that woman loved to pray, in her room—she wouldn't even let me in! Well, that's when I decided, enough's enough, I'll have to knock the mysticism out of her. "Here," I said, "here's your holy image. Here! Here! Look at me, I'm taking it down, it's not so holy now is it? I'll spit on it in a second and what do you think will happen to me? Nothing!" Oh, I thought she'd kill me. But instead, she jumped up, hid her face in her hands, started trembling all over and finally she fell over on the floor, boom. *(finally noticing ALYOSHA, who has grown visibly upset)* Alyosha, Alyosha, what's wrong? Ivan, water. Hurry! Can't you see he's upset about his mother?

IVAN   She was my mother, too, wasn't she?

KARAMAZOV   What? Whose mother? What mother?

Noise and shouting from the hallway.

GRIGORY   *(off)* She's not here, Dmitry!

KARAMAZOV   It's your brother.

DMITRY   *(off)* I know she's in there! Grushenka! Out of my way, old man, out of my way!

KARAMAZOV   He'll kill me. Ivan, save me!

DMITRY bursts in, followed by GRIGORY and SMERDYAKOV.

IVAN   Dmitry—

GRIGORY   He pushed his way in, I couldn't hold him.

DMITRY   Where is she? Where's Grushenka? I know she's here! *(goes into the bedroom)*

KARAMAZOV   He's going after my money! My money!

KARAMAZOV runs after DMITRY. IVAN and ALYOSHA follow.

(off) Hold him, hold him! *(a vase smashes to the ground)* Get him! Help! What are you doing?

SMERDYAKOV   It needn't have come to this. Why, only a few hours before, this same family had tried to settle things in a more civilized manner, at the monastery in our little town, before this man, Father Zossima.

* * *

FATHER ZOSSIMA appears in his room at the monastery.
KARAMAZOV, IVAN, ALYOSHA and DMITRY appear before him.

KARAMAZOV   Ivan, flesh of my flesh, is a most dutiful son, a brilliant young scholar; of Alyosha I hardly need say a word, since he rises with you every morning and prays alongside you all day and night; as for this one, the one from whom I'm seeking justice—through you—he is a most undutiful son.

ZOSSIMA   There's no need to insult the members of your own family.

KARAMAZOV   You're right, reverentialness, but it can't be helped. I've been this way since the day I was born.

DMITRY   Would you be quiet?

KARAMAZOV   Great elder—

DMITRY   I knew this would happen! Reverend Father, forgive me, I'm not an educated man—

KARAMAZOV   And whose fault is that?

DMITRY   —simply a soldier, and I don't know how to address you, but the fact is you've been tricked into meeting with us. All that man—my father—wants to do is make a scene. He always has ulterior motives.

KARAMAZOV   Who's the one with motives? You want facts? I'll give you facts! Dmitry claims I'm cheating him out of his inheritance, when the truth is he's in debt to me, and not a little, but a lot, I have proof! Documentary evidence. I'll tell you something else—the little village where he was stationed up til a few weeks ago? He spent thousands—thousands!—seducing one woman after another—respectable women, too—oh, yes, heard all about it, Dmitry. Can you believe it, Father, he won the heart of a young woman, a girl from a good family, the daughter of an officer—offered to marry her. Next thing you know, he's running around with a certain enchantress by the name of Grushenka— he's already spent a fortune on her, even stole money from his own fiancee to waste it on her, and now he's trying to bully me into giving him more through this bogus claim of an inheritance!

DMITRY   Liar! Hypocrite!

KARAMAZOV   You see how he speaks to his own father!

DMITRY   You accuse me of being involved with this "enchantress," but you leave out the fact that you're after her yourself! Father, I have a number of debts, it's true. That man purchased those debts, and sold them, at a reduced price, to Grushenka, who was then to sue me for the money, threaten me with jail, and all, all with the sole aim of having me out of the way, so that he, that cruel, deceitful, lustful old man could have her for himself. She told me all about it— and she *laughed*.

> *FATHER ZOSSIMA suddenly rises. ALYOSHA supports him by the arm.*

ZOSSIMA Dmitry. Come to me.

> *Before DMITRY, ZOSSIMA sinks to his knees, bows til his forehead touches the floor. He rises.*

Goodbye. Forgive me, everyone, forgive me.

> *ZOSSIMA goes. DMITRY stands a moment in amazement, then bolts from the room.*

KARAMAZOV What was that for? Was that supposed to be symbolic, or what?— Alyosha, where are you going?

ALYOSHA To be with the Father. He's not well.

KARAMAZOV Alright, but then get your things! Your mattress and your pillow! You're not staying here one more night. You're coming home, do you hear?

* * *

> *IVAN and ALYOSHA drag KARAMAZOV out of the bedroom.*

IVAN Are you out of your mind? You want him to kill you?

KARAMAZOV She must be here, he said so himself—Grushenka!

IVAN You know she's not here.

KARAMAZOV She could have come in the back.

IVAN The back door's locked and you have the key, so how could she have gotten in?

> *DMITRY returns.*

DMITRY Where are you hiding her?

KARAMAZOV Son of a bitch. You took my money, didn't you? Now give me back what you just took, you thief! *(rushes at DMITRY)* Give it back!

DMITRY Don't you touch me.

> *DMITRY knocks KARAMAZOV to the floor.*

IVAN Stop it!

DMITRY *(kicks KARAMAZOV in the face)* Filthy pig!

IVAN Stop it!

DMITRY *(kicks KARAMAZOV repeatedly)* Pig! Pig!

IVAN   (*pulls DMITRY away*) Enough! Enough!… You've killed him, you've killed him.

DMITRY   Good. And if I haven't, I'll come back and finish it. A man like that doesn't deserve to live. Look at his face, his *face*, I can't stand it, I'll tear it apart.

ALYOSHA   Get out of here, Dmitry. Go—now!

DMITRY   Alyosha. You're the only one I trust. Was Grushenka here?

ALYOSHA   I swear to you, she wasn't here.

IVAN   Alyosha, help me get him up.

DMITRY   Alyosha, go to Katerina's. Tell her I said "thank you and goodbye." Exactly those words, understand? "Thank you and goodbye." And tell her I'll get her the money somehow.

IVAN   Alyosha!

> *IVAN and ALYOSHA help KARAMAZOV to his feet. His face is covered with blood.*

DMITRY   I'm not sorry. Do you hear me? You have your dreams, well I have mine. I curse you, old man, I curse and disown you!

> *DMITRY runs out.*

KARAMAZOV   (*barely audible*) Grushenka …? Is she here…?

IVAN   Christ. They're both mad. *She's not here.*—He's fainting, come on, we'll take him to his room. Smerdyakov, water, towels, hurry!

Scene 2. Katerina's house.

ALYOSHA with KATERINA.

ALYOSHA   There was so much blood, and Dmitry cursed him.

KATERINA   Oh God. Is he alright, your father?

ALYOSHA   He's recovering. He wanted to press charges, but Ivan talked him out of it.

KATERINA   Where is Dmitry?

ALYOSHA   He ran off. And sent me with a message.

KATERINA   Yes. I knew he would. What is the message?

ALYOSHA   "Thank you."

KATERINA   "Thank you"?

ALYOSHA   "And goodbye."

KATERINA   Are those the words he used?

ALYOSHA　The very ones. He was insistent.

KATERINA　Was he? Well, now that's very interesting. You see, if he had simply said it in passing, without really thinking about it, then clearly he would have meant it, and everything would be over between us. But he was insistent, you say, insistent?

ALYOSHA　He was, yes, why?

KATERINA　Clearly, Alyosha, he was excited, not thinking clearly, and perhaps—yes—afraid of his decision. You see, and by repeating it over and over it's as though he was trying to convince himself of the truth of those words, when in fact it was all merely an act of bravado. Don't you think?

ALYOSHA　Yes, I believe you're right. At least, I hope you are. I'm very worried about him.

KATERINA　You needn't be. I can still help him. Tell me, did he say anything about money?

ALYOSHA　He did. It was the last thing he said: "Tell her I'll get her the money somehow."

KATERINA　Ah.

ALYOSHA　Has he really taken money from you? Forgive me for prying, it's just that…

KATERINA　Don't apologize, darling. Yes, I gave him some money—three thousand rubles—and asked him to post it to my sister in Moscow. It never reached her. It's my understanding that he spent them on Grushenka. I've been trying to think how to keep him from being ashamed over it all. But he won't accept that I'm willing to help him. *(through tears)* Why won't he come to me? Why won't he speak to me, his own fiancée? Don't I deserve that?… It's alright. He'll come to me eventually, once everything is finished between him and Grushenka.

ALYOSHA　He seems fairly taken with her.

KATERINA　It's infatuation, dear—and a Karamazov doesn't stay infatuated for long. In any case, Grushenka is no longer interested in Dmitry.

ALYOSHA　Why do you say that?

KATERINA　I don't. She does. *(calling out)* Grushenka? Come join us, dear, would you? It's alright. I'm with a friend. Alyosha. He knows everything. *(to ALYOSHA)* Wait til you see, Alyosha. She's a lovely person. So good, just divine, and noble, in her own way.

GRUSHENKA　*(appearing)* I've been sort of hoping for an introduction. It's a great pleasure to finally meet Dmitry's little brother.

ALYOSHA　How do you do?

GRUSHENKA   I do fine.

KATERINA   You see? Lovely. Can you believe, this is the first time we've met. It was the oddest thing; I was just about to go to see her, to make her acquaintance, when all of a sudden there she was at my door.

GRUSHENKA   And you, kind lady, took me in. You're so sweet, so pure of heart.

KATERINA   You mustn't say those things, you little devil! Oh but let me kiss your hand, your charming, chubby little hand. *(kissing GRUSHENKA's hand)* Look at this hand, Alyosha. It has brought me such happiness.

GRUSHENKA   Oh my, I'll blush if you keep kissing me like that in front of Alyosha!

KATERINA   It isn't to make you blush that I kiss your hand, dear girl, but to thank you for helping us save Dmitry.

GRUSHENKA   Oh but who said anything about saving Dmitry? You're the one who kept saying that.

KATERINA   We gave our word. We're going to tell him there's another man waiting for us, a Polish officer with whom we've been in love a long time, who's offering us his hand in marriage.

GRUSHENKA   I don't think I exactly put it that way, dear lady. The officer of whom you speak, why, he took up with another woman, a woman of some wealth, not unlike yourself, dear Katerina. All I said was that I heard his wife had died, poor thing, and that he might be sending for me.

KATERINA   But there must be some sort of misunderstanding. You promised.

GRUSHENKA   Maybe I did. But after all, I *am* a little devil. And now I'm thinking, "Maybe I'll take Mitya back." I liked him very much once, for a whole hour. We went to an inn, and had a lovely time. Maybe now I want him forever.

KATERINA   But just five minutes ago, you said something very different.

GRUSHENKA   Well, I'm just a girl who can't make up her mind. I'm not as selfless as you are. Will you let me kiss your hand, as you did mine? *(holds KATERINA's hand to her lips as though to kiss it)* On second thought, angel, I don't think I will kiss your hand.

> **SMERDYAKOV, *observing the scene, laughs; continues to "before, you know."***

I think I'd like to leave you with the memory of how you kissed *my* hand, and how I refused to kiss yours.

KATERINA   You—are an awful person.

GRUSHENKA   Relatively speaking, I suppose. But, after all, I know where your hands have been.

KATERINA   You little bitch.

GRUSHENKA   Oh my. What *will* Mitya say when I tell him what happened here? He might not say anything. He might just laugh. We've laughed about you before, you know.

KATERINA   Get out of this house, you—you—whore!

GRUSHENKA   *Mon dieu!* Now, really, is that any way for *us* to talk?

KATERINA   Get out! Get out!

GRUSHENKA   If you're going to call me a whore, what are you going to call yourself? After all, a whore meets men in the dark for money—and you've done that yourself, haven't you?

KATERINA   You... *(rushes GRUSHENKA)*

GRUSHENKA   Alyosha, do you know the story of how this dear lady met your brother?

KATERINA   Be quiet!

GRUSHENKA   Once upon a time, in a town far away—

KATERINA   Filth!

ALYOSHA intervenes, throwing his arms around KATERINA.

ALYOSHA   Katerina. Please, miss, will you leave?

GRUSHENKA   Oh, don't call me "miss"—call me Grusha. Your brother does.

ALYOSHA continues to hold back KATERINA.

ALYOSHA   Please go.

GRUSHENKA   Alright. But feel free to drop by any time, Alyosha. You've got a sweet face.

GRUSHENKA goes.

KATERINA   Why did you stop me? I'd have killed her! I'd have.... She should be horsewhipped for that... in public! Humiliated! *(pause)* How could he have told her about that night? He's a monster, to have told her that. How could he have told her? How?

Scene 3. The outskirts.

ALYOSHA and DMITRY.

DMITRY   Look, I didn't exactly *tell* Grushenka about the—I may have mentioned, in passing, something about the night Katya came to me for—yes, alright, fine, I told Grushenka the whole story! But I was drunk—

SMERDYAKOV   He'd been waiting for his brother all night, by a tree on the outskirts of town. The last thing he imagined was that his fiancee and his girlfriend would ever meet.

DMITRY   —We were in Mokroi, at this inn—everyone was drunk, the Gypsies were singing, the bears were dancing… only I was weeping. Weeping and kneeling and praying at the altar of Katya. I thought Grushenka understood it. I remember, she even cried herself.—Goddammit! And now she uses it to stab Katya in the heart. These women, these women…. Well, there's no two ways about it. I'm a son-of-a-bitch, even if I did cry that night.

ALYOSHA   Dmitry, please, I don't understand.

>   *Pause.*

DMITRY   You see this? This *bug?* God gave the angels mercy, and the insects—lust. That's what I am. An insect. All of us Karamazovs are insects. Even you, an angel, there's an insect crawling inside you, and one day this insect will make your blood boil. Yes, I'm a bug. A Karamazov…. In the little town where I was stationed, the commanding officer had two daughters, both as comely as they come. I had my hands on one, and my eye on the other, but the one I had my eye on, she wanted nothing to do with me; that was Katya. One night, there was a ball.

* * *

DMITRY   *(to KATERINA, appearing)* Miss Verkhovtsev. Care to dance? *(to ALYOSHA)* She didn't even look at me, just gave me the side of her stuck-up little face. Alright, I thought, I'll get you back. Soon, I had my chance. Her father was caught with his hand in the army's cookie jar, was about to be discharged, disgraced. I sent word through Katya's sister—"come see me in my apartment, I've got some money, we'll straighten the whole thing out." I never expected her to come.

>   *KATERINA knocks at the door of DMITRY's apartment.*

It's open.

KATERINA   *(emerging)* I've come for the…

DMITRY   Hm?

KATERINA   I've come—

DMITRY   Can't hear you.

KATERINA   I've come for the money. For my father.

DMITRY   Yes. Ran into a spot of trouble, hm? Care to dance?

KATERINA   Let me see the money.

DMITRY   *(to ALYOSHA)* There she was, in all her dignity, ready to sacrifice herself. And I… I loved it. I could have done anything I wanted with her—and she'd let me. I could hardly breathe. But I knew, being an honest man, that if I had my way with her, I would have to go to her the next day, offer her my hand. And she would say, "Out!" I could see from her face it was true.

KATERINA   The money.

DMITRY   *(to KATERINA, laughing)* You mean to say, you fell for my little joke? That's all it was. Did you really think I was going to save your old man? I was just having you on, my dear. Tell you what. I'll give you two hundred.

KATERINA   He owes much more than that. Let me have the money!

DMITRY   *(handing her the money)* Take it. All of it. Take it!

> *She takes the money; begins to undress.*

Wait.... Go.

KATERINA   Go?

DMITRY   Leave. Or is this why you came? *(pause)* The door's still open.

> *He makes a deep, respectful bow, to the waist. She returns the bow, forehead to the floor. Then jumps up and runs away.*

(to ALYOSHA) I should've killed myself right there and then; why I didn't, I'll never know. A month later, a package arrived from Katerina. She'd just inherited a fortune, from her aunt in Moscow, and decided to pay me back— with interest.

KATERINA   *Dear Dmitry Fyodorvitch Karamazov: I love you madly, even if you don't love me, it doesn't matter, be my husband. Don't be afraid. I won't get in your way; I'll be the carpet beneath your feet; I want to love you forever; I want to save you from yourself.*

DMITRY   Or something like that, I can't remember it exactly. I wrote her back, I said, "but you're rich and I'm poor, and besides, I can't get to Moscow just now," oh anything to get her off my back. She wouldn't let up.

> *IVAN appears. The scene is a montage: IVAN with DMITRY; IVAN with KATERINA; DMITYRY with ALYOSHA.*

IVAN   What brings you to Moscow?

DMITRY   A mistake.

IVAN   What's her name?

DMITRY   *(to ALYOSHA)* What? What are you looking at? Yes, I told Ivan.

IVAN   Imperious, wealthy, disdainful. Sounds delightful.

DMITRY   He went to see her.

KATERINA   *(holding out her hand to IVAN)* I wouldn't have guessed.

IVAN   Different mothers.

DMITRY   And fell in love with her.

IVAN   *(going for a stroll with KATERINA)* Do you know, even if I lost faith in the woman I love, became convinced that the devil ruled the world in all its chaos, then still I'd want to go on living.

DMITRY   And she with him.

KATERINA   I'd like to get to know her, this woman in whose hands you've placed your faith.

IVAN   So would I…

* * *

DMITRY   So I guess that was another stupid idea of mine. But the way I see it, it's the solution.

ALYOSHA   To what?

DMITRY   To all my problems. Ivan's the man for Katya, not me.

ALYOSHA   But it's you she loves.

DMITRY   It's not love; it's gratitude. I'll pay her back the money and be free of her.

ALYOSHA   She says she'll forgive you the money.

DMITRY   I don't want her forgiveness!

ALYOSHA   But you're going to marry her.

DMITRY   I'm going to marry Grushenka. I'll be her slave, her servant, her errand boy. Goodbye, Alexei. I probably won't see you again, unless it's as a last resort.

ALYOSHA   Of course you'll see me again. I'll come find you tomorrow. I'll make a point of it, only tell me where you'll be.

DMITRY   On the road to disaster. There's only one thing left for me to do. I'm in disgrace, it sits on me, here, here, here! *(pounds himself on the chest)* I could make it all stop if I wanted to, but I won't make it stop. I've lost half my honour; tomorrow, I'll lose the rest of it. Goodbye, Alexei.

ALYOSHA   Don't do anything foolish.

DMITRY   Too late!

Scene 4. Outside the monastery.

ALYOSHA joins FATHER ZOSSIMA as he walks along.

ZOSSIMA   There you are, my quiet one. Tell me, did you see your brother, the one I bowed down to?

ALYOSHA   Father, I did.

ZOSSIMA   Has he calmed down at all since this morning?

ALYOSHA   If anything, he's more upset.

ZOSSIMA   Then why have you returned?

ALYOSHA   Why—to be with you, Father.

>*Several devotees crowd around ZOSSIMA. They try to kiss the hem of his garment; others cry out: "Bless me, Father!—Saint Zossima!— A miracle!"*

WEEPING WOMAN   *(through the crowd)* Father Zossima, I've come from far away! 200 miles. I've been to three monasteries, and they told me, "There's going to be a miracle! Go, go to him"—to you!

>*ZOSSIMA comes to her.*

ZOSSIMA   Why are you weeping?

WEEPING WOMAN   For my son. He was only three years old. He was our last. We had four, and now we've none, I've buried the last of them, and I can't forget him. I see him everywhere, he stands in front of me. I see his little clothes, his shirt, his boots, and my heart breaks Father, I lay out his clothes, I look, and I weep.

ZOSSIMA   Once, a very long time ago, a holy saint spoke to a woman just like you, weeping for her little one. "Don't you know," said the saint, "how fearless these little ones are before the throne of God? There are none bolder in the Kingdom of Heaven. They cry to the Lord, 'You gave us life, and no sooner had we gazed upon it, then you took it away again. Now make us angels! We demand it!'" Rejoice, woman, your boy is with the Lord, among the angels.

WEEPING WOMAN   But what proof is there, Father, that when I die, I'll see him again?

ZOSSIMA   There is no proof. But you can be convinced.

WEEPING WOMAN   How?

ZOSSIMA   Through active love. The more you love others, the more you will believe in the reality of God and the immortality of your soul.

WEEPING WOMAN   Oh, but if I could just look at him one more time, just peek into his room, see him playing in the yard, calling his little voice, "Mother, where are you Mother?"

ZOSSIMA   Weep, then. But know this: your boy is looking down at you from the Kingdom, he rejoices in your tears. Weep, therefore, and let your bitter tears purify your heart, deliver it from evil.

>*LISE HOHLAKOV, who sits in a wheelchair by her mother MRS HOHLAKOV, emits a laugh. ZOSSIMA looks over, annoyed. MRS HOHLAKOV quietly scolds LISE.*

ZOSSIMA   What was your wee child's name?

WEEPING WOMAN   Mikhail, Father.

ZOSSIMA   I will remember him, and your grief, in my prayers.

She is inconsolable—until ZOSSIMA lays his stole over her head, says a prayer, and soothes her.

WEEPING WOMAN   Thank you, Father.

MRS HOHLAKOV   So moving. You know, Father, watching all this, I feel so deeply the love these people have for you.

ZOSSIMA   How is your daughter, Mrs Hohlakov?

MRS HOHLAKOV   You have healed her, completely, with your prayers. Lise, pay attention. For six months, we sought a cure for this sudden illness. No one helped—until you.

ZOSSIMA   Why is she still in her chair?

MRS HOHLAKOV   Her legs are still a little weak, but her night fevers have stopped. Lise, thank the Father, kiss his hands!

LISE rises from her chair with some difficulty, walks toward ZOSSIMA. Then bursts out laughing.

LISE   I'm sorry. I'm laughing at him—at him!

She means ALYOSHA, who looks down, ashamed.

MRS HOHLAKOV   Alexei, pay her no attention. *(holds out a gloved hand to ALYOSHA)* You must come see us sometime. You've been back in town an entire year and have completely forgotten us. It would make Lise very happy if you'd come for a visit. Tomorrow, perhaps?

ALYOSHA   I'd like that.

LISE   Will you help me to my chair?

ALYOSHA walks LISE to her chair as ZOSSIMA addresses the crowd.

ZOSSIMA   Good people, the time has come for me to go. Love thy neighbour.

LISE   *(handing ALYOSHA a letter)* Put this away.

ZOSSIMA   Do not weep for me.

LISE   It's for you, a letter.

ZOSSIMA   In sorrow seek happiness.

LISE   Quickly!

ZOSSIMA   Rejoice!

ZOSSIMA starts away.

MRS HOHLAKOV   Wait, Father—would you bless Lise?

ZOSSIMA   *(jokingly)* She doesn't deserve to be loved, this one. She's been acting badly the whole time. Why have you been laughing at Alexei?

LISE   Because he's forgotten me. He used to carry me around when I was a little girl. He taught me how to read. Now he's afraid of me. And he looks funny in that dress.

>   *LISE hides her face in her hands, laughs. ZOSSIMA blesses her. She kisses his hand.*

Don't be angry with me. I'm just a silly girl.

ALYOSHA   The Father is tired now; he needs to rest.

LISE   Alyosha! You will come see us, won't you?

ZOSSIMA   I'll send him. *(walking away with ALYOSHA)* Alyosha, the time has come for you to leave the monastery.

ALYOSHA   No, Father, I'm not—

ZOSSIMA   This is not the place for you, not now. You will live as a monk in the world. You will take a wife. You will bless life, and you will make others bless it.

ALYOSHA   Am I not to see you again?

ZOSSIMA   Don't put me in my grave just yet. You see, I'm standing, I'm talking. I may have another twenty years in me yet.

ALYOSHA   But Father, teacher, I don't understand: what is ahead of my brother?

ZOSSIMA   You mustn't ask. I seemed to see something terrible this morning, as though his entire future could be seen through the look in his eyes.

Scene 5. Outside the gate to Karamazov's house.

DMITRY approaches SMERDYAKOV, who's on guard.

DMITRY   Soup-maker!

SMERDYAKOV   Sir. You're not to be here.

DMITRY   What did you say to me?

SMERDYAKOV   Only what the master, your father, says I should.

DMITRY   Your master is not my father.

SMERDYAKOV   Don't kill me, sir. I'm faithful as a dog.

DMITRY   You're filthy as one, anyway. Was she here?

SMERDYAKOV   "She," sir?

DMITRY   I told you to keep watch for Grushenka; *was she here?*

SMERDYAKOV   No, sir.

DMITRY   You're lying.

SMERDYAKOV   Honestly, sir; if *she'd* been here, the money would not.

DMITRY   What money?

SMERDYAKOV   I oughtn't to tell you. The master has set aside three thousand rubles for her, a sort of bait, if you will.

DMITRY   Three thousand rubles?

SMERDYAKOV   Neither less nor more. I counted it myself, your father—my master—taking me for an honest soul. The money's under his mattress, in an envelope, tied in a bow, and bearing the inscription, "For Grushenka, my little chicken."

DMITRY   Disgusting old man…

SMERDYAKOV   Beneath the mattress.

DMITRY   Does she know about this money?

SMERDYAKOV   She does, sir, and is sure to come tomorrow night to receive it, on account of the fact that Ivan is being sent away. So there will be no one in the house. She need only remember the signals and the money is hers.

DMITRY   Signals? What signals?

SMERDYAKOV   I've said too much. If the master knew I'd revealed—

    DMITRY grabs SMERDYAKOV by the hair, forces him to his knees.

DMITRY   Speak or you'll never speak again.

SMERDYAKOV   Sir, the master has arranged it so with Grushenka that she may gain entry to the house by tapping twice at the bedroom window *(taps it out)* and then thrice more, at which point the door to the house will be unlocked, and all the riches beneath the mattress hers; the ones above it, too.

DMITRY   *(knocks him down)* Filth!

SMERDYAKOV   Sir, I meant no harm. Please, sir, have done with me, or I'm sure to have a seizure.

    DMITRY lets go.

DMITRY   If you like your life, dog, keep Grushenka out of this house, and send word the second she appears.

SMERDYAKOV   I will, sir, I will.

    DMITRY runs off. SMERDYAKOV addresses the audience.

Not bad for a cook, for a dog, a lackey. "Do I goad you?" No, sir, I live to serve you. I'm honest as the day is long—in a Russian winter. Dog, cur, lackey, filth.

Am I less than he? Why, he's as ill bred as I. And I, too, have dreamt of a better life. That man, *our father*, he sent me once to Moscow, to learn to cook. I learned well, and dreamed I might one day have my own establishment; the food in Moscow is terrible, and the people are even worse. I hate Russia and all Russians.

Scene 6. Mrs Hohlakov's house.

Enter LISE, in a wheelchair, to ALYOSHA waiting.

LISE   Alright, Alexei. Let me have the letter. Quick, before Mother comes back.

ALYOSHA   What letter?

LISE   Oh! I knew you'd say that! It's in your pocket, now give it back.

ALYOSHA   I left it at the monastery.

LISE   You didn't!

ALYOSHA   Yes. I was in such a hurry to come to town that I left it on the nightstand.

LISE   I never should have written it! You know I only meant it as a joke. Now if you really haven't got it on you, then go and get it.

ALYOSHA   I can't today, Lise. I've too much to do.

LISE   You see how little you care about me? You probably laughed out loud when you read my letter.

ALYOSHA   Of course I didn't. I believed everything you wrote.

He produces the letter, reads from it; LISE tries to snatch it away.

"Dear Alexei, They say that paper doesn't blush, but Alexei, this paper is blushing just as much as I am now, all over. Dear Alyosha, I love you, I've loved you since I was a child, when you carried me around on your shoulders. I'll always love you. My heart is yours, on condition of course that you leave the monastery. You must, must, must—"

LISE   I hate you! Now give it back!

ALYOSHA   No. As soon as I read it, I understood that everything you said would come to pass. I was sure of it. When Father Zossima dies, I'll be leaving the monastery. I'll finish my studies, and once you're old enough, we'll marry. I'll love you then. I haven't thought it all through, but Father Zossima told me to take a wife, and here you are, and I don't think I could find a better person than you.

LISE   A cripple... in a wheelchair.

ALYOSHA   I'll wheel you around myself.

He kisses her. She slaps him.

LISE   "Take me," will you? You Karamazovs are all the same. You don't care about anyone but yourselves, ever ever ever! You didn't even come to visit *me*.

MRS HOHLAKOV, IVAN and KATERINA enter, unseen by LISE.

You only came because you knew Ivan was here, and he only came because Katerina was here, and he loves her, and you love her, and everybody loves her! Now give me back my letter! It was just a joke, a joke!

MRS HOHLAKOV   Lise. What on earth is going on? You're supposed to be napping.

LISE   Nothing, Mother. Only take me away from this monster!

MRS HOHLAKOV Lise, you are positively absolutely out of your mind. Sometimes it's hard to believe you're fourteen years old.

LISE   I'm fifteen, Mother!

MRS HOHLAKOV   And in need of your sleep. *(wheeling her out)* Come along now, Lise.

KATERINA   Ivan, don't go just yet.

MRS HOHLAKOV   Julia? Julia, take Lise to her room.

MRS HOHLAKOV takes LISE out, returns during:

KATERINA   Now Alyosha's here, let's hear what he has to say. You see, darling, I've come to an important decision. I wrestled with it all night, and I doubt very much that anything will get me to change my mind. My dear friend and adviser—Ivan—knows about this decision, and he approves.

IVAN   Unquestionably.

KATERINA   Still, I'd like to hear from Alyosha; dear, sweet Alyosha, who I think of almost as a brother. *(taking his hand)* I know that whatever you say will put my mind at ease.

ALYOSHA   Yes, but… what is it you're asking me? I don't really know what we're talking about.

IVAN   The subject is honour, Alyosha. Duty. And maybe something more than that.

KATERINA   Yes, you see, I've decided that even if Dmitry marries that foul, horrid—person—who I'll never forgive—even then, I'll never leave him. I won't chase after him, but I'll keep watch over him, all my life. And when he becomes unhappy with that… woman—and he will—then let him come to me. I'll be the way to his happiness.

IVAN   I've already offered my opinion. From any other woman, all this would sound false and self-pitying, an excellent performance. But coming from you, Katerina, it sounds absolutely sincere, and therefore absolutely right.

MRS HOHLAKOV   I can't agree. She may feel this way at the moment, but what *is* this moment? Nothing but a reaction to yesterday's insult.

IVAN   True, no doubt, but as I was about to say: any other woman would eventually forget yesterday's insult. But not Katerina. It's in her character to never forget it. Just as it's in her character to never forget the promise she made to Dmitry.

MRS HOHLAKOV   A mistake, a horrible mistake!

KATERINA   What do you think, Alexei? Tell me, I have to know. *(in tears)* It's nothing, nothing. I'm just upset over last night. Sitting here with such good friends, it gives me strength. I know the two of you will never leave me.

IVAN   Sadly I have to go to Moscow tomorrow, so I may in fact be leaving you for a good long time.

KATERINA   Moscow? Tomorrow?

IVAN   Yes.

KATERINA   But—

IVAN   There's really nothing I can—

KATERINA   That's wonderful! *(wipes away her tears; completely composed)* Not to be losing you, no that's not the wonderful part. No, it makes me very sad to be losing you. *(Smiling, she takes both his hands in hers.)* The wonderful part is that you'll be able to look in on my sister and tell her about everything that's happened. I was dreading having to write her, but now that you'll be there to explain things, I can send the letter with you. Wait. *(starts off)*

MRS HOHLAKOV   You forgot to hear from the man you think of almost as a brother.

KATERINA   I didn't forget. And there's no need for sarcasm. Of course I want his opinion…. Alexei? Is something the matter, dear?

ALYOSHA   Ivan's going to Moscow and you say you're happy—then you say you're *not* happy, that you're *unhappy* to be losing a friend. But it's all an act, isn't it? You're just playing a part.

KATERINA   What are you talking about?

ALYOSHA   You don't love Dmitry at all… you never have, from the beginning… and Dmitry has never loved you. He admires you, but he doesn't love you…. I don't know why I'm saying this, or how, only that it's the truth, and it needs to be said, because no one in this room is willing to speak the truth. It's Ivan you love, but you're torturing him, all because of this false love for Dmitry. Let me go find him now, and bring him here, and we can resolve everything.

KATERINA You… little… twit! You stupid little religious *idiot!*

IVAN *(laughing)* You're wrong, Alyosha. Katerina's never cared for me. And I've never been her friend, not for a moment. She's too proud to need my friendship. She's only kept me around to spite Dmitry. Believe me, Katya, you're still in love with him, and the worse he treats you, the more you'll love him. You need him to be bad, so that you can be good. That's your tragedy. Mine is that I'll never see you again. *Den Dank, Dame, begehr ich nicht. [Thank you, Madam, I want nothing.]*

MRS HOHLAKOV *(swooning)* Oh! Schiller…

IVAN *(going; turns)* You know, it's a damned shame I pulled Mitya away yesterday. Maybe I should have let him murder the old man after all.

ALYOSHA God forbid.

IVAN Why should He forbid? One snake will devour the other. Serve them both right.—Madam.

    IVAN goes.

ALYOSHA Ivan! Ivan, wait!… It's my fault, my fault! He didn't mean what he said, he was just angry, that's all.

    KATERINA goes into the next room, and can be heard weeping offstage.

MRS HOHLAKOV You've done nothing wrong. You behaved like an angel…. Poor thing. She's so proud; it's such a struggle for her. You must know, Alexei, that I've been praying this last month to find some way to have her give up Dmitry and marry Ivan, who dotes on her, and is such a fascinating young man.

ALYOSHA But listen to her.

MRS HOHLAKOV Never trust a woman's tears, Alexei. I'm never on the side of the woman in cases like this.

LISE *(off)* Mother, Katerina's not well.

MRS HOHLAKOV I'll be there in a minute. *(to ALYOSHA)* This is a good sign.

LISE *(off)* She's having convulsions, Mother! You'd better come, Mother, you'd better come now!

MRS HOHLAKOV Lise, stop, stop, stop that SCREAMING!

    KATERINA stops wailing.

Pardon me. Apparently I'm the one who's screaming…. I do worry about Ivan. He really is so brilliant. Such a gifted student. And so… young.

Scene 7. Karamazov's house.

SMERDYAKOV helps IVAN change for dinner.

SMERDYAKOV   I'm surprised at you, sir.

IVAN   Why?

SMERDYAKOV   Why, that you're not going to Chermashnya.

IVAN   What's it to you?

SMERDYAKOV   Oh, nothing. Just having a little conversation. The fact is, I'm in a terrible position. I don't know what to do.

IVAN   Well?

SMERDYAKOV   It's your father and Dmitry. They're both crazy, no better than children. Any minute now, your father will come looking for me, he'll ask "Has she come? Why hasn't she come?" He'll be up all night with worry. Then, as soon as it gets dark, your brother will show up, holding a gun, he'll say, "Careful, soup-maker, if she comes here and you don't tell me, I'll kill you."

IVAN   It's your own damn fault—spying for Dmitry in the first place.

SMERDYAKOV   I had no choice, really. I'm afraid, sir. In fact, I'm so afraid that I might have a long seizure tomorrow.

IVAN   What do you mean by that?

SMERDYAKOV   It could last for hours, maybe even a day or two, on and off, you know. I had one once that went on for three days.

IVAN   But how can you know you're going to have a fit?

SMERDYAKOV   That's just the thing. You can't tell when one's coming on. But let's say I was on my way to the cellar—I go there almost every day—and I have a fit and fall down the stairs. Do you see?

IVAN   Are you saying you're going to pretend to have a fit tomorrow and be sick for three days?

SMERDYAKOV   Well, I don't know. But if I were to have such a fit—or to fake one, let's say, which wouldn't be difficult for someone who's used to having them—well then, and if Grushenka comes and I don't tell Dmitry, then he wouldn't very well kill me for not having told him, given my condition.

IVAN   He's not going to kill you—not you.

SMERDYAKOV   Well let's say he doesn't. Let's say he kills his father; then I'd be taken for an accomplice.

IVAN   Why?

SMERDYAKOV   Because of the signals.

IVAN   Signals?

SMERDYAKOV   Your father has given me a set of signals to get into the house—all over this business with Grushenka. Only now Dmitry knows.

IVAN   Did you tell him?

SMERDYAKOV   He made me. He kept saying, "You're hiding something from me. I'll break your legs if you don't tell me."

IVAN   You can't let him use the signals to get in.

SMERDYAKOV   But how can I stop him, if I'm going to have a fit?

IVAN   Goddamn it! You can't *know* you're going to have a fit.

SMERDYAKOV   It's just a feeling I have. Sometimes fear brings it on.

IVAN   Then let Grigory know about it; if you're not on duty, he'll be keeping watch.

SMERDYAKOV   But your father told me not to tell anyone about the signals. Besides, Grigory's not feeling well. Not since yesterday. Marta's been giving him a tonic, with alcohol in it. Some she rubs on his back; the rest, he drinks. And as he's a bit of a teetotaler, it helps him sleep.

IVAN   So he'll be asleep and you'll be recovering from a fit that you just know you're going to have.

SMERDYAKOV   You make it sound as though things have been worked out.

IVAN   Have they?

SMERDYAKOV   If anyone is planning anything, it's your brother. He's desperate for money. If your father were to die tomorrow, Dmitry would inherit forty thousand rubles. And so would you.

IVAN   Is that a fact?

SMERDYAKOV   That is a fact. And Dmitry knows it, too.

IVAN   Then why are you suggesting that I go to Chermashnya? If I go away, there'd be no one to stop something from happening.

SMERDYAKOV   Precisely.

IVAN   …What do you mean by that?

SMERDYAKOV   You're in a difficult position, sir.

IVAN   Yes, but one thing's clear. You're a lackey, and an idiot. *(turns to go, then turns back)* I'm going to Moscow tomorrow, if you'd like to know. First thing in the morning. That's all I have to say to you.

SMERDYAKOV   Yes, that's good. That's very good. Only leave an address where you can be telegraphed. In case anything should happen and you need to be sent for.

> *Pause.*

IVAN   And if I were to go to Chermashnya? Would I be "sent for" from there, as well? Well?

SMERDYAKOV   You would.

IVAN   And Chermashnya is not nearly so far away, is that it?

SMERDYAKOV   That's precisely it, sir.

> *SMERDYAKOV is smiling. Suddenly, IVAN begins to laugh.*

Scene 8. Restaurant.

> *IVAN, holding court with several ladies. Laughter. ALYOSHA enters as:*

IVAN   *(to the ladies)* Anyway, are we going to discuss Katerina all night? Well, good evening, Alyosha.

ALYOSHA   Smerdyakov told me you'd be here.

IVAN   And here I am. Odd place for a monk, though.

ALYOSHA   They let me in the back way. Pardon me. I need to find Dmitry. Have you seen him?

IVAN   *(for the ladies)* Am I my half-brother's keeper?

> *The ladies laugh.*

Actually, he's supposed to meet me here. So come, loosen your sandals, join us. We've been having the most fascinating conversation, haven't we ladies, all about the existence of God and immortality; socialism, anarchy, the transformation of humanity into something altogether new. The eternal questions.

ALYOSHA   Yesterday you said there was no God.

IVAN   I was just teasing you. I want to be your friend. You see, I don't have any, and I wonder what it's like. The truth is that I accept the existence of God. Does that surprise you?

ALYOSHA   Unless you're teasing me again.

IVAN   People always think I'm joking.

ALYOSHA   Are you sure Dmitry's coming?

IVAN   …I accept God.

ALYOSHA   One of us should be at the house to make sure nothing else happens.

IVAN   *(overlapping)* I accept his wisdom and his purpose. Oh, I don't pretend to understand it—my mind isn't big enough for that—but I accept that there is an underlying order and meaning to life. What I don't accept, can't accept, is the world he made.

ALYOSHA   Why can't you?

IVAN   The suffering, Alyosha, especially of the children. I collect stories from the newspapers about the sufferings of children. As far as adults are concerned, to hell with them, they've eaten from the tree. It's the innocents that concern me. Here's one tale I added recently to my collection. In the darkest days of serfdom, there was a general who owned great estates; on his main estate he kept two thousand souls. Among them were a hundred boys whose only purpose was to care for the general's two hundred hounds. One day one of these dog-boys, no more than eight years of age, playfully threw a stone that landed on the paw of the general's favourite hound. The dog came up lame; the general wanted to know why. When he was told that the boy had thrown a stone, he found the boy, he looked him up and down, he said, "So it was you." Then he said, "Take him." The boy was snatched away from his mother and kept locked up all night. Early the next morning the general came along on horseback, surrounded by his hounds, his serfs, the boys and a number of hunters. The servants were summoned for a lesson. In front of them all stood the mother of the child. The boy was brought from the lock-up. It was a cold, foggy, gloomy autumn day; a grand day for hunting. The general ordered the child stripped naked; he begins to shiver, numb with terror, not daring to cry.—"Make him run," commands the general. "Run! Run!" shout the dogboys, "Run!" The boy runs.— "Sic him!" shouts the general, and he sets the whole pack of hounds on the child. The hounds catch him, and, before his mother's eyes, tear him to pieces.—I believe the general was later declared unfit to manage his estates. Well—what did he deserve? To be shot? To be shot for our moral satisfaction? Well, Alyosha?

ALYOSHA   Yes, to be shot.

IVAN   Bravo. Even the monk says so… so there must be a little devil inside you.

ALYOSHA   Are you putting me to the test? Why do you tell me these things?

IVAN   Because I love you, and I won't give you up to the church.

ALYOSHA   All I know is that none of us has the right to condemn the criminal for his crime. Let his torment be his punishment.

IVAN   We're all guilty—is that it?

ALYOSHA   We are.

IVAN   Very good, Alyosha; you've learned well from your Zossima. As for me, I only know that there is great suffering in the world, and I want retribution for it, and not in heaven, but here on earth. What do I care for a hell filled with oppressors? I don't want the mother of that boy to forgive her son's murderer. Let her forgive him for herself if she has to, for the immeasurable suffering of a mother's heart. But as for the suffering of her tortured child—she has no right to forgive him. She dare not.

The ladies have by now drifted away.

ALYOSHA Ivan, can I ask you something? Does any man have the right to decide who should live and who should die?

IVAN I don't know about the right to de*cide,* but as to the right to *wish,* that I reserve for myself.

ALYOSHA To wish? For another man's death?

IVAN Why not? But why do you ask? Because of what I said before, about one snake devouring the other? Do you think I could kill the old man myself?

ALYOSHA Of course not. I don't think either one of you could.

IVAN …Well, you'd best be running along. If your Zossima dies without you, you'll never forgive me. If Dmitry shows up, I'll—

ALYOSHA You're so unhappy. In your head and in your heart. "If there is no immortality, then anything is possible." Is that the "way" for you?

IVAN It's the Karamazov way. In any case, it's my credo at the moment; I won't deny it. I won't renounce it.—Will you renounce me?

ALYOSHA kisses IVAN.

Scene 9. Karamazov's house.

KARAMAZOV, a red bandage around his head, and SMERDYAKOV. Enter IVAN, with suitcase.

KARAMAZOV *(seeing the suitcase)* What's this now?

IVAN I'm off.

KARAMAZOV Off?

IVAN To Moscow.

KARAMAZOV Oh?

IVAN Yes, and for good this time. Smerdyakov, are the horses ready?

SMERDYAKOV They're just being brought around, sir.

KARAMAZOV Wait, wait, wait. Why didn't you tell me last night? You came in late. I heard you.

IVAN I was tired.

KARAMAZOV I see. Were you going to leave without saying goodbye?

IVAN I'm saying goodbye now.

KARAMAZOV Well.—Listen, do me a favour, will you? On your way—Ivan—it's only a little out of your way—Chermashnya I mean.

IVAN   I'm sorry, I can't. There's a seven o'clock train to Moscow. If I leave now, I'll only just make it.

KARAMAZOV   There's another train tomorrow, and another the day after that. Humour an old man. If I didn't have something keeping me here, I'd do it myself. Come on now, Ivan, there's a man there said he'd pay me eleven thousand for the woodlands in Chermashnya. But he'll only be there a week. Go talk to him, get him to improve the offer.

IVAN   I haven't got time.

KARAMAZOV   Ivan, have a heart for once. What's a day or two? Where is it you're going? Venice, isn't it? Well, Venice has been there a long time; it'll keep another two days.

IVAN   You don't let up. Are you going to force me to go to Chermashnya?

SMERDYAKOV smiles to himself.

KARAMAZOV   Ah, you'll go, then! You'll go?

IVAN   I don't know. I'll decide on the way.

KARAMAZOV   Nonsense! Make up your mind to do it, and now, now my dear boy. All you need to do is settle the thing and send me a note. That's all I'm asking. Then you go to Venice. Only be sure to come see me again. I'm always glad to see you, my boy. Hee hee! Smerdyakov, a brandy for Ivan. I'll write you a note. *(going)* Pour one for me.

IVAN   It seems I'm going to Chermashnya after all.

SMERDYAKOV   Well, then, it's true what they say—"A little conversation goes a long way."

IVAN downs the brandy, then hands SMERDYAKOV thirty rubles.

IVAN   Here. Ten for you; ten for Grigory, ten for Marta. Be sure they get it.

SMERDYAKOV   I'm nothing if not honest, **though to be honest, I'm nothing.**

KARAMAZOV returns with the note.

KARAMAZOV   Here's the note. Now, I tell you how you know if he's lying, this Jew. You watch him when you give him this note, watch how he reacts. If he strokes his beard, he's lying. Here, take it, take it. *(hands the note)* You haven't seen Dmitry, have you?

IVAN   Not since—no.

IVAN takes the note.

KARAMAZOV   Well, then. Good luck to you. Good luck.

He raises his glass, drinks. He goes to kiss IVAN, who instead holds out his hand.

Yes. Well. Well, you'll come see me again, won't you? I'm always glad to see you, my boy.

> *IVAN gives SMERDYAKOV one last look, then goes. KARAMAZOV shouts after him.*

Christ be with you!

SMERDYAKOV   **Night was falling; all that was left was for me to take a little tumble, and for Dmitry Karamazov to come calling. Soon enough.**

Scene 10. A tavern.

> *DMITRY, drinking, and finishing a letter. As he seals the envelope:*

DMITRY   Glory to God in the world, Glory to God in me, Glory to God in the world, Glory to God in—o, for a small pot of money—and then I would be free. Not exactly poetry; not exactly a poet. Why should I have been born to so lowly a man? A thief, a monster, who cares for nothing and no one but himself—and that hideous face of his. If ever I were to see it again—oh, I'd rip it to pieces, feed it to the dogs. Only they'd gag on it. Three thousand rubles, that's not so much—my own sweet mother left as much and more to me—and he stole it, the thief. And if I had it, oh Glory to God in the world, Glory to God in me, I'd set things right with Katya, and—

> *He writes the last sentence, putting down the last emphatic exclamation marks on the page.*

"Kill me, kill me, kill me!"... *(calling to a waiter)* Boy. How'd you like to make a few copecks? Take this letter to Katerina Verkhovtsev. The address is on the envelope. Tell her I said—. No, don't say anything. Just give her the letter. She'll pay you.

SMERDYAKOV   **Death was in the air that night, all through our little town. Up the hill, in the monastery, the followers of the great teacher, Zossima, gathered in the holy man's room. Alyosha, the poor boy, was exhausted from his sleepless night by the elder's bed, where he'd written down every last word that had fallen from the old man's lips. When death came, it brought with it a rather unpleasant surprise. Instead of a miracle, there came a stench, the sickening odor of corruption, from the body, and maybe the mind, of the great Zossima.**

Scene 11. Various locations.

> *The scene takes place in several locales, starting with GRUSHENKA's apartment. GRUSHENKA, pacing. An open bottle of champagne, and one glass, on the table. An overnight bag.*

GRUSHENKA   Who is it? Fenya, is that you?

Enter FENYA, with ALYOSHA.

FENYA Yes, Miss. With Dmitry's brother.

GRUSHENKA   Alyosha! You picked a great time to drop by. Fenya, keep an eye out for the carriage.

FENYA   Yes, Miss.

FENYA goes.

GRUSHENKA   You don't know how glad I am to see you. I thought it was your brother trying to break in. He didn't send you, did he? No. He wouldn't do that. Everything seems to be happening at once. What's the matter with you, anyway? You look so sad. You're not afraid of me, are you? You're so serious, so *pious.*

ALYOSHA, terrified to speak or move.

Would you like some champagne? I've had a little myself; well, more than a little. You see, my officer's called, he's called. He's waiting for me, in Mokroi, at this little inn where—well, I had a nice time there once. Now I'm going back. If Dmitry knew, he'd—

ALYOSHA   Father Zossima died.

GRUSHENKA   Good God. *(crosses herself)* Was there a miracle?

ALYOSHA   *(shakes his head no)* People came. Expecting one. Not me. Not for the reasons they wanted. A whole year I've been with him. Do you know what it is, to enter the monastery? You submit yourself, you give up your self, and I did, because I didn't want to be a Karamazov anymore. To take, always take, and give nothing back. He taught me, he showed me how not to be bad. And I thought, when he dies, he'll be exalted for that, honoured, his memory cherished. I thought the words he spoke would hover over us and, in time, bring goodness and peace to the world. That would be the miracle. But instead, his body—there was a stench, a horrible… *(in tears)* And everyone crowding around, all the people who'd come for a miracle, mothers and their babies, the sick and the lame, their faces, ugly in horror, and the monks who'd been jealous, jealous because he was good, they began to shout, "There lies the false prophet! It's a sign from God! His teachings were false! Zossima was a sinner!" What am I to do now?

GRUSHENKA   You haven't lost *your* faith, Alyosha? Have you?

ALYOSHA   I still believe in God. I'll always believe. "But as to the world he made…"

He starts to remove his cassock. The scene intertwines with:

The garden outside KARAMAZOV's house. KARAMAZOV can be seen through the window of his bedroom, pacing, drinking brandy. He's still wearing the bandage. DMITRY peers in.

DMITRY   *She's in there… behind the screen… look at him, all done up…*

ALYOSHA   My brothers are destroying themselves. My father, too. Why shouldn't I?

GRUSHENKA   *(She stops him from removing his cassock.)* Oh, Alyosha. Sweet Alyosha. It isn't in you to be bad. I'm the one who's bad. My whole life, I've never done a single good deed, and today, I'm going to pay for it. I wanted to ruin you, Alyosha, that's the God's honest truth. I saw you on the street one time, you wouldn't even look at me, and I thought you despised me.

ALYOSHA   No.

GRUSHENKA   You should.

DMITRY   *Or is he alone?—That's more likely…. No sign of Ivan… the servants in their quarters…*

GRUSHENKA   I really am a bad person, you see. I've only been using Mitya, to stop myself from going back to my officer. I was fifteen when I fell in love with him; I was seventeen when he left me. For the last five years, I've only had one thought—"I'll get you back." I saved my money, I hardened my heart. And as soon as he whistled for me, I knew I'd crawl back to him, like a beaten dog. Well, what do you think, Alyosha: should I forgive him?

ALYOSHA   You already have.

GRUSHENKA   …Have I? But I've grown accustomed to my tears. I might want to keep them forever.

> *Enter FENYA.*

FENYA   Here's the carriage, Miss.

GRUSHENKA   Time to crawl back.

FENYA   What am I to tell Dmitry, Miss? He's sure to come looking for you, ask where you've gone.

DMITRY   *Why is he looking out the window? Looking for her? Then he is alone.*

GRUSHENKA   Don't say a word, only this, that Grushenka loved him once, for a whole hour, and to remember that hour for the rest of his life. Only don't tell him where I've gone. He'll kill me.

> *DMITRY, using the signals: knocks twice slowly.*

He loves me so.

> *DMITRY knocks three times quickly, slips away. GRUSHENKA and FENYA go. KARAMAZOV comes to the window, opens it, looks out.*

KARAMAZOV   *(a half-whisper)* Grushenka? Is it you? Is it you? Where are you my angel? Where are you, my little chicken? Come in, there's no one here—Ivan's gone to Chermashnya, just the way I planned, it's just you and me.

DMITRY   So…

KARAMAZOV   I have a little present for you. Come in, come in… a little envelope, my angel, just for you… all done up in a bow and waiting for you in the bedroom… come in, come in… I'll unlock the door…

> *He disappears into the house.*

DMITRY   Disgusting old man… his face… his *face*…

> *GRIGORY approaches. DMITRY, in shadow, draws his pistol.*

GRIGORY   What's the window doing open? *(goes to close the window, sees DMITRY)* Who is it? Who's there? *(advances; DMITRY raises the pestle)* Is it you?—It is.— *(turning)* Murder! Murder!

> *DMITRY brings the pistol down on GRIGORY's head. The old man crumples to the ground. DMITRY bends down to GRIGORY.*

DMITRY   Christ. Christ, no. No, no, no. Blood… *(with a handkerchief, he tries to staunch the blood)* No, Grigory, no…

> *The scene intertwines with:*

> *The monastery. FATHER ZOSSIMA lies in a coffin. FATHER PAISSY reads the Gospel. A hymn is being sung. ALYOSHA, exhausted.*

PAISSY   *"And the third day there was a marriage in Cana of Galilee. And the mother of Jesus was there. And both Jesus was called, and his disciples, to the marriage."*

DMITRY   Not you, oh Christ, not you, not you, not you…

PAISSY   *"And when they wanted wine, the mother of Jesus saith unto him, They have no wine."*

DMITRY   This blood, it won't stop. I've killed him.

PAISSY   *"Jesus saith unto her, Woman, what have I to do with thee? Mine hour is not yet come."*

DMITRY   Stupid old man, it's your own fault. Lie there, lie there!

ALYOSHA   *(at ZOSSIMA's side) Father…*

> *KARAMAZOV appears at the window.*

KARAMAZOV   Who is it?

PAISSY   *"This beginning of miracles did Jesus in Cana of Galilee—"*

KARAMAZOV   Who's there?

> *DMITRY freezes in the shadows.*

ALYOSHA   *Father…*

PAISSY   *"—and manifested forth his glory—"*

KARAMAZOV   Smerdyakov?

PAISSY   *"—and his disciples believed on him." (to ALYOSHA) He died bowing and kissing the earth. Go, Alyosha. Go, my orphan, he wanted you to be with your brothers.*

SMERDYAKOV   He went outside, longing for freedom, space, openness. He fell to the earth, kissed it. He wanted to forgive everyone, for everything, and to be
forgiven, not for himself, but for all mankind. The night was still and silent. If Fyodor Karamazov had had the opportunity to scream in the town below, his son may well have heard the cry. But there would be no scream.

KARAMAZOV   Who is it?

SMERDYAKOV   And as one brother prepared to spend his last night on earth—

KARAMAZOV   Who's there?

SMERDYAKOV   Another raised a glass, and toasted his future.

IVAN, in a bar on the way to Chermashnya, raises a shot of vodka.

IVAN   *To a new world; a new life; and no looking back.*

SMERDYAKOV   And I?

KARAMAZOV   Smerdyakov?

IVAN   *Scoundrel.*

SMERDYAKOV   I awoke. And went into the garden...

ACT 2

Scene 1. Mokroi. An Inn.

GRUSHENKA, sitting with her OFFICER and his friend VRUBLEVSKY, screams as DMITRY strides into the room, holding a champagne bottle and a wad of bills.

DMITRY   Evening, don't get up. Just passing through, mind if I join you?

VRUBLEVSKY   *(Polish accent)* Please, mister, is private room.

DMITRY   Forgive me, sir, I flew here on wings of—hello, Grushenka—wings of— well, never mind. I thought we'd have a drink, toast our friendship. *(holding up the bottle)* There's plenty more where this came from. And this. *(holds up the money)* We'll make a night of it, hm? Why not, my last night on earth, and I flew here, to spend it in this room, that very table, where I, like you, adored this… Goddess.

GRUSHENKA   Mitya, what's the matter with you? Are you trying to frighten us?

DMITRY   Frighten you? No, no, no. In fact, just pretend I'm not here, or think of me as a bug, nothing more, and in the morning I'll crawl away.

DMITRY turns and seems to be weeping.

GRUSHENKA   Oh, come on now, Dmitry. Don't be like that. I'm glad you're here; really, I am. Come and join us.

OFFICER   Yes. Please, mister, to join us.

DMITRY   Join you? Join you?

GRUSHENKA   Only, why don't you put that money away, hm? Where'd you get so much anyway?

DMITRY   I killed an old lady in the market. *(beat)* Ha ha ha!

Everybody laughs. DMITRY stuffs the money back into his pocket.

Well, about that drink. *(downs it)* Oh. Forgot to pour for you. Here we are. *(as he pours three glasses)* This is just the beginning, gentlemen. There's more champagne on the way, a whole cartload—and food, and wine, and gypsies, just like last time, just like last time! *(calling out)* Trifon, more champagne! *(to the others)* Now—to Poland!

DMITRY, VRUBLEVSKY & OFFICER   To Poland!

They drink.

GRUSHENKA   Mitya—there's blood on your forehead.

DMITRY   *(wiping it off)* Oh. Thought I got it all.

GRUSHENKA   What's happened? Were you in a fight?

DMITRY   Not much of one. *(refilling the glasses)* Now, gentlemen, let's be brothers and drink to Russia, what do you say?

GRUSHENKA   I'll drink to Russia, you'd better pour one for me. We've been drinking tea all night.

DMITRY   Yes, everyone, everyone will drink to Russia!— *(calling out)* Trifon, where's that champagne? *(to all)* To Russia!

DMITRY & GRUSHENKA   To Russia!

> *They drink. The Poles do not.*

DMITRY   What, gentlemen, will you not drink to Russia?

VRUBLEVSKY   *(raising his glass)* To Russia—before 1772.

OFFICER   Yes, is good. To Russia's border from 1772.

> *They drink.*

DMITRY   Oh, I see. Just a couple of morons, aren't you?

OFFICER   Mister!

VRUBLEVSKY   *(shouting)* We love our country, can you blame us?

GRUSHENKA   Be quiet! I won't have any fighting, from any of you!

> *She stamps her foot on the floor, arms akimbo. Beat. DMITRY imitates her, stomps his foot, begins a Russian dance. Stops.*

DMITRY   Come on, let's have some fun!

GRUSHENKA   We were playing faro before.

DMITRY   Faro? Let's play.

OFFICER   Is too lite.

DMITRY   It, what? Too light?

VRUBLEVSKY   Not light, *lite*.

DMITRY   *(to GRUSHENKA)* What are they talking about?

GRUSHENKA   He means late.

OFFICER   Is what I said.

GRUSHENKA   It *isn't*. You see how dull they are? It's always too "lite" to do anything.

OFFICER   My kveen!

GRUSHENKA   You are, you're dull and you want everyone else to be dull. Mitya, before you came they barely said a word.

OFFICER   Is because you are acting, mm, unkind to me, so it makes me sad. *(to DMITRY)* But if you like to play, we play.

VRUBLEVSKY produces the cards, begins to set up.

VRUBLEVSKY   Is good thinking.

DMITRY   Very good teen-kink.

TRIFON enters.

Ah, the champagne. Good man, Trifon. Trifon! Have the gypsies arrived?

TRIFON   The police sent them away after the last time, Dmitry. But I got you some Jews.

DMITRY   Excellent! Wonderful! Send them up, right away! What about the girls? We need singers.

TRIFON   Yes, uh—only they want their money up front.

DMITRY   Smart. *(peels off some money)* Will two hundred rubles do?

TRIFON   Sir, for that, the whole damn village will show up and sing!

DMITRY   Ha ha ha! Excellent, Trifon, excellent! Revels!

VRUBLEVSKY   We are ready.

TRIFON   Faro, is it? I can get you a new deck, if you like, Dmitry.

DMITRY   A new deck? But why? We'll play with these.

VRUBLEVSKY   Sir, pliss to take your seat.

TRIFON   Well, it's a pleasure to see you again.

DMITRY   And you, Trifon.

TRIFON goes.

What's in the bank? Is there enough to cover it?

VRUBLEVSKY   Depends, mister, on how much you will bet. One hundred rubles? Two hundred?

DMITRY   Three thousand! But we'll start with ten. Knave leads.

VRUBLEVSKY turns cards.

SMERDYAKOV   **They played. Dmitry lost. And lost.**

The music, singing and dancing have begun in the next room.

And—

DMITRY   Lost again!—Double again, then, double on the Jack.—Lost!

GRUSHENKA   Mitya…

VRUBLEVSKY   Mister, pliss, you lost first two hundred.

DMITRY   Already? Then another two hundred! Double on the kveen. *(throws the money down)*

GRUSHENKA   *(covering the money with her hands)* That's enough! I don't want you to play anymore!

VRUBLEVSKY   What do you think you're doing?

OFFICER   Stupid bitch!

GRUSHENKA   Don't you talk to me that way.

DMITRY   *(to the OFFICER)* Sir, a word. In the next room, if you don't mind. I think you'll like what I have to say.

OFFICER   *(meaning his friend)* He comes with.

DMITRY   Yes, yes, of course, gladly. March! Won't be a minute.

> *DMITRY and the two Poles go. GRUSHENKA pours herself another glass of champagne. She takes a sip, then downs the rest. Voices are raised, off. TRIFON trails in after them.*

OFFICER   This is an insult! A grave insult!

GRUSHENKA   What's going on?

OFFICER   My kveen, this man —

GRUSHENKA   Stop calling me that! The name's Grushenka!

OFFICER   Grushenka—I came here to forget the past, and forgive it.

GRUSHENKA   Forgive it? Forgive *me*, you mean?

OFFICER   Yes, to show you I am generous. Then, in comes your lover, and offers me, just now, three thousand rubles, if I will leave.

GRUSHENKA   What! How dare you? Is it true, Mitya? Do you think I'm for sale?

DMITRY   Sir, sir—just a minute—first of all, I've never been her lover—

GRUSHENKA   Don't you dare defend me to him! Did he take the money?

DMITRY   He was going to, only he wanted it all now, and I haven't got it.

OFFICER   Grushenka, I am a man of honour. I came here to take you as my wife, and—

GRUSHENKA   Shut up! You came here to take my money!

OFFICER   You're not the woman I knew. You've changed, you have no shame.

GRUSHENKA   Get out! I've been a fool, a fool, all this time. You used to make me laugh, you used to make me cry, and I wasted five years thinking about you, five years!

> *An upbeat song begins in the next room.*

OFFICER   What is this singing? I can't think! Landlord, tell those Jews to be quiet! What kind of filthy tavern you are running?

TRIFON   Filthy? Who's filthy? You—who plays with marked cards!

GRUSHENKA   Calls himself a man of honour.

VRUBLEVSKY   Shut up, fucking whore.

DMITRY seizes him by the throat, forces him to the ground.

GRUSHENKA   Dmitry, let him go. Please, sweetheart, let him go.

DMITRY releases his grip; VRUBLEVSKY falls to the floor. DMITRY turns to stare at the OFFICER. The OFFICER picks up his hat.

TRIFON   Wait. Give him back the money.

DMITRY   No. Let him keep it.

The OFFICER turns to GRUSHENKA. Is about to say something. He and VRUBLEVSKY go.

GRUSHENKA   Let's get drunk! Come on, Mitya, just like last time.

The singing and dancing pick up in the next room. GRUSHENKA drinks another glass.

Mitya, Mitya. *(He goes to her.)* No, go and dance. Go on. Then come back to me. *(He starts to go.)* Mitya, darling, stay with me, don't go. Do you think I could love anyone after you? Do you forgive me? Do you love me? *(They embrace.)* It was from spite I did the things I did—Mitya, my only one, kiss me, won't you kiss me?… I knew when you walked in here, Fenya must have given you my message… I'm yours, Mitya…. Do you know Mitya, if I were God, I'd forgive everyone. I'd say, "Sinners, from this day forth, I forgive you!"…. Mitya, look at them, watch them dance. The world's a good place, isn't it, and everyone in it's good? Except us, we're bad. Or am I good? Tell me I'm good. I have to dance. Dance… round and round… everything's going round and round…

She dances, waving a handkerchief, the music crescendos. She comes to a sudden stop.

… Mitya, help me…

DMITRY picks her up, carries her to the bench. He tries to kiss her.

No, Mitya… not til I'm yours… I'm yours but don't touch me… not that…

DMITRY   Whatever you want. I worship you.

GRUSHENKA   We're not animals… we'll be good… we'll go to Katerina, we'll bow to her, ask her to forgive us. Only don't love her, do you hear? Love me.

The party slowly comes to a halt. KIRILLOVITCH. POLICE CAPTAIN, CLERK and policemen enter.

If you love her, I'll put out her eyes… with a needle…

DMITRY   I love you. Only you. Even in Siberia, I'll love you.

GRUSHENKA   Siberia? What are you talking about? Oh, fine, Siberia, then, wherever you like…only I'm so tired now… there's snow in Siberia… I love a sleigh ride… I want to be far away, with you… only you…

DMITRY   Only you.

GRUSHENKA   Mitya… we're not alone…

DMITRY   We are, darling… just you and me…

GRUSHENKA   But who are they?

DMITRY   *(turns; rises)* Gentlemen…

KIRILLOVITCH   Ex-captain Dmitry Karamazov…

DMITRY   You don't need to say another word, sir. I know why you've come.

KIRILLOVITCH   Would you please step into the next room? We'd like to speak to you.

DMITRY   Yes, I understand. The old man, I killed him, I admit it.

POLICE CAPTAIN   Son of a bitch! You hear that? How calm he is about it all! Monster!

KIRILLOVITCH   Please, Captain, will you let me handle this? Sir, my name is Kirillovitch, chief prosecutor here in—

POLICE CAPTAIN   Look at him, drunk, in bed with a whore, and his father's blood on his hands!

KIRILLOVITCH   Captain, please.

DMITRY   My father?

KIRILLOVITCH   Ex-Captain Karamazov, it is my duty to inform you that you are under arrest for the murder of your father, Fyodor Karamazov, a crime committed on this evening.

DMITRY   No… No, I—

POLICE CAPTAIN   Son of a bitch, you just admitted it!

DMITRY   No—it was Grigory I killed—Grigory!

KIRILLOVITCH   No, sir. Grigory is recovering. Now would you be so kind as to—

GRUSHENKA   It's my fault! He did it for me!

POLICE CAPTAIN   It *is* your fault.

KIRILLOVITCH   Captain for the last time, will you let me do my job! You'll ruin this case before it even begins. There are procedures!

GRUSHENKA   Take us together, together!

DMITRY   Don't listen to her. She's done nothing.

KIRILLOVITCH   Gentlemen, kindly escort the lady downstairs, hold her with the other witnesses.

DMITRY   Let her go, she's done nothing.

KIRILLOVITCH   Sir—

GRUSHENKA   It was my fault! I drove him to it! For money, for money!

> *She's taken out.*

KIRILLOVITCH   Mr Karamazov, will you sit down? Will you sit? We have some questions…

Scene 2. Mokroi.

SMERDYAKOV   **How be it if all are guilty? Surely anarchy will rule the rest of our days…. Poor Dmitry. Stupid Dmitry. So used to having his own way. Fierce, unruly, possessed of an uncontrollable anger—but underneath it all, tender-hearted. At least, that's what the defense attorney would claim. His interrogators would have none of it. The evidence was simply too strong.**

> *DMITRY, KIRILLOVITCH, POLICE CAPTAIN and CLERK.*

KIRILLOVITCH   Captain?

POLICE CAPTAIN   I count eight hundred rubles.

KIRILLOVITCH   Eight hundred. You say you spent seven hundred earlier this night. That makes fifteen hundred. Yet we have heard from a number of witnesses that you had more, much more, when you arrived here tonight.

DMITRY   They're wrong. You searched me—thoroughly—that's all the money I had on me.

KIRILLOVITCH   From where did you get it? *(pause)* Mr Karamazov, it's in your own best interest to answer our questions.

> *Pause.*

DMITRY   I'd like to leave now, gentlemen.

POLICE CAPTAIN   Sit down.

DMITRY   I have an appointment. Is it five yet?

POLICE CAPTAIN   You better sit down.

DMITRY   I didn't kill him. I wanted to, but I didn't.

> *Pause.*

KIRILLOVITCH   Was it jealousy, Dmitry?

DMITRY   What?

KIRILLOVITCH   Jealousy? You've just told us that you wanted to kill your father. Is it because you were jealous of him?

DMITRY   No. It was more than that. Much more.

KIRILLOVITCH   Was it over money?

DMITRY   Yes, money.

KIRILLOVITCH   You felt he owed you money.

DMITRY   My inheritance. But I only needed three thousand. So I only went *after* the three thousand. I wish I hadn't.

POLICE CAPTAIN   Hadn't what, Dmitry?

DMITRY   Hated him.

KIRILLOVITCH   Is that remorse, Mr Karamazov?

> *Pause.*

DMITRY   How was he murdered?

POLICE CAPTAIN   That's what we'd like to know.

KIRILLOVITCH   Captain, please. We found him in the dining room, on his back. His head had been smashed in.

> *DMITRY puts his head in his hand, utters a little cry.*

The murderer entered through the door to the garden. That much is certain.

DMITRY   The door wasn't open. When I was there.

KIRILLOVITCH   Tell us.

SMERDYAKOV   **The interrogation continued through the night. Dmitry got to telling his story, every detail of it.**

DMITRY   I needed money. There was only one person I knew who had it.

* * *

> *DMITRY at MRS HOHLAKOV's.*

MRS HOHLAKOV   Oh, I simply knew you'd come, Dmitry. I've been praying for it.

DMITRY   Perhaps we can be the answer to both our prayers, Madam. I have a proposition, financial. It's not going to cost you a thing, in the end. You see, my mother left me, as part of my inheritance, some land in Chermashnya. I could easily get seven, eight, ten thousand for it, only that man, my father, has put a counterclaim on it. Now, if you buy it from me for, say, three thousand rubles, then—

MRS HOHLAKOV   Dmitry, Dmitry, say no more. If it's three thousand rubles you want, three thousand rubles you shall have.

DMITRY   Madam, you've saved me.

MRS HOHLAKOV   What do you think of gold mines?

DMITRY   Gold mines? I don't think anything of them.

MRS HOHLAKOV   No need. I've thought of them for you, and come to the conclusion that, based on the way you walk, you really ought to be in gold mines.

DMITRY   The way I walk?

MRS HOHLAKOV   Oh you can tell a lot about a man by his gait. Science tells us so, and I'm a great believer in science now, especially after this dreadful business with Father Zossima.

DMITRY   If I may, what does this have to do with the three thousand?

MRS HOHLAKOV   Everything! Find yourself a gold mine, Dmitry, make your millions, and return home a pillar. You'll put up buildings, your name carved across the top of them, you'll help the poor and be blessed by them, create institutions devoted to the study of medicine, science, the arts, become indispensable to the Department of Finance, which is so badly off at the moment.

DMITRY   Madam, please. Yes, gold mines, hm, very interesting, perhaps we can chat about it another time. Now, if you could get me the three thousand.

MRS HOHLAKOV   What three thousand?

DMITRY   The three thousand you just promised me. I need it, you see, to pay back Katerina, to be *rid* of Katerina, to be *free* of—

MRS HOHLAKOV   Oh, my my my, no no no, I haven't any money, not a copeck. I—

DMITRY   Goddammit! Stupid woman!

* * *

> At GRUSHENKA's. FENYA, the maid, screams on seeing DMITRY.

DMITRY   Where is she, Fenya?

FENYA   I don't know, sir.

DMITRY   Tell me, or I'll slit your throat.

FENYA   Don't hurt me, sir… she said to tell you, she loved you once, and to remember that she loved you.

> He eases his grip on her.

She's gone to Mokroi, sir. To be with her officer.

DMITRY   …Ah…

FENYA   He was her first. Now he's sent for her. Please, sir, don't hurt her, don't take another person's life…. Sir, there's blood on your hands, and your forehead. What's happened?… Come, I'll wash you.

* * *

DMITRY   *(to KIRILLOVITCH)* I cleaned myself up. Then went to find her. What else was there to do? I'd done it for her.

POLICE CAPTAIN   Done what, Dmitry?

> *Beat.*

KIRILLOVITCH *(holding up an envelope)* Do you recognize this?

DMITRY   It… it must be the envelope my father left for Grushenka, under the mattress… let me see it—yes, you see? He wrote on it, "to my little chicken." He left three thousand for her.

KIRILLOVITCH Yes. But we didn't find any money in it. It was empty, lying on the floor, by the bed.

> *Pause.*

DMITRY   It's Smerdyakov!!—Don't you see that now? Smerdyakov killed him, then stole the money! No one else knew where the old man hid the envelope.

KIRILLOVITCH   Except you. You just told us it was under the mattress.

SMERDYAKOV   **Stupid Dmitry.**

DMITRY   I didn't *know*, though.

SMERDYAKOV   **Dog.**

DMITRY   I'd only heard about it from Smerdyakov.

SMERDYAKOV   **Cur.**

DMITRY   There's no question that he's the murderer. He must have done it while Grigory was unconscious… he gave the signals, the old man opened the door—

KIRILLOVITCH   You're forgetting one thing: there was no need to give the signals, since the door was already open. Do you see?

SMERDYAKOV   **Lackey.**

KIRILLOVITCH   Grigory insists upon it.

DMITRY   The door.

KIRILLOVITCH   Was already open.

> *Pause.*

DMITRY   Everything's against me. Even God.

> DMITRY *rises; the* CAPTAIN *moves as though to stop him, but* KIRILLOVITCH *makes a sign to leave it go. He waits a moment.*

KIRILLOVITCH   Let me ask you again, Dmitry. From where did you get this money?

DMITRY   Yes. Yes, I'll tell you. My shame, my disgrace. *(beat)* It's mine, in a manner of speaking.

KIRILLOVITCH   Yours?

DMITRY   Fifteen hundred rubles. I had it on me the whole time.

KIRILLOVITCH   But from where did you get it?

DMITRY   From around my neck. Sewn up in a rag.

POLICE CAPTAIN   A what?

DMITRY   A rag, a rag, here, here, here! *(He pounds his chest.)* I'd had it there for a month.

POLICE CAPTAIN   Where is this rag?

DMITRY   Where I left it, I suppose, in the town square.

POLICE CAPTAIN   Why?

DMITRY   That's where I tore it off.

POLICE CAPTAIN   And if we go looking in the town square, we'll find it?

DMITRY   What does it matter?

KIRILLOVITCH   A great deal, I should think. It would be material evidence in your favour. But let's return for a moment to the fifteen hundred. From where did you… obtain it?

DMITRY   You mean "steal it," don't you? Then say that. It was theft, of a *kind*. I took it from Katerina Verkovtsev, my fiancée. I shouldn't even drag her into this, but what can I do now? A month ago, she gave me three thousand rubles to send to her sister in Moscow, only instead of sending it, I spent it—*half of it*. The other half I kept with me, my disgrace, until last night, when I tore it from my neck and spent it.

> *Beat.*

KIRILLOVITCH   May I be so bold as to inquire—have you ever mentioned this to anyone before, this business of the fifteen hundred?

DMITRY   No one.

KIRILLOVITCH   Odd. Absolutely no one?

DMITRY   No one, and nobody.

KIRILLOVITCH   But why make such a secret of it?

DMITRY It's not the fifteen hundred that's the problem—it's the fact that I separated it from the rest of the three thousand.

KIRILLOVITCH But isn't taking the money more important than what you did with it?

DMITRY No! Don't you understand? What I *did* with it was vile…. Let me try to explain. I take three thousand rubles—I spend them. The next morning, I go to Katerina, I say, "I've done you wrong, I've spent your three thousand." Now, is that the right thing to do? No, it is *not*—it's the coward's way out—but at least I wouldn't be a thief; you see? I'd have *spent* her money, but I'd have told her about it, and therefore wouldn't have *stolen* it, per se. Now let's look at a second, more favourable, option: try to keep up with me—I'm getting a little confused myself—the second option: I spend only fifteen hundred, only half. The next day I take her the rest of the money, I say, "Katya, I've wasted half of what you gave me, and I'll waste the other half, so take it, keep me from temptation." Well, what about it, gentlemen? In *that* case, I'd be a real son-of-a-bitch, but not a thief—*not a thief.*

KIRILLOVITCH I suppose there's a subtle difference.

DMITRY A vital one. Every man is capable of behaving badly, but not every man is capable of being a thief; no, you must be überbad to be a thief. Oh, hell, I don't know, I'm not smart enough to categorize things. All I know is that I had no choice but to carry the money around with me, until I could figure out a way to repay her.

KIRILLOVITCH I still can't understand why you set it aside. To what end?

DMITRY What end?… Yes, the end—it all had to do with the old man, my— father. He was after Grushenka, and I was jealous. Every day I thought to myself, what if she comes to me and says, "It's you I love, not him, take me to the four corners of the earth." Well, alright, but I had only forty copecks to my name, so I'd be lost. I didn't understand her then, I thought she wanted money; so when I "obtained" the three thousand, I counted out half of it—like a fiend, frankly— and sewed it up. And *then* I went out and got drunk. With her. She has the most incredible body, but I didn't touch an inch of it. I kissed her baby toe, and nothing else. And she laughed… she laughed… how she laughs.

KIRILLOVITCH I think I'm beginning to understand you, Mr Karamazov. All the same, couldn't you have explained things to Katerina—asked her for a further loan of money?

DMITRY Are you—! Nothing would have been filthier than for me to have gone to that woman for more money!

KIRILLOVITCH Do you not think she would have given it to you?

DMITRY Of course she would have! To show her great contempt for me. She's full of anger, that woman. And do you know something else? I'd have taken it, and then, for the rest of my life… oh Christ. Forgive me. It's been on my mind for such a long time and, now I've told you, I've told you everything. Is it five? You see, last night, the moment I tore the money from around my neck, and decided to spend it, I became a thief, a man without honour. And sentenced myself to die at five this morning. Is it five?

> *Pause.*

POLICE CAPTAIN   When did you learn to sew?

DMITRY   What?

POLICE CAPTAIN   This rag. When did you—

DMITRY   For God's sake, is nothing sacred to you? I've just ripped my heart in two for you, and you're picking at the wounds… oh God, oh Christ. I shouldn't have lowered myself before men like you. You led me to confess. It's all a game to you. Well, congratulations, sir, and to hell with you, to hell with all of you, you're nothing but a bunch of torturers!

Scene 3. Mrs Hohlakov's.

> *MRS HOHLAKOV. ALYOSHA. Two months later.*

ALYOSHA   It wasn't him.

MRS HOHLAKOV   Of course not, dear—it was Grigory who murdered your father.

ALYOSHA   Grigory?

MRS HOHLAKOV   Naturally. After Dmitry knocked him to the ground, Grigory got up, saw that the door was open, went inside and bashed your father repeatedly over the head.

ALYOSHA   But why?

MRS HOHLAKOV   He must have had an aberration. There's a lot of that going around these days, and no wonder, *vous comprenez, cette affaire et la morte terrible de votre papa.* Of course it would have been so much better if it *had* been Dmitry—oh, I don't mean "better" that a son should murder his father— children really ought to honour their parents, don't you think?

ALYOSHA   It wasn't Dmitry. The money they found on him at Mokroi, that was the money he took from Katerina.

MRS HOHLAKOV   But one of the papers, dear, I think from Moscow, said that that was simply preposterous.

ALYOSHA   No. I saw him, the day before my father was murdered. *(beat)* I saw Dmitry, he was very upset and kept pointing to a place on his chest, here, just below his neck, pointing and saying it was his disgrace, and it was the money, the money they say he stole from our father!

MRS HOHLAKOV   You know, I don't think it was a paper from Moscow, I think it was one from St Petersburg.

ALYOSHA   *Mrs Hohlakov. You* must *testify tomorrow.*

MRS HOHLAKOV   I just don't think I'm up to it, dear. My heart.

ALYOSHA   You must make it clear that when Dmitry came to see you, the only thing on his mind was to be rid of Katya.

        Pause.

MRS HOHLAKOV   Is that wool? You look so handsome, and you're the spitting image of your mother.

ALYOSHA   I have a lot to do this morning, Mrs Hohlakov.

MRS HOHLAKOV   Of course. Go and see Lise…. Did she send for you?

ALYOSHA   Yes.

MRS HOHLAKOV   She's had a relapse, you know.

ALYOSHA   …I hadn't heard.

MRS HOHLAKOV   No, well. But then you haven't been around much these last two months.

ALYOSHA   I've been spending as much time as possible with Dmitry. He's very depressed, he—

MRS HOHLAKOV   No need to explain. Do go and see her. I trust you implicitly with her, Alyosha. It's Ivan who's not to be trusted.

ALYOSHA   Ivan?

MRS HOHLAKOV   He's been to see her. Several times. Ever since his return from Moscow. He's changed. I think he's had an aberration. He was always so charming. So intelligent. I thought he was in love with me. Isn't that funny? Not that I had any proof, of course; I've no proof of anything…. He's been telling her things. His writings.

ALYOSHA   Ivan?

MRS HOHLAKOV   All sorts of horrible thoughts. He left a pamphlet for her. I found it under her mattress. "To Lise, my little one." It says in there that everything's a lie, that the afterlife is just a mirage… I'm so frightened, Alyosha…. Alyosha, will there be something, when the birds fly down to my grave, will they carry my soul to heaven?

ALYOSHA   They will. You must have faith. You must believe.

MRS HOHLAKOV   You're just telling me what *he* used to say. The one who *stunk*. You're all the same. I need proof, proof, not homilies, you, you monk in sheep's clothing! There was supposed to be a miracle! But instead—oh, it's all my fault, my fault! If only I'd had the money for Dmitry. But what could I do? It's gone, Alexei, all for her, and there's not a damn thing the matter with her, not a thing!

LISE   Sorry to be such a drain, Mother.

MRS HOHLAKOV   Why, Lise, have you been listening the whole time? I'll leave the two of you to talk. Are you comfy, dear?

LISE   For a cripple.

> *MRS HOHLAKOV goes.*

Going about your duties?

ALYOSHA   I would have been by earlier. You know I would have. Are you upset with me?

LISE   On the contrary, monk. I've been thinking about what a good thing it is that I've decided not to marry you. *(laughs)* You're not fit to be a husband. If I were to give you a note to take to my lover, you'd not only take it, you'd bring his back. *(laughs)* I like you, Alyosha, but I don't respect you. Tell me: what will they do to me in the next world if I commit the greatest sin?

ALYOSHA   God will judge you.

LISE   Good. That's just what I thought you'd say. I want to do something bad.

ALYOSHA   Why?

LISE   So that everything will be destroyed. Wouldn't that be nice?

ALYOSHA   It's not unusual to have this desire—to destroy what's good. Especially at times like these.

LISE   Yes; exactly. Do you know something? Everyone loves the fact that your brother killed his father.

ALYOSHA   He didn't.

LISE   Course they say it's awful, but secretly they love it. I love it.

ALYOSHA   Dmitry is innocent.

LISE   But don't you know, Alyosha? None of us is. He taught that. It's better to be bad, to know evil. Otherwise, how will we know good? *(pause)* Alyosha, is it true what's taught in religion, that one day the dead will rise, and we'll all be together again?

ALYOSHA   Yes, it's true.

LISE   A certain person came to see me, and said it isn't true.

* * *

Enter IVAN to LISE's. LISE's dialogue is to ALYOSHA.

IVAN   Would you like to hear a poem? I call it a poem, but it's more like prose. Anyway, it's a story, and I'm always glad for an audience, even of one.

LISE   *In the darkest days of the Inquisition—*

IVAN   When the streets of Madrid were lit by the burning bodies of heretics—

LISE   *Christ returned.*

IVAN   The people knew it was Him, and gathered round, and demanded a miracle. A little girl, no more than seven, had just died; she lay in her open casket, clutching a bouquet of sweet roses in her hands. He approached and cried—

LISE   *"Rise, maiden!"*

IVAN   The girl rose.

LISE   *The Inquisitor happened to be passing by just then—*

IVAN   Old he was, almost 90, with sunken cheeks and hollow eyes. It is He, the Inquisitor thought to himself.

LISE   *He has returned.*

IVAN   The Inquisitor knew there was danger, and had Jesus arrested and kept locked in a dark dirty cell for three days.

LISE   *Then the Inquisitor came to Jesus. He asked—*

IVAN   "Is it You?" And receiving no answer, said, "Be silent then, and listen. You had your say; now the Pope speaks for you. Why have you come back? You gave men freedom, and it has taken us fifteen centuries to correct your work. And, tomorrow, you will burn."

ALYOSHA   *I don't understand. Was it Jesus or not?*

LISE   *He doesn't say.*

IVAN   What does it matter? Leave realism for a moment, if you can; or say it's the wild deranged imaginings of a ninety-year-old still giddy from a full day of burnings. The important thing is that the old man is finally saying what for ninety years he's only been thinking. "Do you not know that men cannot be happy as long as they are free? Man is born a rebel; how can rebels be happy? And who was it that showed men the way to their unhappiness? Speak! You were given the chance, in the desert, to turn stones into bread, and earn thereby man's undying obedience. But you refused, saying, 'What is this obedience worth if it is bought with bread?' Did you not understand that man needs someone to worship; he craves it. Man is weak by nature. You sought to raise him up, win freely his love. And what is the result? Fifteen centuries have passed, and man is as weak, vicious and worthless as ever. He has not yet learned that in complete submission lay his happiness. And who is to blame?

Who scattered the flock down unknown paths? Who made them proud by lifting them up? Oh, but we shall bring the flock back together, take from them their pride. They will grow timid, no better than children, fearful, quick to shed tears. We shall set them to work at once, but give them bread to sate them, and time for leisure, so that they might enjoy simple songs and innocent dances. We shall even allow them to sin, but only if they expiate their sins, through us. And all will be happy, the millions of creatures on the earth, joyful children all, who shall die in peace, your name on their lips, only to find, beyond the grave, nothing." This secret we shall keep, for it is the way to lead them to their happiness, with the promise of eternal life. And only we, who guard the mystery, shall be unhappy.

ALYOSHA   *And Jesus? Did he say nothing?*

LISE   *Nothing.*

IVAN   The old man waited for the prisoner to speak, even in reproach. But instead the silent one rose, kissed the Inquisitor on his dry, bloodless lips. That was his answer. The old man shuddered, opened the door. "Go, then," he said. "Go, and come no more. Not at all. Never, never!" The prisoner went away.

LISE   *(rising to him)* And the old man?

IVAN   *(kisses her)* The kiss glows in his heart, but nothing can change his mind.... I like you. *(He goes.)*

* * *

ALYOSHA   But this poem, it's in praise of Jesus, not against him. And this idea of freedom, Lise, it's absurd! The Inquisitor is a fraud, a fiction. Who are these people who "guard the mystery"? They don't exist. And what sins is he talking about? None of it makes—

LISE   Alyosha, save me! Save me! I don't want to live. Alyosha, don't you love me a little?

ALYOSHA   I do love you.

LISE   Will you weep for me?

ALYOSHA   I will.

LISE   Take this. *(hands him a letter)* Yes, yes, it's for Ivan. Give it to him. Go, this very second, or I'll set my hair on fire, I will. *I will!*

Scene 4. Katerina's.

This scene takes place at KATERINA's but spans several places and times. It begins with ALYOSHA handing IVAN the letter from LISE.

IVAN   *(ripping up the letter, laughing)* Not yet sixteen and already offering herself to me.

ALYOSHA   What do you mean, "offering herself"?

IVAN   The way all sluts do.

ALYOSHA   Ivan, she's a child, and not well.

    Enter KATERINA.

IVAN   Change the subject.

KATERINA   How is Dmitry?

ALYOSHA   Yes. Dmitry. He sends a message. He asks that you, that we, all of us, speak the truth tomorrow.

KATERINA   Whose truth?

IVAN   "And what is truth?"

ALYOSHA   You've been to see him, haven't you, Ivan? I know you have and gave him to believe that you think he's guilty.

KATERINA   What *else* should Ivan believe?

ALYOSHA   That Dmitry is innocent, that he could never commit this crime, that the truly guilty one walks free.

IVAN   What do you mean by that?

ALYOSHA   You know.

KATERINA   Don't listen.

ALYOSHA   It's Smerdyakov. He's to blame.

IVAN   Why do you say that?

ALYOSHA   Because Dmitry says it, and I believe him.

IVAN   Why?

ALYOSHA   From the look on his face when he told me.

KATERINA   The look?

ALYOSHA   On his face. Our brother could not have done this thing. The evidence is all against him, I know, but I also know Dmitry, I believe in his goodness, just as I believe that if he is punished for this crime, he will become, for the rest of his life, cruel, because we were cruel; he will turn his back on the world, as we turned our backs on him; he will say, an injustice was done to me, therefore I will be unjust. So. Believe in him.

KATERINA   Alyosha. I have a letter. From Dmitry, in which he makes it clear— Ivan, wait—that he intended to kill your father.

ALYOSHA   My brother is not a murderer.

KATERINA Why? Because of the look on his face? And Smerdyakov is? The police interviewed him, several times. They have no proof; where is yours?

ALYOSHA I went to see Smerdyakov.

IVAN What? When?

ALYOSHA This morning. I looked into his eyes, I asked him, did you murder your master?

KATERINA It wasn't him, it wasn't him.

IVAN What did he say?

ALYOSHA *(very upset)* He *spat* in my face.

    Pause.

IVAN Yes…. Very good. So it was him.

KATERINA No, Ivan. It was Mitya, Mitya! You know it yourself, convinced me, even before I showed you the letter.

IVAN No. It was Smerdyakov—and therefore me.

ALYOSHA You?

KATERINA Don't listen to him. He's not well. He's been torturing himself these last two months. He's convinced he's to blame, that somehow he led Smerdyakov on, made him murder your father.

IVAN It's true, it's true.

SMERDYAKOV Maybe I shouldn't have spat; it couldn't be helped. This one, from the moment of his birth, was loved. Everywhere he went, loved. And I? A drunk for a father, and my mother, the village idiot. Little Alexei, the monk in the world, the man of God—came on the pretense of giving me a present, a book: *The Life and Teachings of Father Zossima.* Some of it I couldn't understand; some intrigued me. This, for example: "Hell is the suffering of no longer being able to love."

IVAN You asked me once, "Does any man have the right to decide who should live and who should die?" Do you remember what I said? I said I had the right to wish. I wondered if you thought I was wishing for our father's death. Did you? *Speak.*

ALYOSHA Yes, Ivan. I thought it.

IVAN Yes. And when I said "one snake will devour the other," did you think I meant that Dmitry should kill our father, as soon as possible, and that I was going away so as to let it happen? Tell me, on the grave of your Zossima, tell me!

ALYOSHA Yes, Ivan. I thought that, too.

IVAN Yes. You see? After we said goodbye at the restaurant, I went home. I stood at the top of the stairs. *Listened.*

* * *

KARAMAZOV with SMERDYAKOV.

KARAMAZOV   *(to SMERDYAKOV)* So Ivan's given up on Mitya's fiancee. He's not my son. Never give up on a woman! They always come around in the end. *(clucks)* She'll come. Will she come? Smerdyakov!

SMERDYAKOV   She's sure to come.

KARAMAZOV   I kissed her sweet lips, and fell into her forever.

* * *

A tavern. GRUSHENKA sits with KARAMAZOV.

KARAMAZOV   *(laughing)* That's quite an enterprise you run, Miss Svetlov.

GRUSHENKA   Grushenka will do.

KARAMAZOV   *What* will she do?

GRUSHENKA   Buy your son's bad debts, collect them herself.

KARAMAZOV   A speculator. Well, I'd sooner deal with you than some Jew. What's your offer?

GRUSHENKA   One-tenth their value.

KARAMAZOV   Ha ha ha!

GRUSHENKA   One-tenth more than you're likely to see.

KARAMAZOV   Come come, Miss—Grushenka. Let's not be greedy. What would you say to two-thirds?... *(to SMERDYAKOV)* But, oh, those lips... *(to GRUSHENKA)* One-half.... I could see my way to a quarter.... Sold! For one-tenth!

GRUSHENKA kisses him.

* * *

KARAMAZOV   *(to SMERDYAKOV)* Thus, for a kiss.... Will Grushenka come? If I had my youth again—I was better looking than Dmitry at his age, I can tell you that. And he won't have Grushenka. Now that Ivan's leaving... I'm glad he's leaving. To hell with him! Yes, let him go. Who is Ivan? Where did he come from? People like Ivan, they're like clouds of dust, and when the wind blows—poof—they're gone.

* * *

At KATERINA's again.

IVAN   And as I stood there, I felt, as I never had for that man, such... revulsion. The next morning—

KARAMAZOV   *Christ be with you!*

IVAN   I left, knowing what might happen.

KATERINA   You couldn't have known.

IVAN   And when I heard it *had*, in Moscow, from your sister, I felt… nothing. The whole way back, I thought, "Was it so? Was it?"

* * *

IVAN at the dinner table in the Karamazov house. GRIGORY in attendance.

GRIGORY   Not eating, sir?

IVAN   It's cold. Take it away. *(as GRIGORY reaches for it)* The door was open? You're sure of it?

GRIGORY   Never been more certain of anything.

IVAN   But you weren't feeling well that night. Marta prepared something for you?

GRIGORY   To help me sleep.

IVAN   What was in it, this concoction?

GRIGORY   Will that be all?

IVAN   I asked you a question.

GRIGORY   Some herbs.

IVAN   Anything else?

GRIGORY   Pepper. I can't remember it all.

IVAN   And all of it dissolved in vodka.

GRIGORY   She rubbed it on my back.

IVAN   All of it?… No. The rest you drank. How much?

GRIGORY   Maybe half a glass.

IVAN   Maybe a glass and a half?… Very good. With a glass-and-a-half of vodka in you, you might not only have seen the door to the house open, but the gates of heaven as well.

GRIGORY   I'm a servant. If my betters want to make a fool out of me, I have no choice but to be made a fool of. But I know things. There is a God, there is eternity. The door to the house was open—and you didn't weep at the funeral.

* * *

IVAN, with SMERDAYAKOV, before the murder.

SMERDYAKOV   I'm surprised at you, sir.

IVAN   Why?

SMERDYAKOV   Why, that you're not going to Chermashnya.

* * *

And again at KATERINA's.

IVAN   *(to ALYOSHA and KATERINA)* I let him talk me into it; or did I?

SMERDYAKOV   *If your father were to die tomorrow...*

IVAN   I couldn't stop thinking about it.

SMERDYAKOV   *A little conversation goes a long way.*

IVAN   For two months, these thoughts, they won't go away, why did I go? If the door wasn't open, and I hadn't gone, and Dmitry, but not, and I went away, and why? Why? Is it because I wanted his money? Yes, because I love life—I do, I do! And even if I were to lose faith in the woman I love, become convinced that the devil ruled the world, even then I would want to live, to see the leaves open in springtime, to taste from the cup, to live, to have, to get, to take, to—

ALYOSHA   It wasn't you, Ivan. I know your thoughts, I've had them, too. But it wasn't you.

IVAN suddenly slaps ALYOSHA.

KATERINA   Ivan...

ALYOSHA   If it's God's will that you should hit me, then hit me.

IVAN   *(grabbing ALYOSHA by the shoulders)* I can't stand prophets or epileptics; and I especially hate self-appointed messengers from God. I want nothing more to do with you, from this moment on: never!

ALYOSHA gets to his knees, bows in front of IVAN.

You've seen him, haven't you? In my room, at night, when he comes to me. How did you know?

IVAN goes.

Scene 5. Smerdyakov's.

SMERDYAKOV, in bed.

SMERDYAKOV   He'd already been to see me twice.

IVAN   You don't look well, Smerdyakov.

IVAN picks up the book of Zossima's sayings.

I see you found religion. So he was here.

SMERDYAKOV   You know, you don't look so well yourself. You don't *look* yourself.

IVAN   What did you tell him?

SMERDYAKOV   Your eyes look almost yellow; are you worried about something?
(laughs)

IVAN   Goddammit, you think I want to be here?

SMERDYAKOV   What are you so upset about? Is it because I'm testifying tomorrow? Don't worry. There's nothing to be afraid of.

IVAN   What do you mean by that? What *would* there be to be "afraid of"?

SMERDYAKOV   You really are something, you know that?—Look, I won't say anything against you. In any case, there's no evidence against you. You didn't kill him.

IVAN   …I know.

SMERDYAKOV   Do you?

> *IVAN jumps up, grabs SMERDYAKOV.*

IVAN   Tell me everything, you pig, everything!

SMERDYAKOV   Everything? Alright: here's everything—you killed him.

> *IVAN sinks back down to his chair.*

IVAN   You mean because I went away? Is that what you mean?

SMERDYAKOV   When will you stop? You know the truth—you murdered him. I was only your instrument.

IVAN   You didn't kill him! You're lying!

SMERDYAKOV   You mean you really had no idea?

> *SMERDYAKOV withdraws a wad of bills from his sock.*

Have a look.

> *IVAN unfolds the notes.*

It's all there; you don't need to count it. Three thousand rubles. You can have them if you like.

> *IVAN sinks back down in the chair.*

IVAN   I thought it was Mitya. She showed me the letter. In his own handwriting. Mitya, Mitya!—Wait. Did he help you?

SMERDYAKOV   You're the only one who helped me. "Everything is possible," that's what you said, and you were so sure of yourself. Look at you now. Not so cocky.

IVAN   How? Tell me.

SMERDYAKOV   Very simply, as per your instructions.

IVAN   Never mind that. Give me the details.

SMERDYAKOV   After you left, I had my fit, fell down the cellar stairs.

IVAN   Did you fake it, or was it real?

SMERDYAKOV   Oh I faked it. I faked everything. I *walked* to the bottom of the stairs, screamed and waited for them to find me.

IVAN   But I saw you in the hospital, you were sick.

SMERDYAKOV   The morning after the murder, I had a real fit. Never had a worse one.

IVAN   Alright, go on, then.

SMERDYAKOV   They put me to bed in the servants' quarters. I lay there half the night, moaning, waiting for Dmitry to show up.

IVAN   To come to you?

SMERDYAKOV   No, not to me. I figured he'd climb the fence, the way he did when I wasn't around to let him in, and come into the house, and do something.

IVAN   What if he hadn't come?

SMERDYAKOV   Then nothing would have happened. I couldn't have done it without him.

IVAN   Alright, alright, go on.

SMERDYAKOV   I figured he'd kill your father. After what had been building up the last few days, and the fact that he knew about the signals... I expected it to happen.

IVAN   But then Dmitry would have taken the money.

SMERDYAKOV   Except he didn't know where the money was. I told him it was under the mattress, but it wasn't. I told the old man to hide it behind a painting—no one would have found it there, and he trusted me with money. I'm the only one he trusted.

IVAN   And if Dmitry hadn't killed him, but only beat him?

SMERDYAKOV   He'd have beaten him unconscious, and then again I would have taken the money, and said that Dmitry had stolen it.

IVAN   Alright, then. Go on.

SMERDYAKOV   What's left to tell?

* * *

KARAMAZOV's house and garden.

GRIGORY   Is it you? It is! Murder! Murder!

SMERDYAKOV   *(to IVAN) My heart was pounding; I couldn't stand it. Had Dmitry come? Had he done it? Finally, I got out of bed, went outside.*

KARAMAZOV   Who is it? Who's there?

SMERDYAKOV   *"Christ," I thought, "he's still alive."*

KARAMAZOV   Smerdyakov?

SMERDYAKOV   Yes, it's me.

      GRIGORY moans.

KARAMAZOV   Who's that?

SMERDYAKOV   It's Grigory. *(to IVAN) He was in shadow, so I didn't see him at first. I knelt down, and saw he was covered in blood, unconscious. I thought to myself, "Dmitry's been here." I decided right then to do it.*

KARAMAZOV   What's wrong with him?

SMERDYAKOV   He's fainted. He's drunk.

KARAMAZOV   Take him to the servants' quarters.

SMERDYAKOV   Wait. Grushenka's here. She wants to come in.

KARAMAZOV   My little chicken? Here? Oh! Where? Where is she?

SMERDYAKOV   Right over there.

KARAMAZOV   Where? I don't see her.

SMERDYAKOV   Standing right over there. Open the door for her. *(to IVAN) He didn't seem to believe me. So I tapped out the signals; as soon as he heard them, he ran to the door and opened it. I tried to get in, but he blocked my way.*

KARAMAZOV   Where is she? Where is she?

SMERDYAKOV   She's afraid to come in. She heard voices, and hid in the bushes, there, under the window, go and call to her.

KARAMAZOV   Grushenka, Grushenka are you here? I don't see her, Smerdyakov. You're lying.

SMERDYAKOV   No, look! There she is! She's there, in the bush, laughing at you, don't you see her?

KARAMAZOV   Grushenka?

           * * *

SMERDYAKOV   *(to IVAN)* He believed me then. I picked up the brandy decanter—you know the one, it must weigh two pounds—and brought it down on the top of his head. He didn't make a sound, just sank to the ground. I hit him again, and again—and the third time, I knew I'd broken his skull. He rolled onto his back, face up, covered in blood. There was no blood on me, not a trace. I wiped the decanter, put it back, grabbed the money, threw the envelope to the floor. Then I went back to bed, and started moaning, to wake up Marta. It took a while, but she finally got up; when she saw that Grigory wasn't in bed, she went out to look for him. I heard her scream in the garden, and my mind was at ease.

IVAN   And the door? If my father opened the door for you, it couldn't have been open before, the way Grigory said.

SMERDYAKOV   He only imagined it was open. The man's a mule, I tell you. Just a bit of luck on our side, you see, because without that they probably wouldn't be able to get Dmitry.

IVAN   You contemptible little shit! The only reason I haven't killed you is because I'm keeping you alive for the trial tomorrow. Maybe I'm guilty—maybe I *did* want to see my father dead, but I swear to God—

SMERDYAKOV   To who?

IVAN   ...I swear, I'm not as guilty as you say, I didn't encourage you. Tomorrow, I'll tell everything, confess it all. But you have to confess, too.

SMERDYAKOV   You won't confess. And if you do, it won't make any difference, because I'll deny having said anything about any of this to you. I'll say you're either sick, or you're feeling sorry for your brother and that you're sacrificing yourself to save him, and you made everything up, because you've always hated me, you've always thought of me as nothing more than a servant, a cook, a lackey, even though you've known all along who I was, that I was a brother to you. And if you say these things, who'll believe you? You haven't got the tiniest bit of proof, you haven't got a thing.

IVAN   I've got the money.

SMERDYAKOV   Good. Take it, then. Take it.

IVAN   But why? Why give it to me if you killed him for the money?

SMERDYAKOV   I thought once I might use it to start a new life, in Moscow, maybe. Or another country. That would have been better. It was a sort of dream; I dreamed it because "everything is possible." You taught me that.

IVAN begins to put the money in his pocket.

Wait. Let me see the money.... Alright. *(aside)* **"Stinking Liziveta," that's what they called my mother. The village idiot, she was. No being "got between the sheets" for me, when some hidden lane would do. The old drunk pushed her against the wall, bent her forward, hiked her skirt, did what he had to do. Nine months later, bloated and bleeding, she climbed the fence of the Karamazov house, left me bawling at his doorstep. "Take him." It was Grigory who found me; childless he was, and lo, a miracle. Yes, I was that miracle. "Smerdyakov." That's what Karamazov called me. He thought it was funny.**

"Stinking Yakov," stinking, just like my mother. Who breathed her last as I breathed my first, and in that breath begged for mercy.

Scene 6. Ivan's room.

IVAN stares at an empty chair. ALYOSHA enters.

IVAN   I told you not to come.

ALYOSHA   Smerdyakov's dead. He—an hour ago—he took his own life. I found him, hanging by a nail in the wall. There was a note. "I take my life of my own free will, so as not to cast blame on anyone." Ivan, do you understand what I'm telling you?

IVAN   I already knew.

ALYOSHA   How?

IVAN   You know. *He* told me.

ALYOSHA   "He"? Who is "he"?

IVAN   He made fun of me because I said he was just an ordinary devil and not Satan. I said he goes to the public baths—

ALYOSHA   Let me put this round your head.

IVAN   I love your face, Alyosha, do you know that? He's me. He's everything that's rotten in me. He kept taunting me, saying I believed in him, and that's why I had to listen to him. So clever. "Conscience," he says, "conscience! What is conscience? Just a bad habit. Let's get rid of it." He said that.

ALYOSHA   Not you?… Never mind, Ivan, he's gone, forget about him.

IVAN   He laughed at me. He's spiteful. He told me lies, to my face, about me. "You're going to do something heroic," he said, "something good: you're going to confess to murdering your father—"

ALYOSHA   Ivan…

IVAN   "That Smerdyakov killed him under your guidance."

ALYOSHA   It wasn't you!

IVAN   "You want their praise, you want them to say, 'He's a criminal, a murderer, but what a generous soul, to try to save his brother!'" It's a lie, Alyosha! I don't want the people to praise me, they're scum, they're nothing, I don't want their approval!

ALYOSHA   Calm down, Ivan.

IVAN   And Katya despises me. You're going to hate me, too, Alyosha. And I'm going to hate you back, just as I hate that monster. Let him rot in Siberia, to hell with him, I hate him, hate him, and I'm going to go tomorrow, I'm going to go and stand in front of them and spit in their faces, spit in all their faces!

Scene 7. The courtroom.

IVAN in the witness box, his head bowed, as though lost in thought. The PRESIDENT of the court addresses him.

PRESIDENT   Is there something you wish to say?

IVAN   No... nothing, Your Honour... I... no, I...

PRESIDENT   Mr Karamazov?

IVAN   I have nothing to—it's just, I was thinking about the man who found his wife in bed with a judge, and cried, "Your Honour! Get off her!"—I'm sorry, would you mind if I—let me go, would you, I don't feel well.

He stands up, takes four steps, stops, smiles, walks back.

I'm like a peasant girl, your honour, do you know what I mean? How does it go? "I'll stand up if I want to, and won't if I don't." They were trying to put on her dress, to take her to church for her wedding, and she said—that thing. I read it in some book about the peasants.

PRESIDENT   What's that supposed to mean?

IVAN   Just this... *(pulls out the rubles)* Here's the money... that came from that envelope... *(points to the evidence table)* ...Over which our father was murdered. Where would you like me to put these? Should I give them to the clerk, or...?

The usher takes the money, hands it to the PRESIDENT.

PRESIDENT   How could this money have gotten into your hands if it is indeed the same money?

IVAN   I got it from Smerdyakov, the murderer, yesterday. I was with him just before he hanged himself. He killed our father, not my brother.

DMITRY   He lived like a dog, and he died like a dog!

IVAN   He murdered him, and I encouraged him to do it. After all, who doesn't wish for his father's death?

PRESIDENT   Are you in your right mind?

IVAN   Oh I think so... I'm in the same nasty mind as the rest of you... as the rest of these... hideous faces. My father has been murdered and you all pretend to be horrified! Hypocrites! You all wish for your fathers' death... one snake devours another.... If there hadn't've been a murder, they'd all have gone home disappointed. They want a show! *Panem et circenses.* Not that I should talk! Is there any water? For Christ's sake, give me a drink of water!

The usher approaches. ALYOSHA stands.

ALYOSHA   He's not well, he's not well.

IVAN   Don't worry yourselves. I'm not mad, I'm only a murderer. You can't expect a murderer to be so well spoken. *(laughs)*

PRESIDENT   Witness, your words are impossible to understand. Calm down and tell us what you want to say…. If indeed you have something to say. How can you confirm what you've just reported?

IVAN   Well, that's the problem, isn't it? I can't! I have no proof, no witnesses… well maybe one.

PRESIDENT   Who?

IVAN   *(laughing)* He has a tail, your honour. But don't worry, he's nothing, a pitiful little devil. *(convinced)* He's probably here right now… under the evidence table. Where else would he be?

KATERINA rushes to the PRESIDENT.

KATERINA   There's something I need to say! Right now, this very second!

PRESIDENT   We have heard your testimony.

KATERINA   I have a letter, take it, read it, quickly, quickly, it's from that monster, that man there! *(pointing at DMITRY)* He's the one who killed his father, you'll see when you read the letter. He wrote it to me, told me how he was going to kill him. Don't listen to the other one, he's not well, he doesn't know what he's saying!

PRESIDENT   Witness, are you prepared to answer questions regarding this additional piece of information?

KATERINA   I'm ready!

PRESIDENT   Explain to the court what this is and how it came into your possession.

KATERINA   One morning, three weeks before he murdered his father, he came to see me.

* * *

KATERINA's house.

DMITRY   I need…

KATERINA   Yes?

DMITRY   My father, the son of a bitch, he owes me money. My inheritance. Son of a bitch.

* * *

KATERINA *(to the PRESIDENT)* I knew he was desperate for money, and I knew what he needed it for. That creature. "Dmitry, would you do me a favour, darling? I need to send my sister some money, in Moscow. Three thousand rubles. Would you be a dear and post it for me? You can send it when you like, even in a month would be fine."... How could he not have understood that I was telling him to take the money, to spend it on that woman, to be false to me. I might as well have said, "Here's the money for your creature, take it, take it." I didn't need to. He looked into my eyes; he understood everything that wasn't said, and he took it—he took it!

DMITRY That's right, Katya, I looked into your eyes and I knew what you were doing. You *wanted* to ruin me.

PRESIDENT Prisoner, one more word and I'll have you taken from the court. *(to KATERINA)* The witness will continue.

KATERINA That money ate away at him. He wanted to pay it back, it's true, but he also needed money for his creature. So he murdered his father, stole his money. And the day before the murder, he sent me that letter. He was drunk when he wrote it, I could see that right away; but what he wrote when drunk, he planned when sober.

PRESIDENT Prisoner, did you write this letter?

DMITRY Yes, it's mine, it's mine!

PRESIDENT The clerk will read the letter into the record.

DMITRY We've hated each other for a lot of things, Katya, but I swear I loved you even when I hated you, and you didn't love me back!

SMERDYAKOV *(assuming the role of the CLERK)* "Fatal Katya: Tomorrow I will get the money and repay you the three thousand and say goodbye, angry woman, but goodbye, my love! Let's make an end of it. Tomorrow I'll try to get it from anyone I can, and if I can't borrow it, I give you my word of honour I'll go to my father and break his skull and take the money that's under his pillow, under the mattress, tied in a pink ribbon—but only if Ivan leaves town. If I have to go to Siberia for it, I'll get you back your three thousand. And so goodbye. Forgive me! No, don't, you'll be happier that way and so will I! P.S.—I kiss your feet. P.P.S. Katya, pray to God that someone gives me the money tomorrow, then I won't be steeped in blood! P.P.P.S. Kill me, kill me, kill me!"

GRUSHENKA Mitya! *(to the PRESIDENT)* Now do you see what she is? A serpent! Mitya, she's destroyed you! *(to the court)* Listen to me, he's not the man you want. He told me he didn't murder his father, and I believe him. I've always believed him! Mitya! Mitya!

> *GRUSHENKA tries to get to DMITRY, and he to her, but they are prevented from reaching one another.*

SMERDYAKOV   It was all over but the speeches. Very good speeches they were, too. Copies can be found in the best libraries. The jury deliberated for one hour. And when the first question was put:

PRESIDENT   Did the prisoner commit the murder for the sake of robbery and with premeditation?

SMERDYAKOV   The answer was given, in a clear, loud voice: "Yes, guilty!" And the same answer was given again, and again.

The jurors call out "Guilty! Guilty! Guilty!"

Scene 8. The cell.

ALYOSHA. DMITRY.

DMITRY   I'm just sorry for God.

ALYOSHA   Sorry for God?

DMITRY   Inside the brain, in the nerves of the brain, there are these sorts of little tails and they—they let you think, and contemplate; it has nothing to do with the soul, you see, it's only because of how your brain works. Little tails. Oh, hell, I don't know. It was in some magazine Ivan writes for. A new man is rising, that much I get. So I'm sorry for God. *(pause)* What if they don't let Grushenka come with me? *(ALYOSHA doesn't answer.)* Alyosha. If they try to beat me on the march, or in Siberia, I won't let them. I'll kill someone. You should hear the way they talk to me even now. I'm not fit for suffering. *(pause)* Alyosha, put me out of my misery, will you? Is Katerina coming or not?

ALYOSHA   She said she would. But it's difficult for her.

DMITRY   I guess it is. Christ, tell me what I want. I love Grushenka so much; when she looks at me, she understands. But I want Katya! Or do I? That's the Karamazov spirit!

ALYOSHA   I'm coming with you. You're innocent, and this cross is too much for you to bear. I'll help you bear it.

KATERINA enters.

KATERINA   I came to hold your hands, to squeeze them in mine, the way I used to; do you remember, in Moscow how I'd hold your hands, and tell you over and over how I worship you, that you're my joy?

GRUSHENKA enters during:

(presses his hands to her lips; through tears) Love's over, Mitya! But I'll never forget the past, no matter how much it hurts. I only came so that what might have been *could* be, for just a moment. You love another woman, and I another man, but I'll love you forever; do you know that? Love me, for the rest of your life.

DMITRY   Do you believe I murdered him?

KATERINA   No. Never. Not once. *(turning to GRUSHENKA)* Forgive me.

GRUSHENKA   We're too full of hate for that.

DMITRY   You're not coming.

GRUSHENKA   They won't let me. I offered them money. Everything I have. Still they wouldn't let me.

DMITRY   No.... I have to go alone. Listen. The night I was arrested, as we rode back to town, I fell asleep. I dreamed I was in a carriage, somewhere in the steppes. Snow was falling in big wet flakes. Soon we came to a village. I could see the black huts, and half of them were burnt down. As we drove in, there were peasant women lined up along the road, and one of them, a tall, skinny woman, she looked so old, but couldn't have been more than sixteen, and she held in her arms a little baby, and the baby was crying. And the woman's breasts were so dried up that there wasn't a drop of milk in them. The baby cried and cried, and held out its little arms, with its tiny fists blue from the cold. "Why are they crying?" I asked the driver. "It's the wee child," he said. And there was something about the way he said it, "the wee child," something I liked. There was pity in it. I asked again, "But why is it crying? Why are its arms bare? Why don't they wrap it up?" He said, "Its clothes are frozen and don't keep it warm. They're poor. They have nothing. No bread. Their houses have been burnt down." Still I didn't understand. "Why are those poor woman standing there? Why are they poor? Why is the child poor? Why is the land barren? Why don't they hug each other and kiss? Why don't they sing songs of joy? Why don't they feed the child?" And I felt so much pity, rising in my heart, and I wanted to cry, I wanted to do something for them, so that the child would stop crying, so that the child's mother would stop weeping, so that no one would ever shed tears again from that moment. Then I heard a voice, whispering in my ear, it was Grushenka. "I'm with you," she said. "I won't leave you, not ever." I could see a light, and my heart was so full, and I struggled toward the light, I wanted so much to live, to go on and on and on towards this light, to live, to live. "Where are you?" I cried. "Where are you?" I opened my eyes, and saw that I was alone.

Scene 9. Graveyard.

ALYOSHA and LISE.

ALYOSHA   ...and he said, "Why did I have that dream? Why then?" Then he looked at us, and said, "It was a sign to me; it's for that wee child I'm going. We're all responsible for them, for all the children. So I'm going; because someone has to go." We embraced him one last time, each in our turn. "I forgive you," he said; he said I forgive you. The guards came then, and took him away.

Pause. They have arrived at SMERDYAKOV's grave.

LISE   Is this where they buried the little lackey?

ALYOSHA   Shush now.

LISE   Are you going to say something?

SMERDYAKOV   **They stood over my grave. It hadn't been easy for them to find it, buried as I was in unholy ground. No one had come to my funeral. I imagined what it might have been like, had I been as blessed as Alyosha. Surely the church would be packed; there would be songs, there would be tears.**

ALYOSHA   I have something for you. Your letter. I ought to give it back. Soon I'll leave our town, maybe for a long time, to be with my brothers. One is going away, and the other is very ill, he may even die. I don't know when we'll see each other again. It might be a very long time. But let's promise to always remember how good it once was, when we were together, and I carried you around; how you laughed. Remember that, Lise; it will get you through.

LISE   I remember, Alyosha, I remember.

ALYOSHA   There's no reason to become bad, is there, Lise? Life's sweet when we do good.

SMERDYAKOV   **For me, there was nothing. I do not ask for pity. I took my life of my own free will, so as not to cast blame on anyone. It's just to set straight the record that I've come before you, to say what I was never given a chance to say.**

LISE   I brought some bread; Mother says we're to crumble it onto the grave, and call the birds to come down. Only I don't see any birds, Alyosha; winter's come, and they've all flown away.

ALYOSHA   It's alright. Here, I'll do it with you.

As they crumble the bread over SMERDYAKOV's grave.

SMERDYAKOV   **And is it true what's taught in religion? That one day, the dead shall rise, and be together again? Oh, for that. Then would I gather the fathers before me, and speak to them these words of the apostle—"Fathers, provoke not your children to anger." For what is a father? Is he that man by whom we were "begat"? If so, then he is nothing. But if he is that man by whom we were begat, and who showed us love, and kindness, and in whose arms we found safety, then step forward, fathers, step forward, so that we, your children, may call you so. Until that day, I lie here moldering, vengeance my mattress, sweet memory my pillow. I dare not tell you, ladies and gentlemen, where my spirit has gone; I fear you wouldn't believe me—and, anyway, I have no proof.**

LISE   You can kiss me now, Alyosha.

He kisses her on the lips.

It's better when you're not wearing a dress. *(She laughs.)*

ALYOSHA   I like it when you laugh, Lise. You seem just like a child.

LISE   Alyosha, we'll be happy, won't we?

>   *He smiles.*

>   Alyosha! Look! *(points up)* Fly down, little birds, fly down! *(She laughs.)*

>   *The end.*

THE BEAR

a new version of the vaudeville by Anton Chekhov

Production

The Bear was first produced by Soulpepper Theatre, Toronto, in September 2002 as part of an evening of short plays by and about Anton Chekhov. In the cast were Oliver Becker (Smirnoff), Martha Burns (Popova) and William Webster (Luka). Albert Schultz was the director, with design by Astrid Janson (set and costume) and Paul Mathiesen (lighting). Maria Costa was the stage manager.

Characters

Elena Popova, a widow.
Luka, her servant.
Grigory Smirnoff, a creditor.

Setting

Living room in the house of Elena Popova.

THE BEAR

A drawing-room in the home of ELENA POPOVA, a widow. She is dressed in black and staring at a photograph of her late husband. LUKA, her servant.

LUKA   *(to POPOVA)* But, missus, it just isn't right. You've got to go on with your life. Look outside—it's a beautiful day. The cook's out there, the maid's out there, picking berries, soaking up the sun. Even the cat's outside, chasing birds. You see, they're all pursuing something. But you, missus, you sit here, cut off from the world, like a nun, in black, staring. It's been nearly a year since you set foot outside this house.

POPOVA   Why should I leave, Luka? What have I got to live for? My Nicky's dead. He's dead and buried, and me, I'm buried with him, here, inside these four walls, my grave.

LUKA   Oh nonsense. Nicky—may he rest in peace—is gone, nothing's going to bring him back. You've mourned for him, for a year you've mourned, but now you've got to move on, you've got to pursue something. You can't just go on like this, weeping and staring and wearing black. I lost my wife, but did I sing hymns over her for a year? No. One month, that's what I gave her, and believe me, that was more than she deserved, the little—. *(sighs)*

You don't go anywhere. You don't see anyone. We're like ghosts—we never see the light. And look, the mice have eaten right through my clothes. Missus, you're young and beautiful—for now. But in five years, ten, you'll succumb to the curse of the Russian woman. You'll begin to thicken all over, grow hair on your upper lip, you'll sag and stink and—I don't want to think about it. Live while you're young. Listen, there's a regiment stationed not too far from here, and some of the officers, I've seen them, they're not so bad looking, one or two of them are even what you might call handsome. And every Friday, they have a dance, you see, with live music; a woman like you could easily—

POPOVA   Please, Luka—stop, stop, stop it! None of that matters to me. Life seems so meaningless now. When Nicky died, I swore to myself that I would mourn him til my dying day, never leave this house. *(beat)* I know what you're thinking. He was unkind to me, at times even cruel, unfaithful—but I won't be any of those things. I'll be true to him, and show him what love really means.

LUKA   Missus, you have to stop talking like that. Come outside, take a walk around the garden. Or—better yet—I'll have the stableboy hitch up Toby, we'll go for a little—

POPOVA   *(weeping)* Oh!

LUKA   What? What is it?

POPOVA   Toby! He loved his Toby. He'd ride him everywhere, and he rode him so well. I can see him now, sitting tall in the saddle, so handsome, so graceful, pulling at the reins with those muscular arms of his… man and horse, in unison, riding, riding… Luka, have the stableboy give Toby extra oats today.

LUKA   Of course, missus.

The doorbell rings several times.

POPOVA   Who's that now? Send them away. I'm not home to anyone, anyone.

LUKA   Yes, missus.

LUKA goes.

POPOVA   *(looking at the photograph)* Oh Nicky. Do you see now what love really means? What forgiveness is? I'll love you til the day my heart stops beating. You son of a bitch. You see, I'm still the good little girl you married, I've locked myself away, virtuous to the end. You lied to me, you cheated on me, humiliated me, but I still love you. We made promises, Nicky. And I'm going to keep mine.

LUKA returns, upset.

LUKA   There's a man at the door, says he has to see you.

POPOVA   Didn't you tell him that since my husband died I receive no visitors?

LUKA   I did tell him, but he wouldn't listen, he says it's very urgent.

POPOVA   Then tell him again—I'm not at home to *anyone.*

LUKA   I, I did, missus, but, well he started shouting and pushing his way past me and—he's sort of in the next room.

POPOVA   I see. Well you'd better show him in. Honestly.

LUKA goes.

What is it with people these days? They have no idea how to behave. People think only about themselves, no consideration for others. All I want is to be left alone, in peace. Peace and quiet. *(beat)* Maybe I should go to a convent after all…. I'll have to cut my hair, but—I can still wear black.

Enter LUKA with SMIRNOFF.

SMIRNOFF   Shut your face, idiot. *(sees POPOVA)* Not you—him. *(bows)* Allow me to introduce myself. The name's Smirnoff, Grigory Smirnoff, Lieutenant, artillery, light—retired. I'm uhh terribly sorry and all that but I've—

POPOVA   What do you want?

Pause.

SMIRNOFF   Your late husband, who I happened to have known—

POPOVA   Whom.

SMIRNOFF   Your late husband.

POPOVA   Yes, I know. But you said "who I happened to know." It's "whom."

SMIRNOFF   Alright, have it your way. Your late husband, *whom* I happened to know, before he died, well that goes without—now you've got me all—look, when he died, for which I'm sorry, he owed me twelve hundred rubles, for which I'm also sorry. You see, I have a mortgage payment due tomorrow, and I've come miss—iz—to request that you pay me.

POPOVA   Twelve hundred rubles? For what?

SMIRNOFF   Oats.

POPOVA   Oats... oats...

SMIRNOFF   Yes, oats—you know, *oats.*

POPOVA   Luka, don't forget about the extra oats for Toby.

LUKA   I'll get right on that.

>   *LUKA goes.*

POPOVA   If my husband owes you money, naturally I'll pay it back.

SMIRNOFF   Wonderful.

POPOVA   But not today. I'm sorry, but I don't have that kind of money lying around. My manager's on holiday til the day after tomorrow; when he comes back he'll take care of it for you. Besides, you've come at a difficult time. It's exactly eleven months to the day since my husband died, and I'm really not in the mood to deal with financial matters, if you don't mind.

SMIRNOFF   Oh I do mind. Because I'm really not in the mood to lose my property, which is exactly what will happen if I don't make that payment first thing tomorrow.

POPOVA   And I've just told you, you'll have your money the day after tomorrow.

SMIRNOFF   I don't want the money the day after tomorrow, I want it today.

POPOVA   Well I'm sorry, but I can't pay you today.

SMIRNOFF   Well I'm sorry, but you're going to have to.

POPOVA   I just explained to you, I don't have it.

SMIRNOFF   What you're saying is: you won't pay me.

POPOVA   What I'm saying is: I *can't* pay you.

SMIRNOFF   Is that your final word?

POPOVA   Yes, that's my final word.

SMIRNOFF   Your absolutely final word?

POPOVA Yes, absolutely—Smirnoff—my final word.

SMIRNOFF I see. Well that's terrific. Don't think I'm going to forget this. *(shrugs)* And people wonder why I get upset. Just the other day, my bank manager said to me, "Grigory, why so angry?" Why so angry? That's a good one, when the question really should be, why not angrier? I've been riding around since yesterday morning. I've been to see every single person whom—who—owes me money, and not a single one of them has paid me. Bunch of lousy no good for—oh they were too happy to take my money when they needed it, but now that I need it back, well it's a different story. I haven't slept in a day and a half; yesterday I was so far out of town I had to sleep in some flea-bag Jew-run hotel with a vodka barrel not six inches from my nose. Finally, fifty miles from home, my last hope to get what's mine, and I'm met by a little priss who's "not in the mood to discuss financial matters!"

POPOVA I have made it very clear to you: my manager will pay you when he returns from vacation.

SMIRNOFF I didn't come here to see your manager, I came here to see you. I don't give—pardon the following expression—two shits about your manager!

POPOVA I will not have that language in my house. And I will not be spoken to in that tone of voice. You barged your way in here, sir; you can barge your way out.

POPOVA goes, quickly.

SMIRNOFF *(mimics her)* "I won't be spoken to in that tone of voice"… "my husband died eleven months ago"… "I'm not in the mood to discuss financial muhmuhmuhmuh".… Alright, her husband's dead, she's upset, she's "not in the mood," what's that got to do with me? I've got a mortgage to pay. "My manager's on vacation," good, I hope he's having a wonderful time, son of a bitch, hope he gets typhus. What am I supposed to do now? Go into hiding? Throw myself off a bridge? A dozen people owe me money, and not one of them's paid up. This one's not at home, that one's out of town, another one wants to fight me, another one's got hemorrhoids. And then this one, "I'm not in the mood." Deadbeats, deadbeats! I know what the problem is. Same as it's always been: I'm too nice, I'm too *gentle*, I'm too *sympathetic*. I'm always letting people off the hook, I'm putty in their hands. Well, not anymore. No more Mr Nice Guy. The buck is stopping—right here, right now. I am not leaving this house until I get my money! Look at that—my hands are shaking. That's how angry I am. I'm all worked up. Not breathing too well either. *(calls out)* Hey! Hey, you! Lackey!

Enter LUKA.

LUKA It's Luka.

SMIRNOFF Yeah yeah. Get me a glass of water. *(LUKA starts to go; SMIRNOFF snaps his fingers)* No, make it beer.

LUKA goes.

The *logic,* that's what gets me. Or should I say, the illogic. A man shows up begging for his own money, desperate for it, and the borrower decides not to pay because she's "not in the mood." It's impossible to do business with women. I'd rather shove nitroglycerine up my ass and sit next to an open campfire than— *(a chill runs through him)* And it's cold in here. Or maybe I just have the shakes. I swear I can't get within ten feet of a wuh-wuh *woman* without breaking into a cold sweat. Just looking at them makes my blood start to boil.

LUKA returns with water.

LUKA   The lady of the house is not feeling well, and doesn't want to see anyone.

SMIRNOFF   Oh shut up. Get outta here! Go on!

LUKA goes.

(imitates him) "Not feeling well. Won't see anyone." Fine. You want to play it that way? *(calls off)* I got news for you, lady of the house! I'm staying right here til I get my money. I don't care how "ill" you are, and I don't care how long you stay ill, a week, a month, a year, I am going to be right here. You hear that, Miss Sensitive? I'm not buying the widow act, not today. Oh, and by the way, your dimples don't impress me. I've seen plenty of dimples, okay? *(shouts out the window)* Semyon, unhitch those horses, we're staying awhile! Take 'em to the stable, get 'em fed.... Whoa, watch it, look out, the one in back's caught in the reins! Moron!—What did you say? What did you—you just wait til I get down there, my friend! *(goes away from the window)* Surrounded by idiots!... God, what a day. And this heat, it's unbearable. No one's paying, I can't get any sleep. Now I've got a professional mourner on my hands.... My head. I need a vodka. *(yells)* Hey! Lackey!

Enter LUKA.

LUKA   What is it?

SMIRNOFF   Get me a shot of vodka.

LUKA goes.

Jesus. *(sits, looks himself over)* What a mess. I'm filthy, head to toe. Haven't washed in days, I must really— *(smells his armpits)* Pooh! *(clears the air with his hands)* She must have been impressed. *(yawns)* Not exactly the height of civility to show up at a *lady's* house looking like this, but, well, I didn't see any dress code posted on the door. Besides, I'm a bill collector, not a dinner guest. What do I have to do, put on a suit, present my credentials, bow and scrape?

Enter LUKA with the vodka.

LUKA   Sir, if you don't mind my saying, you're acting somewhat—

SMIRNOFF   *(jumping up)* What?

LUKA   Nothing.

SMIRNOFF   Who do you think you're talking to?

LUKA   No one.

SMIRNOFF   Then shut the hell up, lackey.

LUKA   *(leaving)* What I wouldn't give for a hammer and sickle…

SMIRNOFF   Okay, before I was just mildly upset. Now I'm angry. *(stomps)* Now I could do some damage! Oh yeah. I could tear this place apart. I could really— *(stomps some more, then grabs his stomach)* Ooh… I don't feel so good. *(yells)* Hey! You there! Lackey!

     Enter POPOVA.

POPOVA   *(not looking at him)* Sir, would you please stop shouting? In my time of mourning, I have grown unaccustomed to the sound of the human voice—particularly when it is raised, repeatedly. Now I ask you to respect my wishes and leave me in peace and quiet.

SMIRNOFF   Happily. As soon as you pay me.

POPOVA   I've explained, quite clearly, that I can't get you the money today.

SMIRNOFF   And I've told you, quite clearly, that if I don't get the money today, I might as well hang myself tomorrow.

POPOVA   What am I supposed to do if I don't have the money? Stop being so stubborn.

SMIRNOFF   Me stubborn? You're the one who won't budge, you're the one who's refusing to pay me.

POPOVA   I *can't* pay.

SMIRNOFF   And I can't leave. You say you'll pay me the day after tomorrow? Fine. I'll be right here, waiting. *(He jumps up.)* Do you think this is a joke? Do you think I have nothing better to do with my time than ride around making up some story about a mortgage payment?

POPOVA   This isn't a stable. Would you please stop shouting?

SMIRNOFF   I'm not talking about a stable—I'm talking about my mortgage.

POPOVA   You have no idea how to act in front of a lady.

SMIRNOFF   Show me one.

POPOVA   You are a rude, ill-bred boor. Decent people don't behave this way.

SMIRNOFF   Oh, well how do they behave? Do they speak French? *(with a lisp)* Madame, je vous prie…. *(bad French accent)* Thank you, madame, for not paying, I truly appreciate your unkind behaviour before a desperate man…. Ah, pardon, I am upsetting you, *oui*? We will change ze subject. What a lovely day. Ze birds are singing, it is night, and you look beautiful in ze mourning! *(bows)*

POPOVA You're not only a rude, ill-bred boor—you're also not very funny.

SMIRNOFF *(imitates her)* "You're not only a rude, ill-bred boor, you're also not very funny. You don't know how to act in front of a lady." Listen, lady, I've seen more Ladies than you've seen sparrows, alright? I've fought three duels—for Ladies. I've walked out on twelve Ladies, and had nine walk out on me! Okay? In fact, it may surprise you to hear this, but I'll tell you anyway, there was a time when I played the game, oh yeah, played it to the hilt: I'd meet a woman, get myself all decked out: I'd look nice, smell nice, talk nice, act nice—nice and gentle, I'd be a gentle man—I'd open doors, I'd bow, I'd scrape, I'd kiss hands, I'd swoon, I'd sigh at the moon—sometimes I'd get so carried away I'd even talk about women's rights—and for what? I wasted my time, my breath and my money on Ladies, on "love." I'm done with Ladies! I've had enough. Dark eyes, sudden glances, red lips, dimpled cheeks, the moon, whispers, a hurried breath—not interested! Let me tell you something about Ladies, about women. Present company excepted, of course, all women, rich or poor, old or young, fat or thin, are false, hypocritical, jealous, gossipy, vain, petty, heartless, illogical liars—and as for this— *(points to his forehead)* —you'll find more upstairs in a single sparrow than you will in a hundred *Ladies*. Because beneath that lovely surface, the well-coiffed head, the well-dressed veneer, lurks the soul of a crocodile.

He grips the back of a chair; it breaks.

And the amazing thing about this crocodile is that for some reason it believes that it has some kind of monopoly on love. Now you show me a woman who can love anything but her little lapdog, and I'll fetch you the morning paper. A woman in love knows how to do only two things: whine and complain. And as she's whining and complaining, she's digging her hooks ever more deeply into the poor idiot who doesn't yet know that it *is* just a game, a game he'll never win. Now since you have the misfortune of being a woman, perhaps you can tell me—if you can bring yourself to speak the truth for one second— whether you've ever known a woman who was sincere, faithful, and true? *(beat)* You see, you can't, because, you've never met one, because there isn't one! The only women who are faithful and true are either dead, or nuns. You ask me, there's a better chance of meeting a talking horse than a truthful woman.

POPOVA I see. And I suppose that, in your worldly opinion, it's men who are sincere, faithful and true?

SMIRNOFF Absolutely.

POPOVA Men. *(laughs)* Men are faithful and true. Of course. It all makes sense now. *(beat)* You have no idea what you're talking about! Let me tell you about *men*, or rather, about one man, a man with whom I was very familiar.

SMIRNOFF   Who.

POPOVA   My husband.

SMIRNOFF   Yes, but you said "with whom" you were very familiar, it's "with who."

POPOVA   My late husband was the best of men. I loved him deeply, passionately, devotedly, as only a young, inexperienced woman could. I gave him my youth, my happiness, my life, my fortune—I breathed him in, I worshipped him—and what do you think I got in return? This best of men began to cheat on me as soon and as often as he could. When he died, I found in his desk a drawer full of love letters. He used to leave me alone for weeks on end. And when he *was* home he'd flirt with every woman in the room, right in front of me. He'd spend my money and laugh at me when I tried to talk to him about it. But in spite of it all, I still loved him. I was true to him. I'm still true to him. The day he died, I vowed to shut myself away inside these four walls and wear nothing but black til the day I die.

SMIRNOFF mockingly applauds.

SMIRNOFF   *Brava.* You think I'm an idiot? You think I don't know why you go around wearing that ridiculous costume, "inside these four walls"? It's obvious! You love playing the widow! So mysterious, isn't it, so romantic! You're just waiting for some Romeo to wander by, gaze up at your figure through the window and cry, "There lives the mysterious one, who, for the love of her husband, has buried herself within these four walls." Who do you think you're talking to?

POPOVA   How dare you say these things!

SMIRNOFF   You shut yourself away, but you didn't forget to curl your eyelashes.

POPOVA   How dare you? How dare you!

SMIRNOFF   Keep it down, will ya, I'm not your doorman. I'm just *a* man, and I call it like I see it. So relax, and quit that yelling.

POPOVA   I'm not the one who's yelling, you are. Now leave me alone!

SMIRNOFF   Pay me and I'll go.

POPOVA   You're not getting a thing from me!

SMIRNOFF   Oh yeah?

POPOVA   *(imitates him)* "Yeah!"—Now please leave!

SMIRNOFF   Look, I'm not your husband, and I'm not your boyfriend, so do me a favour, cut the dramatics. Okay? *(sits)* I'm not impressed.

POPOVA   *(beside herself with anger)* Who said you could sit down?

SMIRNOFF   You did.

POPOVA   I asked you to leave.

SMIRNOFF That's not what I heard.

POPOVA Will you please go.

SMIRNOFF Dinner? Wonderful. Or you could just give me my money. *(aside)* Now I'm pissed. Now I'm really pissed!

POPOVA Sir, I have had quite enough of you and your rude behaviour. Are you or are you not going to leave.

SMIRNOFF I are not.

POPOVA Absolutely not?

SMIRNOFF Absolutely.

POPOVA Fine.

> *She rings a bell. LUKA enters.*

Luka, kindly show this "gentleman" to the door.

> *LUKA keeps his distance.*

LUKA Uh. The lady would uhh, appreciate it... if, uhh...

SMIRNOFF *(jumps up)* Shut your mouth! Talk to me like that again, I'll break you in two.

LUKA *(clutching his heart)* Oh. *(falls into a chair)* I can't get my breath!

POPOVA Where's Dasha? Dasha! *(shouts)* Dasha! Pelagea! Dasha! *(rings again and again)*

LUKA Ohhhh! Picking... fruit.... No one's home.... Water!

POPOVA Get out of this house, right now.

LUKA But I don't feel well.

POPOVA Not you! Him! Out!

SMIRNOFF Ask me nicely.

POPOVA *(clenches her fists, stamps her foot)* Nicely! You? You boor! You bear! You bully! You—you—half a man!

SMIRNOFF What? What did you just say?

POPOVA I said you're a boor, and a bear, and a bully!

SMIRNOFF And then what did you say?

POPOVA I said you're half a man.

SMIRNOFF *(approaching her)* "Half a man"? Is that what you said? Is it?

POPOVA Do you think I'm afraid of you?

SMIRNOFF   You think just because you wear a skirt, you can insult me with impunity? Huh? You're going to answer for that.

LUKA   Oh God… oh God…

SMIRNOFF   Pistols!

POPOVA   Do you think I'm afraid of you just because you have a big chest and a bigger mouth? Hm? Well, half man, do you?

SMIRNOFF   That does it! No one insults me, I don't care what you are, a man, a woman—

POPOVA   What if you're half of each?

SMIRNOFF   Alright. If you want to insult me like a man, you can fight me like one. Pistols!

POPOVA   Fine!

SMIRNOFF   Right now!

POPOVA   Fine! My husband happened to have had pistols. I'll get them. You'd better be here when I get back.

SMIRNOFF   Oh I will be.

POPOVA   Good! *(starts to go; turns back)* You don't know what pleasure it's going to be for me to put a bullet through that thick, idiotic skull of yours! You son of a bitch.

> *She goes. SMIRNOFF holds up an imaginary pistol, pretends to shoot her, to LUKA's horror.*

SMIRNOFF   Pow! Right between the—eyes. She really chose the wrong day to pick a fight with me. Mr Nice Guy might have missed, but *this* guy won't. No mercy.

LUKA   Oh God… *(kneels)* Please, you don't need to go through with this. Just leave.

SMIRNOFF   *(not listening to him)* Shame really. That is one hell of a woman. *(imitating her)* "You son of a bitch." *(whistles appreciatively)* And she was glowing when she did said it, too. Her eyes were flashing—whatever *that* means. Didn't back down for a second. I challenged, and she was right there. Blow for blow, so to speak. I have to admit, that's a first for me.

LUKA   Please go.

SMIRNOFF   Yes, sir, that is *some* woman. A woman like that a man can appreciate. No whining, no complaining. She's smoldering, that's what she is—*smoking*. Rub her the right way, she'll burst into flames. Too bad I have to kill her.

LUKA   *(weeping)* Plee-hee-heeze.

SMIRNOFF   Wait a second. What's happening to me? It isn't possible. Is it? I think I sort of like her. I really do. Forget "sort of." Dimples and all, I like her! In fact,

I might even tell her to forget about the money.... And I'm not upset anymore. It's incredible.... She's incredible. She's extraordinary.

> *Enter POPOVA with the pistols.*

POPOVA   Alright, I found the pistols. Now, before we start—you need to show me how these work.

LUKA   Oh, God.... Oh God.... I better get some help... what a day...

> *He goes.*

SMIRNOFF   *(looking over the pistols)* Have you ever held one of these before?

POPOVA   Never.

SMIRNOFF   Well there are many different kinds, of course. There are Mortimers, which are specially made for duels, and use percussion firing.

POPOVA   Oh. Are these Mortimers?

SMIRNOFF   No. No, these are Smith and Wessons... revolvers... triple action... with extractors.... Excellent pieces. The two of them couldn't have cost less than ninety rubles.... Now, you hold it like this... *(aside)* She has the most amazing eyes. I'm on fire.

POPOVA   Like this?

SMIRNOFF   Yes, just like that.... Now you—cock the trigger, and aim, like so.... Put your head back a little.... Yes, good.... Now extend your arm.... That's it.... Then you press this... thingy... with your finger and, well, fire.

POPOVA   Easy.

SMIRNOFF   Yes, well.... The important thing is to remain calm, take dead aim.... Try to keep your hand from shaking.

POPOVA   My hand isn't shaking. Let's get started. Should we go outside?

SMIRNOFF   I suppose. Look. I think I'd better tell you. I'm going to fire into the air.

POPOVA   What? Why?

SMIRNOFF   Well, because I... well it's none of your business.

POPOVA   You're afraid, aren't you? Well, you're not getting out of it that easily. I want satisfaction. I want to put a hole through your skull, your stupid, stubborn, obstinate skull!... You are afraid, aren't you?

SMIRNOFF   Yes, yes you've hit it. I'm afraid.

POPOVA   You're lying. Tell me the truth! Why won't you fight me?

SMIRNOFF   Because... because... because I like you.

POPOVA   *(laughs)* He likes me! He has the nerve to say he likes me! *(points to the door)* Get going.

> SMIRNOFF *loads his revolver in silence, goes to the door. He stops, they look at each other for a moment. He goes to her, hesitantly.*

SMIRNOFF   Look. Are you still upset? I am, too, a little, but in a different sort of—How can I explain this?… Look—I like you! Do you understand? I, oh hell, I love you!

POPOVA   Well I hate you! Get away from me!

SMIRNOFF   God, what a woman!

POPOVA   Stand back or I'll shoot.

SMIRNOFF   Shoot, then! Do it, make me happy, let me die by your hand, your silky hand, before your exquisite eyes… I've gone mad. For you. Make up your mind. *(beat)* Will you marry me?

POPOVA   *(angrily waving her revolver)* Marry you? I'm going to kill you.

SMIRNOFF   Same thing. I'm out of my mind. I don't know what's happening.

POPOVA   Let's go, let's go!

SMIRNOFF   I love you! *(kneels)* I love you as I've never loved anyone! I walked out on twelve women, nine walked out on me, but I never loved one of them the way I love you. I'm weak, I'm jelly, I'm wobbly.… Look at me, I'm on my knees to you, like a fool, offering you my hand. *(grabs her hand; she screams in pain)* Five years ago I took a vow, I swore to myself I would never fall in love again, and now, out of the blue, I'm in love, sincerely, honestly, truly, in love. Marry me. Will you? Yes or no? Yes or— *(beat)* I see. Then it's no. Well. Goodbye. *(goes to the door)*

POPOVA   Wait.

SMIRNOFF   Yes?

POPOVA   No. Leave.… No, wait.… No, keep going.… No, stop.… I can't stand you! Which is to say… don't go! I hate you. *(throws the gun away)* What are you standing there for? Leave!

SMIRNOFF   Then this is goodbye.

POPOVA   Yes. *(yells)* Where are you going? Wait a minute.… Go! Go. I'm so… come to me… get away from me, get away from me! You've made me so mad, so mad.

SMIRNOFF   You're mad? *I'm* mad. *(roughly)* I love you! You think I meant for this to happen? *(He goes to her.)* I came here to beg you for my money, and now I'm begging you to take my hand…

POPOVA   Go.

SMIRNOFF   *(puts his arms around her)* I'll never forgive myself if I—

POPOVA   Take your hands off me! I hate you! I want to fight you! I want to f... to ff... to ff—

A prolonged kiss. LUKA enters, sees them kissing.

LUKA   Oh God.

POPOVA   Luka... tell the stableboy... no more oats for Toby today.

The end.

ENEMIES

an adaptation of the play by Maxim Gorky

Production

Enemies was first produced by Ryerson University, Toronto, in February 2006. In the cast were Maya Boyd-Navazo (Yagudin), Laura Burns (Nadya/Worker), Skye Collyer (Worker/Wife) Chad Connell (Zakhar/Soldier/Worker), Cosette Derome (Soldier/ Worker/Wife), Lauren Ferraro (Cleopatra/Worker), Colin Fletcher (Grekov/Soldier), Ingrid Haas (Paulina/Worker), Janick Hébert (Tatanya), Michael Hogeveen (Mikhail/ Boboyedov/Worker), Nils Hognestad (Nikolai/Worker), Daniel McPherson (Yakov/ Worker), Eric Morin (Sintsov/Soldier/Worker), Chelsea O'Connor (Agrafena), Nicholas Rose (Klatch/Policeman/Worker), Monika Schneider (Pologgy/Worker, Erin Vandenberg (Ribitsov) and Aviva Zimmerman (Levshin). Liza Balkan was the director, with Sean Sullivan as assistant director. Design was by Pat Lavender (lighting), Palmer Watt (sound) and Camellia Koo (scenic and costume). Stage Management by Stephanie Nakamura.

Characters

ZAKHAR BARDIN, factory owner.
PAULINA, Zakhar's wife.
NADYA, their niece.
YAKOV, Zakhar's brother.
TATANYA, his wife; an actress.
MIKHAIL, Zakhar's partner, the managing director.
CLEOPATRA, Mikhail's wife.
NIKOLAI, Mikhail's brother; an assistant district attorney.
AGRAFENA, the maid.
POLOGGY, SINTSOV, clerks at the factory.
GREKOV, LEVSHIN, YAGUDIN, RIBITSOV, workers at the factory.
POLICEMAN
CAPTAIN BOBOYEDOV
CORPORAL KLATCH
SOLDIERS and WORKERS

Setting

Act 1. The garden outside the house of the Bardins. Morning.
Act 2. The main room of the house. The next day.

ENEMIES

ACT 1

The garden outside the Bardin house. A verandah. AGRAFENA makes coffee. POLOGGY speaks to her.

POLOGGY   I know I'm nothing, Fenya. In the, how to put it, the "scheme." Just a clerk, nothing more. I don't do the—you know—hard labour. Still, they were my cucumbers, I planted them myself, with my own hands, and I want restitution. That's right, laugh. If they were your cucumbers, you'd be calling the police right now.

AGRAFENA   If they were my cucumbers, Pologgy, they wouldn't have been stolen.

POLOGGY   Well I very much—

AGRAFENA   Cause I'd have smacked their heads together.

POLOGGY   Well how very civilized.

AGRAFENA   You want something done—

POLOGGY   Just smash someone's head in, hm? Well, then, we're no better than the—you know—the thief himself, if it comes to that.

AGRAFENA   So what? At least then we've still got our cucumbers.

POLOGGY   And what about the law? Justice? Etc? What good is a world without laws? I can't understand it. If they'd done it because they were hungry, well alright then, I could forgive them.

AGRAFENA   Could you?

POLOGGY   Of course I—if a man's hungry, you can forgive him anything. Almost.

    YAKOV enters.

YAKOV   Morning. What brings you here?

POLOGGY   I need to see your brother about a very important matter.

AGRAFENA   He's in a pickle.

YAKOV   Eh?

AGRAFENA   Someone stole his cukes, so he's come to lodge a formal complaint.

POLOGGY   It's a question of rights. Mine. Three men from the shop floor came and helped themselves to the fruits of my labour.

AGRAFENA   He saw them, but did he stop them?

YAKOV Take it up with my brother.

POLOGGY That's what I came to do, Yakov, only he's not up, so I can't *take* it up.

YAKOV Don't get smart. Fenya, I need a word with you.

AGRAFENA Face it, Pologgy, you were born to complain.

POLOGGY So what? If man wasn't meant to complain, why was he given a mouth?

AGRAFENA To shut it up once in a while.

POLOGGY I thought maybe you of all people would understand.

AGRAFENA You remind me of a bug I once crushed.

>   *POLOGGY steps away, waiting for ZAKHAR.*

YAKOV Listen, Fenya. Did I—yesterday—did I...

AGRAFENA Yes.

YAKOV Who?

AGRAFENA Several people.

YAKOV Goddammit. Why do I do that?

AGRAFENA Which, get drunk, or insult people?

YAKOV Both.

>   *YAKOV pours himself a glass of wine. AGRAFENA sighs.*

Don't worry. It isn't vodka. Come on now, don't you feel a little bit sorry for me?

AGRAFENA I don't understand it. When you're sober you're so sweet and nice, just an everyday nice guy. You don't act like a—well a—

YAKOV Rich son of a bitch?

>   *Sound of someone splashing in the river.*

Any sign of my wife?

AGRAFENA That's her now. Out for her swim.

YAKOV Her morning ablutions. *(beat)* You do feel sorry for me, don't you?

AGRAFENA You need help.

YAKOV What do you think that's gonna do for me?

>   *MIKHAIL enters, excited.*

MIKHAIL Zakhar? Where's Zakhar? I should have figured he wouldn't be around. Pour me a glass of milk, will you? A cold one. Morning, Yakov. Have you heard?

Those sons of bitches—excuse me—are threatening to stop work unless I fire Lyshenko.

YAKOV   So fire him. The man's a moron.

MIKHAIL   Yes, but he's our moron.

YAKOV   That's it, Mikhail, stick to principles.

MIKHAIL   It's my principles or their demands. It's a slippery slope, my friend. You think they'll stop at that? No. Today it's "fire the foreman," tomorrow it's "jump into this vat of acid."

YAKOV   "Tickets! Who needs tickets?"

MIKHAIL   I'm glad you find it so amusing. I knew I shouldn't have taken my vacation. I just felt something was brewing. It's your brother's fault, him and his heartfelt liberalism. He reads too many pamphlets, that boy, and all from the wrong people.

YAKOV   Well, the right people don't put out pamphlets—they put out newspapers instead.

MIKHAIL   *(looks at his watch)* Nearly ten. They said they'd strike at noon. Yes, a good job your brother's made of it. The men are completely confused.

YAKOV   Doesn't sound like it.

MIKHAIL   This is what comes of compassion. You've got to be firm with people. The common man doesn't want authority; he can't handle the responsibilities that come with it.

> *SINTSOV enters.*

What is it, Mr Sintsov?

SINTSOV   Some of the workers have formed a committee, sir.

MIKHAIL   A what? Committee?

SINTSOV   That's right, sir, and they're demanding to meet with the owner.

MIKHAIL   Oh, "demanding," are they? Tell them to go fuck themselves.

> *PAULINA enters.*

PAULINA   How pleasant.

MIKHAIL   Can't be helped.

PAULINA   It's not the first time I've heard you swear. What's the occasion?

MIKHAIL   These workers, these—what do they call themselves? The "proletariat." Once upon a time, Paulina, they made requests; now it's "demands."

YAKOV   I like the one about the acid baths.

MIKHAIL   Take one yourself, why don't you?

PAULINA   I don't see why you need to be so hard on them.

MIKHAIL   Incredible. You *don't* see it, do you?

SINTSOV   What should I tell the men?

MIKHAIL   To wait. Go on.

> *SINTSOV goes.*

PAULINA   Interesting face.

MIKHAIL   Hm?

PAULINA   I say he has an interesting face. How long has he been with us?

MIKHAIL   About a, I don't know, year.

PAULINA   He seems very—well-bred's not the word.

MIKHAIL   No, he's—

PAULINA   High-minded.

MIKHAIL   What?

PAULINA   I say he's—never mind. Who is he?

MIKHAIL   He makes forty rubles a month.

PAULINA   That isn't what I—

MIKHAIL   What?

PAULINA   I say I—

MIKHAIL   (*checking his watch*) Look at the time. He's a clerk. Nothing more. (*looks around; sees POLOGGY*) What do you want?

POLOGGY   Beg your pardon, Mr Skrubitov. I've come to see Mr Bardin.

MIKHAIL   What about?

POLOGGY   As regards to, uh, that is to say in connection with certain rights of mine which have been trampled upon.

MIKHAIL   (*to PAULINA*) This man's been with us barely six months, and in that time he's lodged half-a-dozen complaints, against everything, the sun, the moon, the frogs in the pond.

POLOGGY   Yes, well they, they, you know, with their throats.

MIKHAIL   "Croak"?

POLOGGY   Prec—ackly.

MIKHAIL   You're an idiot.

POLOGGY   Sir, I—

MIKHAIL   And a boor.

POLOGGY   I merely—

MIKHAIL   Get back to the office. Now!

POLOGGY   Thank you, sir.

POLOGGY bows, leaves.

PAULINA   *(teasing)* It's a wonder you don't carry a bullwhip.

MIKHAIL   It'll be my naming day soon, maybe someone will give me one as a present. *(checks his watch)* Your husband's taking his sweet time.

PAULINA   You can blame it on your brother. They're finishing up last night's chess game.

MIKHAIL   You can't be ser—with what's going on at the factory? Oh that's perfect. You know what? No good will ever come of this country. You know why? Two reasons. One: we're surrounded by anarchists. Two: nobody wants to work. Three: there's no respect for order, for law, for authority.

PAULINA   That's far more than two reasons.

MIKHAIL   Anarchists!

PAULINA   Besides, how do you expect people to have respect for "law, order, authority" when soldiers are going around shooting people in the streets?

MIKHAIL   Those weren't people, they were—

PAULINA   Not people?

MIKHAIL   Rioters, socialists—anarchists.

PAULINA   Mothers and their—

MIKHAIL   They shouldn't've—

PAULINA   Their babies.

MIKHAIL   They shouldn't've been there in the first place.

ZAKHAR and NIKOLAI enter.

ZAKHAR   Provoking my manager again, dear?

PAULINA   Well, he's—good morning. Nikolai.

NIKOLAI   Paulina.

ZAKHAR   Mikhail.

MIKHAIL   Yes, yes, good morning, nice of you to show up. Would you like to hear the news, or did you want some tea first?

ZAKHAR   Mikhail, a vacation's supposed to relax you.

MIKHAIL   It did. Now I'm back and not happy, not—

ZAKHAR   You don't—

MIKHAIL   Not at all!

ZAKHAR   You don't say.

NIKOLAI   What's on your, you know, your mind?

MIKHAIL   The men, the workers, the proletariats, they've given me an ultimatum—yes, you heard me right—fire Lyshenko or we strike. At noon.

ZAKHAR   Lyshenko?

MIKHAIL   At noon.

ZAKHAR   Well, that's not a bad—

MIKHAIL   Huh?

ZAKHAR   Not a bad idea.

MIKHAIL   I'll—Christ!

ZAKHAR   Listen. The man's a—listen. He's brutal, on the men, yes, and the women, brutal, he—

MIKHAIL   Zakhar—

ZAKHAR   He beats people, he—and the women, what he does, it's—disgusting.

MIKHAIL   Look, what exactly happened here when I was gone? Hm? Are you all the same people you were when I left, or have you been replaced by—

ZAKHAR   Mikhail—

MIKHAIL   You've been replaced by duplicates, made of jelly. Before I went on vacation, I had the factory running like a tight ship. I come back and it's full of holes, it's listing to one side. Book clubs! Lectures! Trips to the theatre! And all of it paid for by the company.

ZAKHAR   Calm, calm down.

MIKHAIL   Thanks for the advice. It's taken you one month to undo what it took me eight years to create. I had those men working like machines. Yes, and they understood that that's what—they knew what was—they liked it. They appreciated being appreciated, they—and why? Because there was one man, with a vision of how, and that man was me, with a vision of, and now you come along, with your lib, liberal uh uh views, and you cock up the gum up the—book clubs? What the fuck is—sorry, I'm—oh crap.

NIKOLAI   Relax.

MIKHAIL   Don't tell me to re—I'm under, I've been under*mined* and you tell me to—

NIKOLAI   Okay, don't relax. Burst a vessel, drop dead of an aneurysm.

MIKHAIL   Good!

ZAKHAR   This is… really, Mikhail.

PAULINA   Do you really believe what you're saying? You ought to listen to yourself.

MIKHAIL   Yes, good, then *somebody* would.

YAKOV   *(hoisting his glass)* A real pickle.

MIKHAIL   The last time the Lyshenko question came up, I told the men quite clearly, I said absolutely not, I said I'd sooner close down the factory than fire Lyshenko. They took me at my word, you better believe it. Then this morning I find out that you told one of their leaders—that instigator Grekov—that you yourself wanted to get rid of Lyshenko.

YAKOV   He did?

MIKHAIL   Be quiet!

ZAKHAR   He's a horrible man, always looking for fights. I saw someone with a black eye just the other day.

MIKHAIL   Did you investigate? *(referring to NIKOLAI)* Look, you have a lawyer on staff, why not let him look into these alleged incidents?

NIKOLAI   Agreed. It would certainly show the workers that we take their complaints seriously.

ZAKHAR   I can't agree. It's clear to me what sort of a man Lyshenko is. I want him out.

MIKHAIL   But—

ZAKHAR   You can't treat people like that and expect them to love you back.

MIKHAIL   *Love?* Oh, I see. Now, we're running some sort of, what, workers' paradise? Why don't we just go down there with some blankets and pillows, hm? "Mind your back now. Let me do that for you. Here, rest your feet a while." We're running a business, goddammit!

ZAKHAR   *(gently)* I'll ask you not to raise your voice to me.

MIKHAIL   I'm not the one raising my voice, sir. Your precious workers—or, should I say, their representatives—are threatening to shut us down. Now, what would you like to do about it?

ZAKHAR   Is Lyshenko so important to you?

NIKOLAI   It seems to me—if I may—that we're speaking here not about an individual, but a principle.

MIKHAIL   Precisely, yes—thank you. It comes down to this very simple equation: who's running this show? Us, or them?

ZAKHAR   I don't um… entirely disagree with your pos—your position…

MIKHAIL   Thin edge of the wedge, Zakhar. I even found a few pamphlets lying around. They smacked of socialism.

PAULINA   "Socialism"? Here? You must be joking.

MIKHAIL   My dear Mrs Bardin, you may find all this very cute and non-threatening. Children are cute and cuddly, too—as long as they remain children. Then they hit puberty. They stink, they get hairy and they're bursting with emotions they don't know what to do with.

ZAKHAR   Well… what do you suggest?

MIKHAIL   Close it down. Lock em out. Cut em off from their needs. When the food starts to run out, things will get back to normal.

Meanwhile, YAKOV has one more drink, then slinks off.

Oh, the men will want to hold out longer. But empty stomachs and women's tears will bring them back to their senses.

PAULINA   To their knees, you mean.

MIKHAIL   So be it.

PAULINA   They're not dogs.

MIKHAIL   Neither are they equals.

ZAKHAR   Alright, stop it. *(beat)* Do you really think it's necessary?

MIKHAIL   Give me an alternative.

ZAKHAR   Let me—

MIKHAIL   One that doesn't involve firing Lyshenko.

ZAKHAR   I was going to say, let me speak to this "committee" of theirs.

MIKHAIL   I don't think so. You'll give in to them, and then I'll look like a fool. Look, let me level with you: you're not handling this very well. You're, what's the word—fucking up.

ZAKHAR   Try to understand, would you? I got into the business through blood, not ambition. I'm still new at it. I just want to make sure we do the right thing. And please don't think it comes out of some romantic notion of the noble worker; to tell you the truth, with one or two exceptions, I don't really like their company. You know what I like? Peasants. So calm, so trusting, so undemanding. *These* people, they're, I don't know, arrogant.

MIKHAIL   They've been spoiled.

ZAKHAR   Perhaps. Things changed shortly after you left. They began to get more aggressive. And there were stories in the press about us, very unflattering stories.

MIKHAIL   Who cares about the press? *(checks his watch)* Ten-seventeen. Either we close the factory or I resign. If the former, our losses will be nonexistent; the warehouses are full and there won't be a problem shipping our goods out. If the latter, good luck to you.

> *Pause.*

ZAKHAR   Do we have to decide this very second?—You're right. Stupid of me. Nicky?

NIKOLAI   My brother's right. Civilization stands or falls on moments such as this.

ZAKHAR   Then you think we should close down? That's a shame. I'd like to think it over—be patient, Mikhail. Give me, say, ten minutes. Will that do?

MIKHAIL   It should.

ZAKHAR   Paulina?

PAULINA   *(following him out)* This is awful, just awful.

ZAKHAR   I wish I could have stayed at the winery. The peasants are much more pleasant to deal with…

> *PAULINA and ZAKHAR go.*

MIKHAIL   "The peasants are much more pleasant to deal with." Mincing little turd. He says that after what happened down south? Idiot!

NIKOLAI   Relax, Mikhail. You'll have a heart attack before you're forty.

MIKHAIL   Can't be helped. My nerves are shot. I'm drinking *milk*. I'm going to the factory.

> *Takes a revolver out of his pocket, checks the chamber.*

They despise me, thanks to that moron. What am I supposed to do? Let it go to hell? We'll lose everything we have if that place goes under. He doesn't care, he was born with a silver spoon up his ass.

NIKOLAI   Do you really think it could go under?

> *SINTSOV returns.*

SINTSOV   The committee is waiting for you.

MIKHAIL   You hear that? "Committee!" I told you to tell them to wait.

SINTSOV   I did, sir. Only there's a rumour going around, something about a lockout.

MIKHAIL   *(to NIKOLAI)* Hear that? How did they find out?

NIKOLAI   Yakov left very quietly.

MIKHAIL   That fucking drunk. *(to SINTSOV)* And you, coming up here every five minutes. Did somebody give you the day off?

SINTSOV   It's the bookkeeper, sir. He asked me to fetch you.

MIKHAIL   "Fetch me"? Do I look like a stick?—What's so goddamn funny? Did I ask you to laugh?

SINTSOV   I think I can laugh if I want to.

MIKHAIL   You're not paid to laugh. You're a *clerk*. Now wipe that shit-eating grin off your face. *(pause)* Well?

> *TATANYA enters.*

TATANYA   What's all the shouting about? Oh, it's you. I might have known. You want to be careful, Mr Director. There's a little vein that pulsates in your forehead when you're in a rage. Most unpleasant. *(to SINTSOV)* Good morning, Matvey.

SINTSOV   Tatanya—Miss Bardin. Feeling alright? Not too tired, I hope.

TATANYA   Not at all. My arms are aching after all that rowing, but otherwise I'm fine. I feel it right here. Look.

SINTSOV   You probably don't use those muscles very much.

TATANYA   Maybe you could rub them a little for me. Are you heading back to the office? I'll walk you to the gate. There's something I need to tell you.

SINTSOV   I'm all ears.

TATANYA   You talked a lot last night, and you said a lot of fascinating things. But something didn't sit right, and I figured out why—you spoke too emotionally, and your hands were flying all over the place. If you want to convince people about something, you need to be more centred in your body, and you have to learn to modulate your voice...

> *TATANYA and SINTSOV are gone.*

MIKHAIL   Can you believe that? I'm trying to put that petulant little prick in his place, and that bitch starts giving him *acting* lessons. And he, *he* flaunts it. Did you see the look he gave me as he left? Like he's *in*.

NIKOLAI   She's funny, huh? Gorgeous, dresses well, very fuckable. But then she goes chasing after a man without a penny to his name. She's a, she's a, not a gold digger, the opposite.

MIKHAIL   Her way of spreading democracy. "I feel so drawn to the common man," she says. Soon it won't be just democracy she's spreading. Then again, with that drunk Yakov for a husband, who can blame her? Serves me right for going into business with these people. Weaklings, each and every one. They have no idea how to treat these men.

NIKOLAI   It's a good thing you're in charge.

MIKHAIL   It *would* be a good thing.

NIKOLAI   Soon enough.

MIKHAIL Oh yes.

NIKOLAI Here she comes again. God*damn*.

MIKHAIL What?

NIKOLAI Just—.

TATANYA returns.

TATANYA So quiet. All shouted out this morning?

AGRAFENA returns.

AGRAFENA Mikhail? Zakhar wants to see you.

MIKHAIL About fucking time. *(He goes.)*

NIKOLAI We've been discussing democracy.

TATANYA No wonder he's—

NIKOLAI Yes?

TATANYA Cranky.

NIKOLAI Hm? No, it's not that, it's—he's, well it wouldn't interest you.

TATANYA No?

NIKOLAI What I mean is—

TATANYA Don't bother. I'm an actress, and shouldn't speak of politics.

NIKOLAI That's not what I meant.

TATANYA I'm sure. You know, he reminds me of a cop, your brother.

NIKOLAI A cop?

TATANYA Mm, one in particular. He always seemed to be on duty at this theatre I worked at. Very tall, very thin and his eyes just sort of, sort of *bugged* out, you know?

NIKOLAI Not sure I see the resemblance.

TATANYA Oh, it wasn't physical. No, you see, he, like your brother, was always in a hurry. He never walked, he *ran* and he never just *smoked* a cigarette he... sucked it.

NIKOLAI My brother doesn't smoke.

TATANYA No but he does—

NIKOLAI What?

TATANYA Nothing. Anyway, the policeman, he always, he was never sure where he was going.

NIKOLAI And this, and that reminds me, you, of my brother?

TATANYA   In a—

NIKOLAI   But how did, that's remarka—how did you know he didn't know where he was going?

TATANYA   Who?

NIKOLAI   This policeman.

TATANYA   I don't know, I just—it's a feeling. You know why? Because he was always doing everything so, so quickly and—when a person is, well calm, he you know, you have a pur, a purpose, a goal which, and this cop, he didn't, he just, he wanted it all, you know and he took everything with the wanting of it all in his mind, his heart, if he had a heart, which I doubt. It was like there was something in the back of his, or the front of his, no the back, which was uh egg, egging him on, you know?

NIKOLAI   No.

TATANYA   His his his need to be, uh, *free, of*, of everything he, ooh, damn I can almost, it's almost—you know, when you have a thought, you know what you want to say and you don't, you can't ex*press* it.

NIKOLAI   Yes.

TATANYA   You do?

NIKOLAI   Yes, because I'm having a thought I can't express.

TATANYA   Right now?

NIKOLAI   This very second.

AGRAFENA   I'll be down by the river—if you need me. (*She goes.*)

TATANYA   Tell me.

NIKOLAI   Couldn't possibly. Let's get back to the policeman.

TATANYA   There's not much left. He was run over by a horse and carriage. That came out funny. He—well.

> *PAULINA enters.*

PAULINA   I don't know what's going on around here today. No one's sleeping, or, I mean eating, everyone's in a bad mood, mainly from lack of, I think, sleep, and Nadya, you won't believe it, she went out this morning to pick, guess, mushrooms.

TATANYA   Heavens.

PAULINA   Yes, her and Cleo. And I said to her, explicitly, no mushroom picking, and it's just so, everything's so—

TATANYA   You eat too much.

PAULINA   I what?

TATANYA   You eat. Too much.

PAULINA   Why do you talk to people like that?

TATANYA   Like what?

PAULINA   In that, with that fash—that tone.

TATANYA   My tone is perfectly, it's calm.

PAULINA   Yes, exactly, it isn't normal. It's, oh it's very easy, isn't it, to be "calm" when a thousand people aren't depending on you for their, their *liveli*hood.

TATANYA   Then don't.

PAULINA   Don't—?

TATANYA   Let them be free, *set* them free—

PAULINA   Well that's—

TATANYA   Give them the factory.

PAULINA   The—?

TATANYA   Yes.

PAULINA   Why not give them the land while we're at it?

TATANYA   Yes. Good, now you're getting it. Then you'll be at peace. You'll be free of this burden and in a hundred years or so, you'll see—well, you won't see, but your grandchildren will—a new way of, a higher order of being will have evolved.

NIKOLAI   *(applauding)* Oh very good. Which play is that from?

PAULINA   You shouldn't say things like that, Tanya. Zakhar's already so up—he's upset, this whole thing with the lock-up.

NIKOLAI   Lock out.

PAULINA   It's so maddening, the workers have gone, they've gone mad. And think how hard it will be, and the children, they all have children.

TATANYA   Then why let it happen?

PAULINA   Tanya, really, you're out of your league.

TATANYA   Well.

PAULINA   Your depth. If we don't lock them up—out—they'll strike, and that will be a thousand times worse.

TATANYA   How?

PAULINA   Tanya, Tanya, we can't give in to their demands, which in fact aren't demands.

TATANYA   They're not?

PAULINA   No, they're just ideas being bandied about by the socialists, who are fomenting rev—revolution among the, you know, the workers, filling their ideas with—heads with ideas they don't understand and making them go around shouting out slogans and—things like that which, and I don't even pretend to understand it, I'm just, it's just, if you think about it, take a look around, not just here, but all over the world where, yes, there's socialism, but at least it's, it's part of the social um thingy fabric and it's carried out out in the open. But here, here, it's all done in secret, they whisper in the corners, and they don't understand, not a single one of them, that there's no place for socialism in a monarchy.

TATANYA   But that's—

PAULINA   What we need is a really good constitution. Don't you agree, Niki?

NIKOLAI   *(laughs)* Here's the way I see it. I see it like this. Socialism is very dangerous. No question. And it's bound to find adherents here in, in a country which, where there's no, well let's say *foundation*. We've never built on anything in this country—we build, yes, but only to destroy. We're a country of all-or-nothings. That's our basic, I would say, flaw.

PAULINA   Yes, exactly, thank you. Oh, well put. We're extremists.

TATANYA   Especially you and your husband.

PAULINA   What!

TATANYA   And Mr Public Prosecutor here.

NIKOLAI   Thanks for the promotion.

TATANYA   The—?

NIKOLAI   I'm only Mr Assistant Public Prosecutor.

PAULINA   I really would like to know where you get, where you, what gives you the right to say what you—

TATANYA   Oh relax darling. You've got to either learn to play your part well or give it up altogether.

PAULINA   My *part?*

TATANYA   Your part, everybody's part. You know what it seems to me? It seems to me that life around here is like amateur theatre. The roles have been badly cast, no one has any real talent, everyone overacts, chews up the scenery, what little there is, and the play is impossible to follow.

NIKOLAI   That's very good. And everyone's bored by the whole thing.

TATANYA   And we have only ourselves to blame.

   MIKHAIL enters.

MIKHAIL   Nikolai. A word. *(takes him aside)* It's done, but we need to—

NIKOLAI   Done?

MIKHAIL   We've closed it down. Can you send a note to the Vice-Governor, he's a friend of mine, ask him to send soldiers.

NIKOLAI   He's my friend, too.

MIKHAIL   Huh? Oh, alright. Now look, I'm going to see these little pricks about their "demands." You send that note, only don't let anybody else know, alright?

NIKOLAI   You love this, don't you?

MIKHAIL   Which?

NIKOLAI   *This.*

MIKHAIL   You might be right.

MIKHAIL goes.

PAULINA   So it's done.

NIKOLAI   Seems that way, doesn't it?

PAULINA   He's got a lot of spirit, your brother.

NIKOLAI   It's not spirit—it's raw nerves. *(He goes.)*

NADYA runs in.

NADYA   The most incredible thing just happened, Auntie. The two of us were out for a walk when— *(looking off)* —Grekov, don't go! Cleo, don't let him get away! Aunt Paulina, we were just coming out of the forest when we stumbled across three workers.

PAULINA   You see, Nadya? You see? I *told* you not to go mushroom picking and you—

NADYA   Wait, it's—

PAULINA   Were they drunk? Did they touch you?

CLEOPATRA enters, followed by GREKOV.

CLEOPATRA   *(entering)* Disgusting, the lot of them.

NADYA   They weren't, though! Not at all. No, no, you're taking it all wrong. They said, listen, they started bowing and smiling and, oh, they were so courteous, they said, "Good morning, ladies," and all that, and you know, not even the men on this side of the river say that every day.

CLEOPATRA   I'm going to speak to my husband, you may depend upon it, to have them—

NADYA   No, Cleo.

CLEOPATRA   To have them fired, oh yes.

GREKOV (*smiling*) May I be so bold as to—why?

CLEOPATRA It isn't your place to speak.

GREKOV Not even to ask a question?

PAULINA Who exactly is this?

NADYA This is Grekov, the one who saved us.

CLEOPATRA What happened is—

NADYA Let me tell the story. They, we were coming out of the woods, when—

CLEOPATRA You said that already.

NADYA They came up to us, they said, "How about joining us for a song?"

PAULINA They didn't!

NADYA Oh, they didn't mean anything by it, Auntie. Nothing bad, anyway. They said, "We heard you can sing," they weren't scary at all, they even said, "It's true, we're drunk, but we're nice drunks, not like the foreman." And it's true—they're always so sad, so sullen when they're sober.

CLEOPATRA Luckily, this young man came along and—

NADYA I'm telling it! Cleo started yelling at them—

CLEOPATRA I was hardly yelling.

NADYA Up*braiding*, then. And you didn't need to, you didn't. And then one of them, I forget his—he's tall and thin and—

CLEOPATRA Yes, *him.*

NADYA —And he took her hand and said, in such a sweet voice, a sad voice, he said, "You're such a pretty lady, so kind, it gives us pleasure just to look at you. Why then do you scold us? Have we done anything to upset you?" It was so beautiful, and he spoke from the heart.

CLEOPATRA Yes, yes, but tell them about the other one.

NADYA I was just about to, oh!

CLEOPATRA He wasn't so sweet.

NADYA No, he wasn't, he was a brute, and he said, "Don't bother with them, they're a bunch of pigs!" And then he spit on the ground, and he was talking about us—me and Cleo—us, pigs! Ha ha ha!

TATANYA (*laughing*) And this is amusing to you?

NADYA Well I—ha ha ha!

TATANYA You enjoyed being called a pig, I see.

PAULINA You see? You see? This is what happens when you run into the woods.

GREKOV   If you'll excuse me.

NADYA   What? No! No, please don't go. Have some tea. Please. Please!

> *Pause. CLEO shrugs. TATANYA hums. PAULINA looks away.*

GREKOV   Maybe not.

NADYA   Oh don't be shy. Everyone here's really very nice.

PAULINA   Nadya!

NADYA   But he can't go, I haven't even finished telling the story.

CLEOPATRA   Then I will.

NADYA   But—

CLEOPATRA   *En bref*: this young man happened along just then and talked his friends into leaving us alone. Then he walked us home. The end.

NADYA   Oh but that's so boring, putting it that way! *(to Grekov)* Sit down, sit down.—Auntie, ask him to join us. Why's everyone wearing their masks of disapproval?

PAULINA   *(not getting up)* Young man, I'm very grateful to you.

GREKOV   Not at all, Miss. Least I could do.

PAULINA   Yes, well, it was good of you to make sure that nothing untoward happened.

NADYA   Auntie!

GREKOV   Nothing untoward was *going to* happen.

NADYA   Exactly! Honestly, why do you have to insinuate such—

PAULINA   Don't take that tone with me, young lady.

NADYA   I'm not taking any tone, I'm just saying what happened, and it's not exactly like Cleo said it—it was different. He came along, and his friends were really happy to see him. All he said to them was, "Leave these ladies alone," and they were all so happy to see him. "Grekov! Grekov's here!" They all shouted. "Where have you been all night," they said.

GREKOV   Now now, you're turning me into some kind of hero.

NADYA   Oh, not me—them. They look up to you, Grekov, and it's obvious why.

PAULINA   That's quite enough, Nadya. If only you could hear yourself, you'd know how ridiculous you sounded.

NADYA   If I'm so ridiculous, why are you all sitting there looking at me like a bunch of owls? Laugh if I'm so funny.

CLEOPATRA   *He is.*

NADYA   Are you?

GREKOV   Not at all.

CLEOPATRA   Then why are you smirking?

PAULINA   Never mind. Young man, you did a valuable service. Take this and run along.

GREKOV   That isn't necessary.

NADYA   Aunt Paulina!

PAULINA   What's the matter with you? There are ten rubles in my hand.

GREKOV   I, too, can count.

>   *Silence.*

PAULINA   Well—aren't you going to—I mean—

CLEOPATRA   Just who in hell do you think you are, anyway?

GREKOV   Just a worker. I'm a fitter. That's what I do, all day long. I fit. What do you do?

CLEOPATRA   Insolent little—

PAULINA   Why won't you take this money?

GREKOV   Because I don't want it.

CLEOPATRA   No, no, it's something else he wants.

GREKOV   I want nothing.

CLEOPATRA   Little Nadya.

NADYA   How can you say that?

PAULINA   Cleo, please—

GREKOV   How old are you, Miss?

CLEOPATRA   I beg your pardon? How old am I? Is that what you asked me?

GREKOV   Yes.

CLEOPATRA   A lady never reveals her age.

GREKOV   Yes, but you're no lady.

CLEOPATRA   What?

NADYA   Grekov, wait—don't be angry—she didn't mean it, don't be upset.

CLEOPATRA   Who do you think you are?

GREKOV   Never mind, never mind. You can't help it.

NADYA   It's the heat. It's making everyone so cranky. Maybe I told it all wrong.

GREKOV Doesn't matter how you tell it—she wouldn't have got it anyway. None of them would have.

NADYA No, wait, listen to me…

NADYA and GREKOV go.

CLEOPATRA How dare that little lackey—how dare he—speak to me that way!

TATANYA You shouldn't have said what you said.

CLEOPATRA He's a dog.

TATANYA *(to PAULINA)* And you, offering him a tip.

CLEOPATRA I'm going to speak to my husband about him, you can count on that.

PAULINA And Nadya, walking off with him. What am I going to do with her?

CLEOPATRA I want him thrown out!

TATANYA The factory's closed.

CLEOPATRA We'll open it for five minutes, just long enough to have him thrown out.

PAULINA Would someone go and get Nadya? Tanya, there's a dear.

TATANYA goes.

CLEOPATRA "You're no lady." And those drunks, whistling at us. These socialists of yours are getting bolder by the hour.

PAULINA What makes you say they're socialists?

CLEOPATRA All the best workers are socialists. And you give them book clubs! They whistled at me, too. On Thursday I had to go into town, and they whistled. At me.

PAULINA Insulting. They might have frightened the horses.

CLEOPATRA Zazhar's to blame for it all—yes, it's true. He doesn't put enough space between him and the men—acts like he's their friend or something.

PAULINA Well he's—

CLEOPATRA That's what Mikhail says, anyway.

PAULINA He has a big heart, that's all. He wants to be good and kind, to everyone, even the commoners. It's good for them, it's good for us.

CLEOPATRA And what do you think?

PAULINA Well, when it comes to the peasants, yes, it's a good idea. But they're a different breed: they take the leases, pay the rent, keep to themselves. But these people, I can't—

NADYA and TATANYA return.

Nadya! What is *wrong* with you? I'm sorry to be so—but that was completely improper, completely—

NADYA   Who's improper? You! You sat there and totally missed the—all of you did, just sat there like lumps. And offering him *money*. How insulting, how stupid.

PAULINA   Stupid!

NADYA   *(to CLEO)* And why did you have to say that thing about—

CLEOPATRA   Please, you're giving me a headache.

NADYA   —About him liking me? That was a terrible thing to say, you should be ashamed, you hear, ashamed!

PAULINA   Nadya—

NADYA   I'm not finished. You, Aunt Paulina, you travel all over the world, you make impassioned speeches about the rights of the worker, and then when you've got one in your own backyard, you don't even invite him to sit down for tea!

PAULINA   I won't hear another word out of you! Just how much insolence do you think one person can take?

NADYA   And what about you, Cleopatra? Oh yes, really living up to your name now, aren't you?

CLEOPATRA   I've had enough.

NADYA   All the way back you were sweet talking him, but the second we showed up—

CLEOPATRA   And what did you expect me to do? Fall down on the ground and kiss his filthy feet? Just who do you think you are to speak to me, to speak to any of us, this way? I suppose this is your idea of *democracy*, Paulina—letting anyone say anything, no matter how rude or ill-informed. Or maybe it's—no, it isn't democracy, it's worse, it's *humanism*. Do you know what humanism is? It's the well-off beating each other up over who better understands the peasants they love to trample. You're all a bunch of fools. There's only one man among us who has the answer to all this, and that's my husband. Just you wait, when Mikhail comes back, it's you who'll have a lot to answer for.

PAULINA   Please, Cleo, don't listen to her. It's the heat, it's affecting her—

NADYA   You're the ones suffering from the heat.

CLEOPATRA   It *isn't* the heat, and it isn't Nadya, not *only* Nadya—it's the bunch of you, you're all to blame for this mess!

CLEOPATRA goes.

PAULINA   I don't know what to say to you any more. When your mother called me to her deathbed, entrusted me with your upbringing—

NADYA   Don't you speak to me about my mother.

PAULINA   Nadya, what is *wrong* with you?

NADYA   You never say the right things about my mother! You don't know what she wanted.

PAULINA   She was my *sister*, my dear, so I think if anyone knew her—

NADYA   You don't know anything!

PAULINA   Nadya!

NADYA   You're rich, you've never had to understand a thing, and my mother was poor and you hated her for it. You don't understand anyone, not even Aunt Tanya.

PAULINA   I'll ask you to leave. Now!

NADYA   *(going)* Good! I can't stand being here one more second, I can't stand always being right and you wrong!

PAULINA   This is your doing.

TATANYA   Oh really.

PAULINA   Yes, and forgive me for saying so. It's from all these boat rides and so on, and the way you insist on talking to her as though she were an adult.

TATANYA   Well she's—

PAULINA   She's a child.

TATANYA   Why don't you have a drink? It'll calm your nerves. Maybe Nadya's just a little bit right, hm? I mean about the way you dealt with our hero, not letting him sit, did you think you'd have to fumigate the chair after he sat on it?

PAULINA   Don't be insulting. I won't stand for it, to be accused of per—of looking down on the workers, no.

TATANYA   Fine. And by the way I don't take her anywhere.

PAULINA   What?

TATANYA   Nadya. Boat rides, you said. Well, it isn't true, she goes where she wants to go and there's no stopping her.

PAULINA   As if a girl her age could go off and do these things without being told.

TATANYA   Now look—

YAKOV returns.

YAKOV   The workers are revolting.

PAULINA   What?

YAKOV   I said the workers are revolting. Ba-doom-*sha*.

PAULINA   Would you stop it, Yakov?

YAKOV   They're gonna set the place on fire, and throw us all into the flames, like rabbits.

TATANYA   Have you been drinking already?

YAKOV   I haven't stopped. You know who—whom?—I just saw? Cleopatra. Fucking cunt.

PAULINA   For God's sake.

YAKOV   Well that's what she is. The look she gave me. Tell me something, is there anyone around here she *hasn't f*ucked?

TATANYA   You.

YAKOV   Exactly. Least not that I remember.

TATANYA   Oh, you'd remember.

YAKOV   Yer right, cause I'd be dead. She'd swallow me up and spit me out into a thousand pieces.

PAULINA   *(walking about)* I'd like to know what's going on around here. Everything's falling apart, it's incredible, incredible, I just don't understand…

YAKOV   Not that I'd mind.

TATANYA   Mind what?

YAKOV   Being spit into a thousand pieces.

TATANYA   Please shut up. Your brother's coming.

YAKOV   That's nice. You can't stand me, can you? Don't answer. It's fine. You think I don't get it? I wouldn't love me either. But, if it's all the same, I'm still deeply in love with you. Yes I am. And that's why I drink. To forget, my love, my duck, my ducky wucky, that—

TATANYA   Be quiet. You stink. Christ, you stink.

ZAKHAR   *(entering)* Has the lockout been announced?

TATANYA   *(on her way out)* I wouldn't know. I'm going for a swim.

    TATANYA exits.

YAKOV   To answer your question, Zee, nothing's been announced—but the workers know anyway.

ZAKHAR   How?

YAKOV   I told them.

PAULINA   You did? Why?

YAKOV   Why not? They like to know things, and I like to tell em. They like me, see, because I'm the boss's brother and a stinking drunk. Yes, they take one look at me and suddenly all that talk about the equality of men makes a lot of sense.

ZAKHAR   Yakov, I—look, Yakov, I've got nothing against you hanging around the shop floor, but you can't say the things you've been saying about how we manage things.

YAKOV   Bullshit, who says I do?

ZAKHAR   Mikhail.

YAKOV   He's a liar. I've never said a thing about the management. Or the mismanagement.

ZAKHAR   He also says that you've brought in vodka on occasion.

YAKOV   More lies. I do not bring in vodka—I send for it, and not on occasion but always.

ZAKHAR   Think about what you're doing—you're the owner's brother and—

YAKOV   That's not my only fault.

ZAKHAR   You should start—. I see. Fault. Well. I won't say another word, then. No. It's fine. Must be something in the air today.

PAULINA   Yes, you should have heard Nadya just now.

POLOGGY   *(running in)* Excuse me, sorry to—but someone's just shot Mikhail— Mr Skrubitov.

ZAKHAR   What?

PAULINA   *Shot?*

POLOGGY   Yes, killed him. The workers surrounded him and Mikhail he kicked one of them and then someone, I don't know who, stepped forward, put a gun to his stomach and fired.

PAULINA   Killed?

POLOGGY   He fell down in a heap.

ZAKHAR   Did you see for yourself that he was dead?

POLOGGY   Well, not—no.

ZAKHAR   Did someone send for a doctor?

POLOGGY   I don't—

ZAKHAR   Yakov! Get down there.

YAKOV   Down where?

ZAKHAR   For Christ's sake.

YAKOV   But...

ZAKHAR   Never mind, never mind, here they are.

    *MIKHAIL is led in by NIKOLAI and the workers YAGUDIN and
    LEVSHIN. A POLICEMAN follows.*

MIKHAIL   Goddamit, let me go, leave me alone.

NIKOLAI   Did you see who it was?

MIKHAIL   What? I can't, I don't know, where am I?

NIKOLAI   Who was it?

MIKHAIL   You're hurting me. Let me go. He had red hair, I think. I need to sit, to
lie, to—

NIKOLAI   Red hair?

MIKHAIL   Yes. Let me sit.

NIKOLAI   *(to the POLICEMAN)* You hear? Red hair.

POLICEMAN   Yes, sir.

MIKHAIL   What does it matter? Christ, I'm dying. Oh fuck, *fuck!*

LEVSHIN   We shouldn't bother him right now, sir.

NIKOLAI   Shut your mouth, Levshin! Where's the doctor? We sent for a doctor—
well what are you looking at? Is the doctor coming or not?

MIKHAIL   Quiet... quiet... it hurts.

LEVSHIN   Yes, yes, just rest now, sir. Keep your strength. The doctor's coming,
you'll be fine.

NIKOLAI   Sergeant, send everyone away who has no business here.

POLICEMAN   You heard the man. Clear out. Come on, come on, you're taking up
precious oxygen...

YAGUDIN   Money—always money.

POLICEMAN   I'll begin rounding up the redheads, sir.

NIKOLAI   Yes, yes good.

    POLICEMAN goes.

ZAKHAR   Where's the doctor?

NIKOLAI   Misha?... Misha! Misha, hold on. Misha, the doctor's coming...

ZAKHAR   He's fainted is all. From loss of blood.

NIKOLAI   No.

ZAKHAR   Check his pulse, have you checked his pulse?

NIKOLAI   It's your fault.

ZAKHAR   Me?

PAULINA   That's a ridiculous thing to say.

NIKOLAI   You! You!

PAULINA   Ridiculous and cruel.

NIKOLAI   You! You! You!

CLEOPATRA returns.

CLEOPATRA   Where is he? Misha? Misha! Answer me. Open your eyes, darling. Why won't he answer? Mikhail? Mikhail!

LEVSHIN   He took out his pistol, miss. He turned it on them, and they used it against him.

NIKOLAI   Shut your filth! Get the fuck out of here!

LEVSHIN   You shouldn't talk to me that way, sir.

CLEOPATRA   Why? Why?

PAULINA   *(to CLEOPATRA)* Darling…

CLEOPATRA   Don't touch me! It's because of you this happened.

ZAKHAR   You can't say that, why do you say that?

CLEOPATRA   You let them get away with things. You let them get bolder, and bolder. They never would have dared even talk back before, but now, because of you, they did this, this. There's blood on your hands, your hands are dripping with blood, the blood of my husband.

ZAKHAR   Please, please. Can't you see she's upset?

CLEOPATRA   Upset? Crying? Good! Have a good long cry, cry all his blood out your eyes you murderers!

NIKOLAI   Cleo—

CLEOPATRA   Murderers! Murderers!

ACT 2

A large room in the Bardin house. Through the glass windows can be seen the verandah, where soldiers guard a group of workers. It's pouring rain.

YAGUDIN, LEVSHIN and RIBITSOV meet in private.

LEVSHIN   It's for the good of the cause, Pavel.

RIBITSOV   Right.

LEVSHIN   For the good of humanity, for all of us, our souls.

RIBITSOV   Okay.

LEVSHIN   The people are lifting themselves up, with their minds, they're listening and reading and talking and thinking.

YAGUDIN   It's true, Pavel.

RIBITSOV   Fine, sure, whatever, but what's with all the, you know, talk. There isn't a lot of time. They've rounded everybody up. Everyone with red hair, and everyone suspected of once having had red hair. I already said I'd do it.

LEVSHIN   It's not a game. If you're going to do it, you've got to understand *why*. You're still a young man, and they're going to put you away for a long time for this.

RIBITSOV   Don't worry about it, I'm planning on escaping.

YAGUDIN   Well, you never know. You're too young for the mines.

LEVSHIN   We can't count on that. The point is, are you ready to face the worst?

RIBITSOV   I said I was.

YAGUDIN   You don't have to decide just like that. It's an important decision, it's going to affect your whole life. Think it over at least.

RIBITSOV   Think it over, there's nothing to think. The man's dead and somebody's got to pay the price.

LEVSHIN   You're right, you're right, and if nobody—listen—confesses, then the rest of us will be under suspicion. And you know what'll happen then? They'll pick anyone, not anyone but someone who's really needed for the cause.

RIBITSOV   Sure, I get it. You don't see me sweating, do you? You made a deal with Zakhar: you supply the killer, he leaves the factory open. Just cause I'm young, don't mean I'm stupid. We're like some chain or something, we're all links in it.

LEVSHIN   Yes, yes, a chain.

YAGUDIN   Your hands. Come, both of you. Is it decided?

RIBITSOV   It is for me. No one's depending on me for food or a clean bed, so it makes sense that I'm the one to go. It's too bad anyone has to take the fall over that piece of shit.

LEVSHIN   That's why he died the way he did. Good people die good deaths.

RIBITSOV   Right. Anything else?

YAGUDIN   That's it, Pavel. When will you tell them?

RIBITSOV   Tonight's as good a time as any.

LEVSHIN   So soon?

RIBITSOV   Why wait?

LEVSHIN   It's up to you, of course. God be with you.

YAGUDIN   Be strong, brother.

> *RIBITSOV goes.*

LEVSHIN   He's a good kid. There's plenty more where he came from, too.

YAGUDIN   No different from raising crops. Plenty of sunshine, fresh water.

LEVSHIN   We may get out of this mess yet.

YAGUDIN   It's a heavy price.

LEVSHIN   No question. At least he'll have the consolation of knowing it was for his comrades.

YAGUDIN   Yes. And Yakov—he's agreed to hide the gun?

LEVSHIN   Yes. That fool Akimov. What made him go and pull the trigger? What does killing get you? Shoot one dog and the boss buys another.—Goddamn it!

YAGUDIN   What?

LEVSHIN   This fucking life.

YAGUDIN   Who's coming?

LEVSHIN   Don't worry. Just the maid.

AGRAFENA   *(entering)* Just the maid who let you in. *(beat)* Vodka? The troops have arrived. They're bringing the men across now.

LEVSHIN   We'll slip out in a minute.

> *Enter TATANYA and NADYA.*

TATANYA   Oh.

LEVSHIN   Evening. We were told to report to the house.

NADYA   It's alright, Levshin. You're welcome here. You too, Yagudin.

TATANYA   Yes. Have your drink.

NADYA   It's been so quiet, I can't get used to it. Why is it, Aunt Tatanya, that people speak in whispers when there's a dead body in the house?

TATANYA   I don't know.

LEVSHIN   Collective guilt. If you don't mind my saying.

TATANYA   How's that?

LEVSHIN   On account of we all feel responsible for the man's death.

TATANYA   Is that right?

NADYA   But not everyone dies the way—well, that way.

LEVSHIN   No. Not everyone dies by the bullet, but everyone dies because of actions taken by others. And we don't even know we've done it, not until the man's lying dead in front of you. That's when you begin to sense your own part in it. You feel shame, fear, because, after all, it's yourself you're looking at.

NADYA   That's such an awful thought.

LEVSHIN   Well, today it's awful; tomorrow it's forgotten. And we all start pushing each other around again.

TATANYA   How should we change then, hm?

LEVSHIN   By getting rid of money.

TATANYA   *(laughs)* Really.

LEVSHIN   Bury it. Then there won't be any reason to push each other around.

TATANYA   So simple.

LEVSHIN   It's a start.

> *Commotion outside as the workers are led to the verandah by the soldiers.*

NADYA   What's this?

> *NADYA and TATANYA go.*

YAGUDIN   Really get under your skin, don't they?

LEVSHIN   The young one's not so bad.

YAGUDIN   No? Is that why you were trying to teach her things?

AGRAFENA   Why not? She could stand to hear the truth; they all could.

YAGUDIN   Keep dreaming. Come on, Levshin. We'd better talk to Sintsov.

LEVSHIN   Yuh. *(to AGRAFENA)* Thanks for the tea.

> *YAGUDIN and LEVSHIN head out as BOBOYEDOV and NIKOLAI enter.*

BOBOYEDOV   Yes this will do fine for the interrogations. Excellent, and you, sir, you'll be acting in your official capacity as—

NIKOLAI   Of course.

BOBOYEDOV   —As assistant prosecutor?

NIKOLAI   That's right, Captain Boboyedov. Fenya, call in the corporal.

> *AGRAFENA goes.*

BOBOYEDOV   We'll bring them in *en masse*, the chief suspects anyway, and in the middle we'll put what's his name, their leader, that clerk.

NIKOLAI   Sintsov.

BOBOYEDOV   That's the one. Nice man, the owner. Charming. Too charming— not cut out for this sort of work, know what I mean?

NIKOLAI   I agree.

BOBOYEDOV   His sister-in-law.

NIKOLAI   Eh?

BOBOYEDOV   I say his sis—his sister-in-law, she's something else.

NIKOLAI   An actress.

BOBOYEDOV   Yes. Saw her once in the north, oh she was good, played a, played a, well a whore. She was good.

> *KLATCH has entered.*

Klatch.

KLATCH   Everyone's been searched, sir.

BOBOYEDOV   And?

KLATCH   Nothing. The murder weapon's been—

BOBOYEDOV   Mm hm.

KLATCH   Hidden. Seems to me the police inspector was a bit too uh casual in his approach.

BOBOYEDOV   Too quick, you mean, too quick.

KLATCH   Yes, I—

BOBOYEDOV   They're always too damned quick. And you searched the premises? The workers' barracks and so on?

KLATCH   We did, sir. Found a few interesting items behind the religious paintings in Levshin's room, sir.

BOBOYEDOV   Good, take them to my room.

KLATCH   Very good, sir.

BOBOYEDOV   Oh, and Klatch.

KLATCH   Sir.

BOBOYEDOV   Well done.

KLATCH   Thank you, sir.

> *KLATCH goes.*

BOBOYEDOV   Good for the morale, give him a boost, and why not, he deserves it, the man has a nose for, an eye for, he finds things. He's good, he's sharp. Looks like a dolt, no question, but he gets in there, like a wolfhound.

NIKOLAI   Yes.

BOBOYEDOV   Bloodhound.

NIKOLAI   Good, even better. Now here's the thing, there's a—Captain?

BOBOYEDOV   All yours.

NIKOLAI   There's another clerk who, well I think you ought to talk to.

BOBOYEDOV   Don't you worry about that, we'll talk to the bunch of them, the clerks, the, not the clerks, the whole cabal.

NIKOLAI   What I mean is—there's one named Pologgy, he's—not that he's under—

BOBOYEDOV   Uh huh.

NIKOLAI   Under suspicion, but—

BOBOYEDOV   Okay, and his name's—

NIKOLAI   Yes, Pologgy, but I think he can be of of of *use.*

BOBOYEDOV   Good. In the sense that—

NIKOLAI   He has information, I think.

BOBOYEDOV   Excellent, yes, I'll speak with him.

NIKOLAI   We already did.

BOBOYEDOV   *(beat)* Good.

> *CLEOPATRA enters.*

CLEOPATRA   Another glass of tea? Captain?

BOBOYEDOV   Hm? Oh, Miss—yes, how lovely, how. Yes. It's—I have to tell you, it's beautiful around here, the country. And do you know something? Coincidentally, I happen to know Miss Lugovya.

CLEOPATRA   Do you?

BOBOYEDOV   Well, "happen to know" isn't quite—I saw her perform once.

CLEOPATRA   She's always performing.

BOBOYEDOV   She must be good.

CLEOPATRA   Mm. Tell me, did you find anything?

BOBOYEDOV   Any—

CLEOPATRA   During the searches?

BOBOYEDOV   Ah, yes. Don't you worry. We'll find it all. No matter the—yes, whatever's there, we'll—yes. And if there's nothing to find, we'll find that, too.

CLEOPATRA   My husband never took it seriously, you know.

BOBOYEDOV   "It."

CLEOPATRA   These pamphlets. He said "Flyers don't make a revolution."

BOBOYEDOV   Mm. Would that it were—

CLEOPATRA   Yes.

BOBOYEDOV   True.

CLEOPATRA   He said, "Broadsides are secret orders issued to idiots by fools."

BOBOYEDOV   Yes, good, funny. But wrong.

CLEOPATRA   It seems that way, because they've gone from words to action.

BOBOYEDOV   And will be punished severely for it, have no fear on that that that score.

CLEOPATRA   I'm glad to hear it. It was a great relief to see you arrive.

BOBOYEDOV   Was it?

CLEOPATRA   Very.

BOBOYEDOV   Part of our job of course is to reassure people.

CLEOPATRA   It's so nice to meet someone so at ease with himself.

BOBOYEDOV   Well—

CLEOPATRA   With his work. It's a rare thing.

BOBOYEDOV   We all feel the same way, the men in the Special Unit.

CLEOPATRA   How lovely.

BOBOYEDOV   May I ask a question that may seem slightly inappropriate?

CLEOPATRA   Please.

BOBOYEDOV   Do you happen to know where Miss Lugovya is performing this season?

CLEOPATRA   No, I—sorry. No.

CLEOPATRA and BOBOYEDOV exit. TATANYA and NADYA enter from the verandah.

NADYA   Did you see the way Grekov looked at us?

TATANYA   Yes.

NADYA   I feel so horrible. Nikolai! Why are these men being held?

NIKOLAI   They are persons of interest in the investigation into the—

NADYA   All of them?

NIKOLAI   —the murder of my brother yesterday morning.

NADYA   But that's—

NIKOLAI   And I would ask you not to consort with them during the investi—

NADYA   Consort!

NIKOLAI   Yes.

NADYA   Don't worry!

TATANYA   What about Sintsov? Has he been arrested as well?

NIKOLAI   Of course.

NADYA   Seventeen people, rounded up, and for what?

NIKOLAI   Young lady—

NADYA   Their wives are standing by the gate, and their children, too, and they're all crying, wanting to see their fathers, and the soldiers keep poking them back and laughing. Can't you at least tell them to treat those people with a little dignity?

NIKOLAI   That's not my department. Corporal Klatch is in charge of crowd control, go squawk at him if you have to.

NADYA   I will!

NADYA goes.

TATANYA   Now look, Czar Nikolai—

NIKOLAI   That isn't the least bit funny.

TATANYA   It's what my husband calls you.

NIKOLAI   That doesn't make it any funnier.

TATANYA   You need to relax.

NIKOLAI   My brother was killed yesterday.

TATANYA   What's it to you?

NIKOLAI   I *beg* your—

TATANYA   Don't pretend to care about your brother's death. You've never felt sorry for another human being a day in your life. You know how I know?

Because I'm the same way. I recognize it in you. Your brother died suddenly, practically in your arms, and all you could think about was rounding up the suspects. You didn't feel genuinely, humanly sorry for him for one second. It isn't *in* you.

NIKOLAI   Interesting. *(beat)* What do you want?

TATANYA   Want?

NIKOLAI   From me. What do you want?

TATANYA   Why do I have to want something? I'm just talking to you. I'm making an observation, that you and I are the same sort of, I don't know, creature. Yes, creature, cold blooded monsters of the deep—all we both want is a really good part to play. We both have hard hearts, otherwise we couldn't pretend to be people we're not. Tell me something, do you really want to be a prosecutor? Is that the role you want to play?

NIKOLAI   Stop this, whatever it is you think you're doing.

> *Pause.*

TATANYA   *(laughing)* I'm not very good at this. You're right, I did want something—to make you feel better, to be charming and pleasant, but you know, as soon as I saw your face I decided to insult you. You make me want to do that, you make me want to hurt you, always, no matter what you're doing, sitting standing talking saying nothing at all, there's something about the way you look or, no, the way you, what you pro*ject,* that makes me want to scratch your fucking eyes out, it's, you know what it is? You *judge* people, that's it, silently, staringly, you judge, you judge, because you think you're better than the rest.

NIKOLAI   And you say we're the same?

TATANYA   The very. And now I'm going to ask you something.

NIKOLAI   Yes, and I know what it is you want to ask me.

TATANYA   Well?

NIKOLAI   You want me to spare Sintsov.

TATANYA   But you're not going to, are you?

NIKOLAI   Oh no, he's far too involved in this.

TATANYA   You like this, don't you?

NIKOLAI   I'm not one to hide.

TATANYA   No. Nor am I. So you see we really are alike. Mean and petty, cruel, vindictive. Is Sintsov under your control, your jurisdiction?

NIKOLAI   Completely.

TATANYA   And there's nothing I can say or do to get you to change—

NIKOLAI   Nothing.

TATANYA   To change your mind.

NIKOLAI   You've already said a number of things.

TATANYA   But I haven't done anything.

NIKOLAI   What is it you would do? Hm? What would you be willing to do?

TATANYA   I don't like your tone.

NIKOLAI   That's a shame. You're a beautiful woman, you could have anything you want, lead any sort of life you—yes, if only you—well but you have your let's say your eccentricities. You only get away with them because you're beautiful.

TATANYA   Is that your judgment?

NIKOLAI   It's my observation, of you, your character.

TATANYA   And Sintsov.

NIKOLAI   Is fucked. He goes to jail. Tonight, because you—no, not you, because the others—never mind. He's done, unless you were willing.

TATANYA   I've told you.

NIKOLAI   Think it over.

TATANYA   And if I did? Would you release him? Tell me the truth, for once in your rotten life.

NIKOLAI   Perhaps.

TATANYA   That's what I figured. We're both a couple of soul destroyers.

> *NIKOLAI goes. PAULINA, ZAKHAR and YAKOV enter.*

ZAKHAR   That's really enough, Yakov.

YAKOV   Zee, you're completely misunder—

ZAKHAR   I really don't want to hear it.

PAULINA   Besides which, he's right.

TATANYA   Who's right, and about what?

YAKOV   These two, treating me like *I'm* the enemy.

ZAKHAR   Now you're overplaying it.

YAKOV   Well I—

PAULINA   The fact is—

ZAKHAR   The fact is we've got to deal with reality.

YAKOV   What the hell were we dealing with before?

PAULINA   Everyone's pointing their fingers at us—at us!—As though this whole—this—yes, even you Yakov. I mean it's shocking, shocking to hear it coming from you.

YAKOV   I never said a goddamned—

PAULINA   You *thought* it.

YAKOV   Thought it?

ZAKHAR   Yes, listen to her.

YAKOV   Oh I'm listening.

PAULINA   Was it our fault the soldiers came? We didn't ask them to take over the property.

YAKOV   But you—

PAULINA   And we didn't ask the Special Unit to move in, either, and turn our house into a bloody interrogation cell.

YAKOV   The fact is over a dozen of our men have been arrested for—

ZAKHAR   And you're blaming me for that!

YAKOV   No, not—

ZAKHAR   You're not?

YAKOV   I'm only *saying*—

ZAKHAR   You're only *saying*, you're only *saying*, your whole life you've only been *saying*, but take a look at what you're doing for a change.

YAKOV   Zee, please, I'm on your side.

   CLEOPATRA returns, in a hurry.

CLEOPATRA   They have him, if you care.

TATANYA   Him, who?

CLEOPATRA   The shooter, they found him, he confessed, they're bringing him here now.

YAKOV   Christ sake.

PAULINA   Who is it, not—

CLEOPATRA   A boy, just a boy. I didn't catch his name, but they're bringing him, they're bringing him. I hope he rots, I don't care how old he is, or young he is, or if knows black from white, right from young, I hope he—where's Nikolai? Have you seen him? Has anyone seen Nikolai? *Useless.*

   CLEOPATRA exits.

PAULINA   Thinks she's in charge now.

ZAKHAR   I just wish they'd—

PAULINA   She was always a bully and now—

ZAKHAR   I want this over with.

PAULINA   And so *rude.*

ZAKHAR   I just want things to go back to normal.

PAULINA   Normal?

ZAKHAR   The way they were. They're strange people, I can't—. One minute, they're like children, the next like animals. Ill-mannered, greedy. I thought I knew them a little, but I don't. Sintsov seemed clear-headed, but it turns out he's a socialist. Grekov's full of himself, making grandiose speeches. And then there's Levshin. I saw him in the garden this morning, I said, Look, you've got to drop those strange ideas of yours, about doing away with money and bosses and all the rest of it, what's that going to get you? I tried to explain that I wanted to do what was right. He said he understood, but I could see he didn't. Just as I can see that they have no idea what it means to have killed a man. It's all so…. Well.

> *NADYA returns.*

NADYA   Aunt Tanya, they won't *listen* to me.

TATANYA   Who won't, dear?

NADYA   The soldiers, the, the one in charge, that *Corporal,* he, all he did was smile his stupid smile and say, "Oh, we're very gallant, Miss," and then he, well he didn't hit one of his men but I think he does and only didn't cause I was standing there, oh, it's such a, and they won't let the women, they're all crying and they won't let them see their husbands. Uncle, will you please, please will you tell them, go and see them, they'll listen to you, you're a man—

YAKOV   Is he?

NADYA   Tell them to—

PAULINA   *Yakov.*

ZAKHAR   Nadya.

NADYA   Tell them to let them see their—what are you waiting for?

ZAKHAR   It isn't that—

NADYA   You're just standing there!

ZAKHAR   It isn't that easy, now calm down.

NADYA   Calm down calm down? They're in *tears* out there and you say—

ZAKHAR   Alright, Nadya, al—it won't do any good, but al*right.*

> *ZAKHAR goes.*

PAULINA   Why must you always upset people?

NADYA   Me? You're the one who—

PAULINA   Stop it, Nadya, stop this ridic—

NADYA   Alright then it's all of us. There, isn't that more like—yes—you and me and Uncle and oh the whole rotten bunch of us! We're useless, we're stupid, we're, you know what we are? *Leeches.*

TATANYA   Nadya.

NADYA   Look at those men out there, look at them. Why have they been arrested? Because of *us*. They have to suffer so that we can lead our splendid little lives.

TATANYA   Alright, Nadya, now listen, I want you to be quiet. Can you be quiet?

NADYA   What is it?

TATANYA   I want you to sit down and get hold of yourself.

NADYA   I won't sit down.

TATANYA   Then stand and get hold of yourself, and listen to me when I tell you this, which you won't like but I'll say it anyway, and it's that you don't understand a blessed thing going—you see? I said you wouldn't like it—but it's true, you don't know what's happening here and there's nothing you can do to make any of it change.

NADYA   Just let it all happen, is that your advice?

TATANYA   What exactly do you think—

NADYA   I won't *not* do anything, and you can say whatever you want, but I won't listen to you, and I won't get *hold* of myself either.

PAULINA   Your mother was right, you know, when she—

NADYA   My *mother.*

PAULINA   When she—yes—said you couldn't be controlled.

NADYA   She *was* right, only she was proud of that fact.

PAULINA   Oh Nadya.

NADYA   She was proud to have raised a daughter who wouldn't be—who wouldn't—who'd stand *up*. Because she was salt of the earth, she earned the bread she ate, and you? You don't even know where the bread you eat is made.

PAULINA   At the bakery.

NADYA   You don't care!

PAULINA   Do you really think your mother would approve of the way you speak to your elders?

NADYA   She would, she would, and don't use that elder trick on me, it doesn't mean anything—being old doesn't give you the right to be stupid.

PAULINA   Do you hear? This is your influence.

TATANYA   Well I—

PAULINA   Tell her she's insolent.

TATANYA   You're insolent.

PAULINA   I—.

> *PAULINA goes.*

NADYA   Perfect. She'll go and tell Uncle Zee I've been rude again, and he'll come back and read me the riot act, only he'll make it so boring you'll wonder where the riot is.

TATANYA   You're going to have to figure out a way to live in this world, my dear.

NADYA   I don't want to live in *this* world—not *this* one. Even the wallpaper's trying to escape. Look at it, sagging and peeling and puffing, just like the people who live here. I was standing on the veranda just now, trying to talk to that idiot officer, and Grekov was out there, you know, smoking and just watching us. He was laughing, with his eyes, I could see, and I thought, But you're going to go to jail. You see? People who live the way they do, they're not afraid of things the way we are. We're afraid of everything. We wake up and right away we start to shake and cry at the terrible things coming our way, we're always looking over our shoulders and we have to worry about every little thing we say. But them, they're happy, they're laughing. I look at them and I feel so ashamed. I'll never forget those two, Grekov and Levshin, I know I won't. Tanya, I…

TATANYA   Yes, dear?

NADYA   Here comes that idiot again! Grr woof woof!

> *BOBOYEDOV returns.*

BOBOYEDOV   Careful now, or I'll throw you into the back of the van and take you to the kennel with all the other little puppies.

NADYA   I'm no puppy. When will you let those men see their wives and children?

BOBOYEDOV   Hm. How about never? Do you like that answer? After all, I'm playing the villain in this piece, so I have to say things like that, don't I, and twist the ends of my moustache.

TATANYA   Why don't you let us twist them for you?

BOBOYEDOV   There, you see? A little bit of humour and you've softened me right up. The truth is, the men will be allowed to say goodbye as they're being led away.

NADYA   That's it?

BOBOYEDOV Best I can do.

NADYA It isn't, though. You can do whatever you want.

BOBOYEDOV Within the limitations of the law.

NADYA What does that have to do with it? Let them—

BOBOYEDOV "What has the law got to"—my, my what a bold thing to say.

NADYA Stop talking to me like I was a child.

BOBOYEDOV Were you ever a child? You keep changing on me. When I came in, you were a dog. Now you sound like a revolutionary.

NADYA I am.

BOBOYEDOV Careful little girl, I may have to arrest you.

NADYA Let them see their families.

BOBOYEDOV The law is the law.

NADYA Then it's a stupid law!

BOBOYEDOV You really ought to watch your tongue. If you're really not a child, as you say, then you'll know that laws are made to protect the people.

NADYA The state, you mean, *from* the people.

BOBOYEDOV For the sake of order, without which, no state could exist, and the state i*s* the people.

NADYA But what good is order, the state and all these laws when all they do is make the people unhappy? It's ridiculous! You don't know what you're talking about!

> *NADYA goes.*

BOBOYEDOV She's a handful. She really ought to watch what she's saying, though, it could get her into all sorts of—her uncle is a liberal, isn't he?

TATANYA How should I know? And besides, what's a liberal?

BOBOYEDOV Someone who says all the right things, and does all the wrong ones. But you must know a lot of liberals, being in the arts.

TATANYA You'd be surprised.

BOBOYEDOV I'm glad to hear it. Allow me, by the way, to compliment you on your fine acting in Voronezh, Miss Lugovya.

TATANYA Thank you kindly.

BOBOYEDOV You didn't happen to notice me there, did you? In Voronezh? I was sitting right next to the Vice-Governor.

TATANYA Oh, was that you?

BOBOYEDOV   Yes, yes, of course I didn't hold quite the same position then that I—you're teasing me.

TATANYA   Fraid so. There are officers in every town, and anyway it's a little hard to see who's sitting out there from the stage.

BOBOYEDOV   Is it?

TATANYA   Those bright lights.

BOBOYEDOV   I hadn't realized.

>   *KLATCH, from the verandah.*

KLATCH   They're bringing him in, sir, the one who did the shooting. Where do you want him?

BOBOYEDOV   In here. Bring them all in. The prosecutor, too. *(to TATANYA)* You'll have to excuse me. Duty calls.

TATANYA   I understand. Only—

BOBOYEDOV   Miss?

TATANYA   Would you mind if I watched? I won't get in the way.

BOBOYEDOV   It's a little unusual.

TATANYA   Think of it as returning the favour. You've seen me perform, now I'll see you.

BOBOYEDOV   Interesting way to put it. Perhaps you could give me a few pointers.

>   *BOBOYEDOV goes. AGRAFENA enters. RIBITSOV, his hands tied, is brought in by two workers. Behind them, LEVSHIN, YAGUDIN, GREKOV, KLATCH, other workers and soldiers enter.*

RIBITSOV   What the fuck? Why'd you tie my hands?

LEVSHIN   Come on, fellas.

RIBITSOV   Take it off.

LEVSHIN   If he was going to run away, he—

RIBITSOV   Now, you pricks!

LEVSHIN   Easy, friend. Come on, boys, there's no need to humiliate the man, is there?

KLATCH   Do it.

AGRAFENA   That's not him.

KLATCH   Hm?

>   *BOBOYEDOV and NIKOLAI enter during:*

AGRAFENA   That can't be him. You've got the wrong—listen—he was on the river when the shooting happened, I saw him myself, I was down by the river when it—.

LEVSHIN   Fenya…

AGRAFENA   Well, say something. Tell them it wasn't you.

RIBITSOV   It *was* me.

AGRAFENA   What? No.

LEVSHIN   Don't you think he knows better than you?

RIBITSOV   It was me alright. I shot him.

AGRAFENA   You're lying! Why are you doing this? You were there, you were singing, I remember that, I know it, I saw you.

RIBITSOV   I *was* on the river, but not til later.

BOBOYEDOV   Just a minute. *(eyeing the prisoner)* This is him?

KLATCH   Yes, sir.

AGRAFENA   No!

BOBOYEDOV   Klatch, see the lady out.

AGRAFENA   Hands off!

NIKOLAI   Leave her alone, Klatch. Fenya, let the man do his job. If you want to stay, let him do his—alright?

BOBOYEDOV   Thank you, sir. *(to RIBITSOV)* What about it? Was it you who shot the managing director?

RIBITSOV   That's right.

BOBOYEDOV   Why?

RIBITSOV   He was a bad man. He treated us badly. So I shot him.

BOBOYEDOV   There it is.

> *YAKOV enters, tanked.*

NIKOLAI   What's your name?

RIBITSOV   Pavel Ribitsov.

NIKOLAI   Uh huh. Now, Fenya. What were you saying?

AGRAFENA   He's not the one. It couldn't be him. He was on the river when the shooting—I swear it! I *will* swear it. I remember seeing him, sitting in his boat and singing.

NIKOLAI   You're sure it was him?

AGRAFENA   I looked right over at him. He was rowing, yes, and singing.

RIBITSOV So what?

NIKOLAI You don't deny it?

RIBITSOV Not a bit. I was upset. I had to do something.

BOBOYEDOV So you sat in a rowboat and sang? After you'd just killed a man?

NIKOLAI You do realize, don't you, that making false statements, that shielding criminals, that these things are punishable under the law?

RIBITSOV Now I feel bad.

NIKOLAI I see. So you pulled the trigger?

RIBITSOV That's right.

BOBOYEDOV Animal.

AGRAFENA He's lying.

LEVSHIN Why don't you learn to keep your place?

NIKOLAI Quiet.

LEVSHIN She's interfering with the investigation.

NIKOLAI And what do you think you're doing? For all I know, you're involved in it yourself.

LEVSHIN Me? You must be joking. I killed a rabbit once and couldn't sleep for a week.

NIKOLAI Then keep your mouth shut. *(to RIBITSOV)* Where's the gun?

RIBITSOV Don't know.

NIKOLAI Describe it.

RIBITSOV You know. It was a gun.

NIKOLAI How *big* was it, can you at least tell me that? About like this? Maybe bigger?

RIBITSOV That's about right. No wait. Little less. Yes, that's it.

NIKOLAI I see. Bogdan.

> NIKOLAI and BOBOYEDOV go aside. AGRAFENA goes.

Something's going on.

BOBOYEDOV With?

NIKOLAI Don't you see it? They're using this boy.

BOBOYEDOV How?

NIKOLAI To—we'll have to find out. Talk to him a little more—exert a little pressure. Leave him for now, let him sweat a bit.

BOBOYEDOV   I don't understand. He's confessed to the whole thing.

NIKOLAI   They're using him. I don't know why, just—they don't want us to take the shooter. Probably someone higher up in the organization.

BOBOYEDOV   Uh *huh*. You think?

NIKOLAI   It's a conspiracy, no question.

BOBOYEDOV   I'd never have—but yes, yes.

NIKOLAI   Have Klatch take the boy out, keep him away from the others. No visitors, none. No one's to talk to him.

BOBOYEDOV   Yes.

NIKOLAI   No one.

     NIKOLAI goes.

BOBOYEDOV   Klatch!

KLATCH   Sir.

BOBOYEDOV   Take this one out. Keep an eye on him.

KLATCH   I'll keep both.

BOBOYEDOV   Good man.

KLATCH   Let's go. On the double!

LEVSHIN   Can we say goodbye?

KLATCH   Make it quick.

LEVSHIN   Take care of yourself.

YAGUDIN   Goodbye, Pavel, goodbye.

RIBITSOV   I'll be fine. So long.

     RIBITSOV is led out.

BOBOYEDOV   How well do you know him?

LEVSHIN   Well enough. We work together.

BOBOYEDOV   How convenient.

LEVSHIN   What?

BOBOYEDOV   What's your name?

LEVSHIN   Yefim Levshin.

BOBOYEDOV   *(to TATANYA)* I hope you're taking notes. *(to LEVSHIN)* Tell me— Levshin—and truthfully now.

LEVSHIN   Of course truthfully. Why would I lie?

BOBOYEDOV   Oh I'm not suggesting you would.

LEVSHIN   But you said "and truthfully," implying—

BOBOYEDOV   Don't be clever. I hate cleverness. Now tell me, honestly, what's hidden behind the religious paintings in your house? The truth, quickly!

LEVSHIN   Nothing.

BOBOYEDOV   You're sure about that?

LEVSHIN   Quite.

BOBOYEDOV   That's a pity. You just said you wouldn't lie and you, within seconds, lied. Like a child. Caught redhanded. Take a look at these, Levshin, take a look—what are these?

LEVSHIN   How should I know?

BOBOYEDOV   Are you blind?

LEVSHIN   A little. It's so dark in the factory, it's affected my eyesight.

BOBOYEDOV   Then let me help you out. They're pamphlets. Outlawed pamphlets. Would you like to know what's written in them? Calls to sedition. Yes, calls to bring down the government, our government, calls to rise up against the czar. And they were found in your house, behind the paintings, the religious paintings, in your room. Now. Would you like to amend your previous answer?

LEVSHIN   No.

BOBOYEDOV   No. Then you deny these are yours?

LEVSHIN   No. They could be mine. Who knows?

BOBOYEDOV   You're lying again.

LEVSHIN   Not really. You asked me what was hidden behind the paintings, and I said nothing, which is the truth, because I knew as soon as you asked me that you'd taken whatever had been there to begin with.

BOBOYEDOV strikes LEVSHIN.

BOBOYEDOV   I told you not to be clever. You're trying to confuse me, with your words, your fucking words. You treat me like an idiot, and if you do again, I'll break your fucking hands. Now where did you get these books from? Answer me.

LEVSHIN   You'll think I'm lying and you'll hit me again.

BOBOYEDOV   Answer me.

LEVSHIN   I don't remember, and anyway what does it matter? You shouldn't worry about these things.—Are you going to hit me again? In front of the lady?

BOBOYEDOV   Alright.—Yes, I'd quite—I forgot myself for a moment.—Which one of you is Grekov? Alexei Grekov?

GREKOV   Present.

BOBOYEDOV   Were you arrested in Smolensk on charges of spreading revolutionary propaganda among the workers?

GREKOV   Yup.

BOBOYEDOV   Well, that's a shame. So young. So talented.

GREKOV   So what.

BOBOYEDOV   (*to the soldiers*) Take these gentlemen back onto the verandah. Getting a little stuffy in here. Dmitry Viripayev? Uh huh. Andrei Yagudin? Pleasure to meet you…

> *The soldiers take the men out, BOBOYEDOV following with the list in his hand.*

YAKOV   Those are good people.

TATANYA   Who?

YAKOV   The men.

TATANYA   Oh. So you found something to look up to. To revere.

YAKOV   Well?

TATANYA   Yes, the simplicity of the—the nobility of the—

YAKOV   What the hell are you saying?

TATANYA   They're not—what—*real*. They're sacrificing one of their own. But did you see them? The look in their eyes? So calm about it all. They're doing it without passion. They think it's heroic but it's not.

YAKOV   They believe in their cause, they're on a path—that calm in their eyes is the calm at the centre of a hurricane.

TATANYA   No. It's contempt. For us.

YAKOV   You're wrong, Tanya. Pity, maybe.

TATANYA   They're using us. Sintsov asked me to hide something for him.

YAKOV   And did you?

TATANYA   I *wanted* to.

> *ZAKHAR enters.*

ZAKHAR   Bunch of idiots these policemen, trigger happy idiots, just itching to show everybody who's boss. It's a show trial, a pig circus, and that Nikolai, christ, "Czar" doesn't begin to—he's a Napoleon is what he is.

YAKOV   You're only upset—

ZAKHAR   A tyrant.

YAKOV   —Because they're doing it in front of you and not in some closed door courtroom.

ZAKHAR   I didn't *ask* for this.

YAKOV   Don't you understand what's going on? Don't you get it? And in your own house.

ZAKHAR   Yes, I get it. I see the *significance*. But what am I supposed to do? We've been attacked, and when you're attacked you have to defend yourself.

YAKOV   Very good, then don't pretend to be offended by it all.

ZAKHAR   I just want a place to... I'm not made for this...

>   *ZAKHAR goes.*

YAKOV   So you're not going to help them?

TATANYA   I tried. I begged Nikolai for mercy.

YAKOV   Really. On your knees?

>   *NIKOLAI and CLEOPATRA return.*

NIKOLAI   It's clear, no doubt, they bribed him.

CLEOPATRA   Yes, but who did it? Those idiots couldn't have come up with something like that.

NIKOLAI   Clearly.

CLEOPATRA   *(calling)* Captain Boboyedov! *(to NIKOLAI)* Someone with a good head on his shoulders.

NIKOLAI   Sintsov?

CLEOPATRA   Who else?

>   *BOBOYEDOV returns from the verandah.*

BOBOYEDOV   How can I be of service?

NIKOLAI   I'm convinced the boy's been put up to it.

BOBOYEDOV   Oh?

NIKOLAI   Listen...

BOBOYEDOV   *(going)* Oh, I see... you don't say... my my...

>   *NIKOLAI walks out with BOBOYEDOV, whispering. YAKOV makes his way out to the verandah, but overhears the following conversation.*

CLEOPATRA   *(seeing TATANYA)* Tanya. Have you been here the whole time?... Sintsov's been arrested.

TATANYA   Yes.

CLEOPATRA   Don't you think that's good?

TATANYA   You don't care what I think.

CLEOPATRA   Or feel?

TATANYA   Either.

CLEOPATRA   You sympathized with him. No? Well, don't fret. And don't look so glum. Your face seems to have fallen.

TATANYA   Must be the weather.

CLEOPATRA   Listen, you can talk to me. I know I'm not the sweetest person in the world, but I come by my bitterness honestly. I've seen things, things have been done to me. And I know that the best friend a woman ever had was another woman.

TATANYA   What's on your mind?

CLEOPATRA   I want to—I like you. I like the way you hold yourself, the way you pre*sent y*ourself, your speech, your manners, your dress, everything, you're just so—and the way you are with men, it's—I hate you. You see? I *want* to like you, but I hate you, not always, just at times.

TATANYA   Alright—why?

CLEOPATRA   I don't know you. I wish I—who are you exactly?

TATANYA   That's—

CLEOPATRA   I can't figure it out. You see, I need to *know* people, I need to have a picture of them in my mind, and if I don't it's because that person isn't sure of what she wants, and that makes her dangerous.

TATANYA   This is getting—

CLEOPATRA   Listen. I *want* to be your friend. Why? Because we *ought* to be, to survive, we ought to be close, be friends, be—because you see what's happening? They're insinuating themselves on us, they're getting inside us, in our homes, between us, slinking up between us, whispering things to us, and soon, when they've lulled us to sleep with their stories, they'll take from us everything we've—yes, it's true, listen, haven't you seen it on the faces of the men they arrested? *They* know what they want. *They* live close to one another. *They* trust each other, and I hate them for it. And then I look at us, at the way we live, with such contempt for one another, we don't believe in anything beyond our own selfish selves, and it's every man for himself, yes, and I'll have the biggest castle and fuck you for trying to take it from me. You see, you see, we need to surround ourselves with these men, these soldiers, Special Unit *men,* while they, the workers, look at them, they need only themselves.

TATANYA   Cleo—

CLEOPATRA   They're stronger than us. That's why they're going to win. I'm so afraid. Aren't you?

TATANYA   Were you happy before? With your husband, I mean.

CLEOPATRA   Why?

TATANYA   Just curious.

CLEOPATRA   No. He never thought about me. He was always too busy…

PAULINA enters.

PAULINA   Have you heard? It turns out Sintsov was only pretending to be a clerk and, well not pretending but, well yes pretending. And Zakhar was going to make him assistant bookkeeper. He feels so betrayed. Can you imagine? Someone like that? Well it doesn't matter now, but—well it's just strange to think, your own enemies can be living under your own roof without your having the slightest idea.

TATANYA   Thank you, God, for not making me rich.

PAULINA   You won't feel that way when you're poor. Cleopatra, they want you to try on your funeral clothes.

CLEOPATRA   Yes. Alright. Only my heart, I suddenly felt this awful tightness.

PAULINA   Would you like some drops?

CLEOPATRA   I think so.

PAULINA   They'll do the trick.

CLEOPATRA   Yes and—yes.

CLEOPATRA goes.

PAULINA   I'll join you in a second, dear. *(to TATANYA)* Can't you be a little more delicate with her?

TATANYA   Me?

PAULINA   Don't take what I'm saying as—it was good of you to talk to her, only try to calm her down instead of getting her so upset.

TATANYA   But I—

PAULINA   We needn't talk about it again. I'll go and give her those drops.

PAULINA goes. TATANYA looks out to where the men have all been lined up.

TATANYA   It isn't right.

YAKOV appears.

YAKOV   It's really unpleasant eavesdropping on people.

TATANYA   Have you been there the whole time?

YAKOV   People sound so ridiculous when you overhear them. I wonder what someone would say if they could listen to me now. Probably the same thing—pathetic. For example, when I say, "I'm leaving."

TATANYA   Are you?

YAKOV   Oh yes.

TATANYA   Where are you going?

YAKOV   Anywhere that isn't here. And so farewell.

TATANYA   Goodbye. Drop me a line.

YAKOV   I hate this place.

TATANYA   Still here?

YAKOV   And you? Will you stay?

TATANYA   No. You're smiling.

YAKOV   I was just thinking—we'll probably never see each other again.

TATANYA   And that's funny to you.

YAKOV   No, not—no.

> *TATANYA kisses him on the forehead.*

Like I was a corpse.

> *YAKOV goes. TATANYA almost follows, but stops herself. NADYA returns.*

NADYA   Oh Tanya, come into the garden with me, please, please. I've been crying all day, and my head's pounding.

TATANYA   You don't need to cry.

NADYA   But it's all so awful, and confusing. I can't make—I don't know who's right, who's—I thought Uncle was a good person, a kind person, but now I don't know. When he talks to me I feel so stupid, just like I'm five or something, and when I start thinking about what I'd like to say to him, all these questions I have, I begin to realize I don't understand anything, not really.

TATANYA   If you keep asking questions, my sweet, you'll end up like them— (*meaning the workers*) —And God help you if you do. You're not built for that.

NADYA   Well, what *am* I "built" for? I must be good for *something*. Well, what's so funny? I can't just go around the rest of my life breathing through my mouth, looking and sounding like some idiot who just woke up in the middle of the night.

TATANYA   Oh no no no, I'm laughing because.... Come on, come on...

> *NADYA and TANYA cross paths with ZAKHAR on their way out.*

ZAKHAR   You haven't seen Yakov?

TATANYA   He's gone.

ZAKHAR   Gone? Where?

TATANYA   He doesn't know.

    PAULINA enters.

PAULINA   Zee, you've got to deal with the peasants.

ZAKHAR   Which, what?

PAULINA   They want more time to pay the rent.

ZAKHAR   Christ, I can't deal with this right now, I'm looking for, I can't find Yakov.

PAULINA   Yakov? Try a ditch, my dear. Now about the peasants—

ZAKHAR   I can't—tell them to go to the office.

PAULINA   The office is closed.

ZAKHAR   Why?

PAULINA   Everything's closed, the house is upside down, the samovar hasn't been heated since this morning, it's—I tell you, we're living in a madhouse.

ZAKHAR   And Yakov's disappeared.

PAULINA   Well—and forgive me for saying this—but it may be for the, don't you think, the best.

ZAKHAR   The—? Yes. You're—yes. He's become a pest, a real, he's annoying, when he's drunk, which is always, he's become one of those annoying drunks, always prattling on, prattling, prattling—

PAULINA   That's just the word for it—

ZAKHAR   Getting in people's faces and insulting them, and always so dark and—.

PAULINA   My dear.

ZAKHAR   I can't remember the last time he was sober.

    SINTSOV is brought in from the verandah by soldiers and KLATCH, who is observing SINTSOV very closely, especially his hands. PAULINA looks him up and down, then goes.

Shame it's come to this, Mr Sintsov. A damn shame.

SINTSOV   Don't let it bother you.

ZAKHAR   Oh but it does bother me, sir, it does. You see I happen to have been brought up to believe that people deserve sympathy from one another, even when one person has betrayed another, has proven himself unworthy of that person's, of *my* trust, it's—we're human beings, after all, and when I see someone less fortunate I—well I just want to do what's right. That's just the way I feel about it. Goodbye, Mr Sintsov.

SINTSOV So long.

ZAKHAR That's all you want to say?

SINTSOV Pretty much.

ZAKHAR And you don't feel—you don't think I've mistreated you in any way?

SINTSOV Mmmmnope.

ZAKHAR I see. Well. I see. Goodbye then. Your remaining salary will be sent to you. *(on his way out)* This is really—my house has become a prison.

> SINTSOV *laughs.* KLATCH *kicks his feet out from under him and* SINTSOV *goes down in a heap.*

KLATCH Watch your step.

SINTSOV I hope you enjoyed that.

KLATCH The fun's just beginning.

> BOBOYEDOV *enters.*

BOBOYEDOV What have we here?

KLATCH He slipped.

SINTSOV Clumsy of me.

BOBOYEDOV Klatch, help him up.

KLATCH Yes, sir.

BOBOYEDOV Mr Sintsov, you're being sent into town.

KLATCH But this isn't Sintsov.

BOBOYEDOV I'm sorry.

KLATCH No, sir. This is—I know him. His name's Maxim Markov. Took me a while to—he used to work at the Bryansk factory. We arrested him there two years ago. Take a look at his left thumb. Do you see?

BOBOYEDOV No nail.

KLATCH I remembered that. So you escaped? Changed your name. Very good.

BOBOYEDOV Is this true, Mr Sintsov?

KLATCH Markov, sir.

SINTSOV Markov, Sintsov, Fuckov, what's it matter? I have rights.

BOBOYEDOV   Ah, you have *rights*. Good. Yes, we'll be very careful around you, sir, because you're obviously you're not a man to be trifled with. He's all yours, Klatch. Keep your eyes on him.

KLATCH   They've been on him.

BOBOYEDOV   We'll keep him here for the trial.

SINTSOV   Trial?

KLATCH   Quiet.

BOBOYEDOV   I'll have the men brought in. Sharp now, Klatch!

BOBOYEDOV goes.

KLATCH   It really is a pleasure to see you again.

SINTSOV   I'm happy you're happy.

KLATCH   And why not? I'm always glad to see an old friend.

SINTSOV   Haven't you had enough? Tracking people down like dogs? Ever think what it does to you? To your soul?

KLATCH   Oh my soul's very, very content. And I don't think of you as a dog at all.

SINTSOV   I wasn't referring to myself.

KLATCH   Oh, I'm the dog then? Well, this dog's going to get a nice little pat on the head, maybe even a promotion.

SINTSOV   All because of me? I'm flattered.

KLATCH   Tell me, where've you been hiding this whole time? Not here.

SINTSOV   Oh, you don't need me to tell you that, do you?

KLATCH   No. You're right. We'll find out. You remember that fella worked at Bryansk, the one with the glasses? The name escapes me. Died in jail, you know. Oh—maybe you hadn't heard. Yes, it was very, very upsetting. He got sick, and then he died. A real loss to the cause, I guess.

SINTSOV   There are plenty of us, don't you worry.

KLATCH   Oh, I'm not worried. The more the merrier.

SINTSOV   Dog.

KLATCH   I'm not gonna hit you. Not here. Too many people watching.

BOBOYEDOV, NIKOLAI, and CLEOPATRA return.

NIKOLAI   I should have known.

CLEOPATRA   So we have the leader.

SINTSOV   Really, Captain, this is a hell of a way to conduct an investigation.

BOBOYEDOV   Keep your mouth shut.

SINTSOV   Why don't you just put a stop to this? Hm?

CLEOPATRA   He shouldn't be allowed to speak.

SINTSOV   It's completely illegal what's going on here.

BOBOYEDOV   Klatch, keep him quiet would you?

KLATCH   Gladly.

> *KLATCH puts a bag over SINTSOV's head. PAULINA, ZAKHAR,*
> *TATANYA and NADYA return, POLOGGY behind them.*

NADYA   What are you doing?

BOBOYEDOV   Keep out of this, miss.

TATANYA   Is that necessary?

BOBOYEDOV   Quiet, please. If you'd like to stay—quiet.

> *RIBITSOV is brought in.*

NIKOLAI   Let's begin. Pavel Ribitsov?

RIBITSOV   Uh huh.

BOBOYEDOV   "Uh huh." You don't answer "uh huh," you fool, you say, "Yes, Your Honour."

RIBITSOV   Okay. What he said.

NIKOLAI   Do you maintain that it was you who killed the manager?

RIBITSOV   I told you once. How many times I gotta say it?

NIKOLAI   Do you know a man named Alexei Grekov?

RIBITSOV   Who?

NIKOLAI   That fellow right there.

RIBITSOV   Him? Oh, is that his name? Yeah, he works at the factory.

NIKOLAI   Then you know him?

RIBITSOV   I don't "know him" know him, I just, yeah, I see him, I see him as much as anybody sees anyone else down there.

NIKOLAI   Alright. But you wouldn't say you know him well, that you spend time with him, that you're his friend?

RIBITSOV   We're all friends, we hang out together, you know how it is.

NIKOLAI   No. I'm asking you to tell me "how it is."

RIBITSOV   I just did.

NIKOLAI   Mr Pologgy. Step forward, sir.

POLOGGY   Yes. Should I stand here or sit behind the table, or—?

NIKOLAI   Right there is fine, Mr Pologgy. Now, sir, would you be so good as to share with us your observations about the relationship between these two men, Alexei Grekov and Yefim Levshin?

POLOGGY   Yes. Yes, it's a—how to put it? They're very close. Very good friends, I would say. Grekov is one of the leaders down there. He's very, how to put it, bombastic. He's very insolent, oh yes, towards anyone in authority. And then there's Levshin, who speaks very eloquently but is, in my opinion, not a man to be trusted, oh no no no.

NADYA   *(sotto)* Stoolpigeon.

> *POLOGGY looks at her a moment. NIKOLAI has also heard.*

NIKOLAI   Go on, Mr Pologgy.

POLOGGY   Well, sir, these two men—Grekov and Levshin—they work hand-in-hand with Mr Sintsov. He's the link, you see, gets on with everybody. He's not your typical worker, sir, I could see that from the day I first saw him. He's more of a thinker, if you will—not that the workers don't think, but Mr Sintsov, he reads a lot of books, and on every subject you can imagine. His room is just across the hall from mine. A very nice room, with plenty of space and—

NIKOLAI   Only the most pertinent details are required, Mr Pologgy.

POLOGGY   Oh these are pertinent details, sir. You see, he needs all that space, on account of the meetings.

NIKOLAI   Meetings.

POLOGGY   Oh yes, quite regular meetings, with all sorts of people, sometimes Grekov and his group, sometimes Levshin and his, and once in a while, they all come in together.

NIKOLAI   What about it, Grekov?

GREKOV   I don't know what he's talking about.

NIKOLAI   As usual.

NADYA   That's right, Grekov, don't take part in this!

ZAKHAR   Nadya—

BOBOYEDOV   Quiet!

> *Noise and voices on the verandah.*

NIKOLAI   Those with no need to be here will be asked to leave.

NADYA   But this is our house.

BOBOYEDOV   Klatch, what's going on out there?

KLATCH   Can't tell, sir. Someone's trying to break through.

NIKOLAI   Well who is it?

NADYA   This is our house, do you hear?

KLATCH   Don't know, sir. They're all gathered around him.

BOBOYEDOV   Get out there and find out.

POLOGGY   Shall I continue?

NADYA   Traitor!

POLOGGY   I wanted to speak about the theft of some property of mine…

NIKOLAI   That's enough! If you've no business here, leave!

NADYA   This isn't your house, it's our house, our house!

ZAKHAR   Go Nadya. Leave now!

NADYA   I will, and gladly, to be away from you, to be away from all of you!

NIKOLAI   Tell those soldiers to mind the door.

NADYA   You're heartless, all of you, contemptible people. You're miserable and I hope you stay that way, all of you, til the end of time!

> *The doors burst open. A great mass of people, and in the midst of them YAKOV, brandishing a gun.*

YAKOV   Fuck you, Czar Nikolai! Fuck you!

> *YAKOV shoots. People duck for cover. Screams. YAKOV keeps shooting.*

Fuck you! Fuck you! Fuck you!

> *He runs out of bullets. A moment as people survey the damage. NADYA has been shot.*

TATANYA   Nadya?… Nadya!

NIKOLAI   Take him.

PAULINA   What's happened?

TATANYA   She's been shot.

PAULINA   Nadya! Nadya!

NIKOLAI   Get away from her, all of you. Give her room, give her room goddammit. Nadya?

TATANYA   It's alright, darling.

YAKOV   No, no, not her…

NIKOLAI   A doctor, a doctor…

TATANYA   Don't cry sweetheart, you'll be fine.

PAULINA   Sweetheart, don't close your eyes. Stay awake, sweetheart.

TATANYA   You'll see, you'll be fine.

PAULINA   Keep your eyes open.

TATANYA   Everything will be fine.

NIKOLAI   Get these men out of here. Do you hear me? Get them out!

> *The soldiers don't move. The workers stand about. SINTSOV has long since removed the hood from his face.*

What are you waiting for? That's a direct order!

TATANYA   Do you hear, Nadya? They're going to win...

NIKOLAI   I said get these men out of here!

TATANYA   They're going to win.... Nadya.... Nadya...

> *The end.*

AFTER THE ORCHARD

a new play inspired by Anton Chekhov's
The Cherry Orchard

Production

After the Orchard was first produced by the National Arts Centre, Ottawa, in September 2005. In the cast were Ellen David (Caroline), Paul Dunn (Jeremy), Jerry Franken (Jack), Peter Froehlich (Len), Carolyn Hetherington (Aunt Faye), Niki Landau (Donna), Nicola Lipman (Rose), Patrick McManus (David), Michelle Monteith (Trish), Harry Nelken (Morris), Alex Poch-Goldin (Sasha) and Philip Warren Sarsons (Andrew). Marti Maraden was the director, with design by Christina Poddubiuk (set and costume), John Munro (lighting) and Peter McBoyle (sound). The assistant director was Abebe Addis, Laurie Champagne was the stage manager and Jane Vanstone Osborn was the assistant stage manager.

Characters

ROSE LEVY, a widow.
LEN, her brother.
FAYE, Rose's sister-in-law.
SASHA, Rose's eldest son.
CAROLINE, Sasha's wife.
JEREMY, their son.
DAVID, Rose's middle son.
ANDREW, the youngest son.
DONNA, Andrew's wife.
JACK SKEPIAN, a real estate agent.
MORRIS, owner of a nearby cottage.
TRISH, Morris' granddaughter.

Setting

Act 1. Living room of a modest Ontario cottage; mid-July.
Act 2. The backyard; one week later.
Act 3. In the garden; end of summer.
Act 4. The living room; that fall.

AFTER THE ORCHARD

ACT 1

Living room and kitchen of a modest Ontario cottage. A door leads to the backyard, and the lake beyond. It's mid-July. JACK SKEPIAN, waits, looking out the window. The silence is broken by the loud drone of a cicada. DAVID LEVY, enters, holding a coffee cup.

DAVID   Still waiting, Mr Skepian?

JACK   Hm? Oh, you scared me, you young rascal.

DAVID   Thought you might have heard me come in.

JACK   Lost in thought.

DAVID   The country air does that to you.

JACK   I suppose that's true. Is that why you come up here, then?

DAVID   Actually, it doesn't have that effect on me. In fact, Mr Skepian, with me it's just the opposite—I come up here to gather my thoughts. It's in the city where I feel lost.

JACK   Isn't that funny? Well, different strokes, eh?

DAVID   Indeed.

JACK   Look, call me Jack, would you?

DAVID   Yes, alright. *(getting his coffee)* Sure I can't offer you a coffee?

JACK   I'd better not.—But would you mind if I make a little observation? I've been waiting here, oh, forty minutes I suppose. And in that time you've come in three times for coffee.

DAVID   I don't really drink it. It's just an excuse to leave my desk. There's a coffee maker in the guest house, but if I used it, I wouldn't be able to go through my ritual, you see, of letting the coffee go cold, getting up from my desk, walking back to the main house, pouring out the cold stuff, filling my cup again—

JACK   Writer's block, is that it?

DAVID   If only. No, my problem is I write too damn much. Too many words. They just pour out of me. The trouble is, I don't know when to stop, when to say "it's finished," and walk away.

JACK   Well, you're making a living at it. That's good, I suppose. *(pause)* Tell me, do you ever have your plays put on at the little theatre here? They do some very good things. Very funny. I saw one last year, took my daughter, it was about this young woman who worked in a flower shop, and was about to be married, only it turned out that her sister was dating the same man. Well, naturally, the second man was the first man's twin.

DAVID   That's good.

JACK   It was very funny.

> *DAVID stares into his cup of coffee.*

But, um, are you working on a play at the moment?

DAVID   No. I'm working on television at the moment.

JACK   Ah, now that's smart; that's where the money is.

DAVID   Yes.

> *Pause.*

JACK   You think she'll remember me?

DAVID   Course. She used to talk about you all the time. That's why the name rang a bell the minute you introduced yourself. "Jack Skepian, the one that got away."

JACK   Is that how she put it?

DAVID   Something like that. A simple twist of fate and I'd be calling you Dad instead of Jack.

JACK   Well.

DAVID   How long did you date?

JACK   Not long. A month or so, perhaps. A month in the summer, August in fact, just before I left for—well, I had a job out west. Your mother was going to stay in town, go to technical college, so I couldn't really ask her to wait for me. I remember telling her that. I could see from the expression on her face that she probably wouldn't. And really how could I ask her to? How do you ask someone to put her life on hold for you? Well. She cried. I cried. We walked for block after block, all along Harbord, and down Spadina, we just kept walking. We may have held hands, I don't remember. Then we were at the waterfront and had to stop. I remember there was a tanker out in the distance, and I think we didn't say a word, just watched it inch forward on the horizon. *(pause)* She was the belle of the ball, let me tell you, not a prettier gal for miles around.

DAVID   Still is.

JACK   I don't doubt it. And of course that fall, she met your father. I got to know him a little when I came back. Wonderful man.

DAVID   Yes. *(pause)* That was quite a walk.

JACK   Yes.

DAVID   All up and down Spadina?

JACK   Mm.

DAVID   It's funny, I—I'd forgotten til you just mentioned it—my father—well, before he became ill—I was going to write a piece for a magazine about him. We were going to go for a walk together, all along Spadina, he was going to tell me what the street was like back in the 40s when he came.

JACK   Your father was a wonderful storyteller.

DAVID   Boy, ain't that the truth. One of his best was about how, after the war, when he came over, a fresh-faced kid, missing his family—all of them back in England—a Jew in a city where there weren't that many, at least none that he knew, or none that he could find—and one Sunday morning, feeling lost and depressed, he went looking for a cup of coffee. That's all he wanted, a cup of coffee. So he started to walk, all along College—

JACK   Yes. And a Sunday in Toronto then—

DAVID   Nothing open.

JACK   Ghost town.

DAVID   And the more he walks, the more depressed he gets, and he's thinking, "I just want to be home, I want to be with my family, I just want to go home." Well, he gets to Spadina, he turns the corner, and—what does he see?—He sees shop windows full of Stars of David, and menorahs and tallises... he sees delis and he sees men in felt hats and païs... and he thinks, "I'm home."

> *Pause.*

JACK   Course it's all Chinese now.

> *DAVID sees TRISH sweeping up outside.*

DAVID   Excuse me. *(slides open the door)* Trish, you don't need to do that.

TRISH   I don't mind. The garden's so overgrown and, well, I just think your mother would like it if it were a bit neater.

DAVID   Well, I'll come help you in a minute.

TRISH   It's fine. You're working. I like to do it. Hello, Mr Skepian.

JACK   Ms Siegel. What a nice surprise. I haven't seen you for a year, maybe longer. I hear all kinds of things about you. Your grandfather tells me you're out to change the world.

TRISH   Not just now. I'm only trying to fix up the garden. *(to DAVID)* The tools are all in the shed, you know. Just the way he left them. It's a little strange to—. Anyway, I'll just get back to it.

DAVID   Don't do too much, alright? It's pretty hot out.

TRISH   Not in the garden, though. It's shady. Did you know that the shade from just one elm tree has the cooling power of four air conditioners?

JACK   Well, you learn something useless every day.

TRISH   Do you think they'll be here soon?

DAVID   Any minute, I expect.

TRISH   I'll just tidy up a bit.

>   *She goes off. DAVID slides the door shut.*

JACK   Ha. "Air conditioners."

>   *DAVID is staring out.*

It is a nice garden, though. Tell me, how long's it been since your father passed on?

DAVID   Three years this August.

JACK   Is that a fact. Goodness. You know I only heard about it after the shiva. Otherwise, of course, I would have come.

DAVID   You sent a card, though. My mother appreciated that.

JACK   Yes, I did send a card. She mentioned it, did she?

DAVID   Of course. Of course.

JACK   Tell me, how's she getting on?

DAVID   Most days she's fine. It took her two years to start getting rid of his things. And for a long time she wouldn't come up here. He built this place with his own hands. She came up once about a month after he died and it just about did her in. This is the first time she's been back—you picked an interesting time to drop by.

JACK   Well, I'm up here every so often. She still has the house, in Toronto?

DAVID   No. She didn't want to leave it, but it became too much for her to keep up. We finally convinced her to sell. She got a good price, though, enough for a condo and then some.—She's alright.

>   *The sound of two cars pulling up outside.*

Here they are.

JACK   Look at that, I'm shaking like a schoolboy. Funny, isn't it, I suddenly got so nervous, a shot of adrenaline just— *(puts a hand on his stomach)* Do me a favour, would you? Don't introduce me. I'll just stand there, I won't say anything. I want to see if she recognizes me. It's been such a long time. I saw her once at a wedding, but that was twenty years ago. I meant to call her after that, but, well.

>   *JACK and DAVID go outside. The stage is empty. A motorboat speeds by in the distance.*
>
>   *Offstage noise increases. Enter ROSE, SASHA, CAROLINE, ANDREW, DONNA, LEN, JACK and DAVID. Voices, off—a babble, none of it*

heard very clearly: "Put a light on."—"Ow."—"Watch it, dumbkopf."—
"Careful, careful."—"Jack?"—"In the flesh."—"I can't believe it."—
"I brought one percent milk."—"We're drinking soy."

ROSE   Who moved the couch?

SASHA   What are you talking about?

ANDREW   Ma, where do you want this stuff?

ROSE   The couch is supposed to be there, against the wall. I don't like it here.

SASHA   Where do you want it?

ROSE   Where it always was.

> *SASHA begins to move it.*

Sasha, careful, with your back.

SASHA   My back's fine.

ROSE   David, Andrew, help him. And what used to be here? The bookcase, the one your father made.

DAVID   I took it into the guest house.

ROSE   No, it doesn't belong in the guest house.

CAROLINE   *(calling off)* Jeremy!

SASHA   Who said you could put it in the guest house?

ANDREW   The nerve! Ow!

ROSE   Be careful! And where are all the books?

DAVID   I put them in boxes, in the shed. Mom, they're just old paperbacks—no one's looked at them in years, I was going to donate them to Goodwill.

ROSE   No, I don't—Just put everything back. I want everything the way it was.

CAROLINE   *(calling off)* Jer-e-my!

DONNA   I can bring in the books.

ROSE   I don't want you carrying nothing, the boys can get it.

DAVID   "Anything," Mom, you don't want her carrying any—

SASHA   *(about the couch)* Like this, Ma?

ROSE   Back a little.

SASHA   Who moved it in the first place?

DAVID   Shoot me.

CAROLINE   Where did Jeremy disappear to? I asked him to help unload.

LEN   Who's hungry?

ROSE   We just ate.

LEN   You call that a meal? David, we stopped at that little burger place—and it was packed, like always!

CAROLINE   Sash.

LEN   Half an hour I stood in line.

CAROLINE   Sash, the kids are standing on the dock without life jackets.

SASHA   So tell em to put em on.

LEN   Ah, they're fine, they're fine. Those burgers were terrible. Not the way they used to be, but still people stood there, and it was hot, too, and the line-up went right outside, almost to the highway.

DONNA   They were dripping with grease, I could only eat half.

ROSE   Mine was good.

LEN   Rose, I'm telling you, the quality's gone way down. But it's a habit with people—you come up here for the weekend, you've got to stop at the burger place.

CAROLINE   (*calling outside*) Jordan! Adam! Life jackets!—I don't care! They're in the trunk, get them and put them on or you can just come inside!

ANDREW   No, please, anything but that. Then mine'll want to come in.

CAROLINE   I don't see Jeremy.

LEN   The drive up was terrible. Used to be you could make the trip in ninety minutes. But, look, we left at one, and it's almost four! That's twice the usual time.

SASHA   Well there's twice the usual cars.

DONNA   Mom, why don't you rest, you look a little tired.

ROSE   I tried to sleep on the way up, but I couldn't. And all last night I was tossing and turning. I started watching a movie at one, and I couldn't stop.

LEN   What movie are you watching at one in the morning?

ROSE   (*overlapping after LEN's "watching"*) I don't know, something about a spy, but I couldn't stop watching. And I was so nervous about coming up here. But now that I'm here, and my children are with me—and Jack, I can't believe you're here.

CAROLINE   (*going*) Boys!

JACK   (*handing her the flowers*) Brought these for you.

ROSE   Oh, they're nice. Someone put them in water.

DONNA   Here, Mom, let me.

JACK   Rose, I was sort of hoping we could catch up or something.

ROSE   I'd like that. We'll go into the garden.

JACK   Oh fine, fine.

ROSE   Jack, I can't get over it. We were kids together.

JACK   Yes, it's funny, isn't it? *(as they leave:)* I was telling your David—we were having a lovely talk—I was saying to him that the last time I saw you, we walked down to the water. And now, here we are, and it's good Lord forty, forty-five years later, and we're meeting at the edge of the water again. Well, it's just a little coincidence, isn't it?...

> *They've gone. SASHA has drifted out by now. LEN follows ROSE and JACK out. DONNA fusses in the kitchen, then goes. ANDREW and DAVID remain.*

ANDREW   I'm exhausted. The flight back was a nightmare. No, check that. The whole trip was a nightmare. What a stupid idea. Mom was practically in tears the whole time. She kept talking about "the last time we were here," or "This is the house where he was born."

DAVID   Well, it was good of you to go.

ANDREW   You don't know what I've been through. The whole time we were in London, it was freezing. The food was terrible. And Caroline never shut up; kept trying to patch things up. But everything she says is just a trick. I don't know why they had to come. On top of it all, London must be the most expensive city in the world—worse than Toronto. That didn't matter to Mom. She insisted on paying for everything. Meanwhile, I'm trying to keep her from bursting out crying every five seconds.

DAVID   I know, I know.

ANDREW   *(beat; sighs)* Did you talk to the guy from the planning office?

DAVID   Yeah.

ANDREW   And?

DAVID   There's no way around it; the cottage is too close to the water.

ANDREW   So what are we supposed to do? Pick it up and move it back?

DAVID   Well. Yes. We have until Labour Day. I got a couple of quotes. One says seventy-five, another says ninety.

ANDREW   *Thousand?*... Where are we supposed to get that kinda money?

DAVID   Believe me, I've been asking myself the same question. I was thinking Mom could put in some of what she got from the house, and the three of us could—

ANDREW   "What she got from the house?" David, there's nothing left from that. She has no money.

DAVID   How's that possible? She cleared thirty thousand from the house.

ANDREW   I'm telling you. I was at the condo a few weeks ago, took a look through her bank statements—there's just a few hundred dollars in there. And she's still trying to pay her taxes from two years ago. One night in London, after the kids had gone to bed, Sasha starts talking to Mom about the cottage, about how much it must be worth by now, how Dad always saw it as an investment.

DAVID   No, he didn't. He never saw it that way. He always said he built this place for—. Anyway, it's not really up to Mom, is it? Dad left it to the three of us; did Sash forget that, or what?

ANDREW   I don't think so. I just think he wanted her blessing.

DAVID   Her blessing's got nothing to do with it. We're not selling.

> *Beat.*

ANDREW   I don't know.

DAVID   What do you mean, "you don't know"? You love this place.

> *JACK sticks his head in.*

JACK   Sorry. Left my briefcase somewhere. Sorry.

> *He goes. DAVID stares after him.*

ANDREW   What?

DAVID   Nothing. It's just—he dropped by all of a sudden. Mom hasn't been here in three years, and the day she comes back there's a real estate agent with an armload of flowers.

ANDREW   …I wouldn't put anything to it.

> *Beat.*

DAVID   You think Sash might have called him?

ANDREW   Sash? Why?

DAVID   Just—no, you're right.

ANDREW   Why would he do something like that?—Look, the two of you ought to talk things over. Whatever's between you, just talk about it, just sit down and be honest with each other.

DAVID   What's the point? You know how he is—it's impossible to have an honest conversation with him.

> *DONNA returns with a load of books.*

DONNA   With who?

DAVID   Santa Claus.

DONNA   …Drew, would you mind looking after the kids? I want to go for a swim.

ANDREW   Sure. Now?

DONNA   Well. Never mind. *(to DAVID)* Where's Liz and the kids?

DAVID   Stayed in Toronto. I came up here to get some work done.

> *Some jet skis go by.*

ANDREW   God I hate those things.

DONNA   Why don't you go have a nap?

ANDREW   Yeah. *(lies on the couch)*

DONNA   I didn't mean there.

ANDREW   I'm too tired to go upstairs. I'll just close my eyes a minute. Besides, I love this couch. It's a great couch.

DAVID   The springs are going.

ANDREW   It's got character.

> *DONNA, at the window, about to head out.*

DONNA   Oh, Jeremy's down there. He's such a great kid.

> *Silence. SASHA comes in, wearing a jogging outfit.*

SASHA   Who died?

DONNA   We're just having coffee. *(beat)* Are those the sneakers you picked up in London?

SASHA   "Sneakers"? They don't really call them that anymore. Anyway, I'm going for a run. Anybody wanna join me? *(sees ANDREW has fallen asleep; creeps up to him)*

DONNA   Leave him alone, he's tired.

> *SASHA bends down and barks loudly in ANDREW's ear; ANDREW wakes with a start, upsetting a coffee cup.*

DAVID   Nice going.

SASHA   Now look what you did.

ANDREW   What happened?

SASHA   Don't know. You were barking in your sleep. That's a sign of creeping dementia. Runs in the family, you might want to have it checked out. Remember how they found Zaydie Levy wandering down the 401 one day? "Just going for a walk." Anyway, now that you're up, you wanna go for a run?

ANDREW   *(lying back down)* Sure.

> *SASHA does some stretches. Sound of a distant train.*

It's three years since Dad died. We were all in this room, just like this, when they took him away. I started to get the shakes, and someone sat me down. Every muscle in my body seized up. Donna, you sat with me, calmed me down. A train was passing by then, too. I can't believe it's been three years, though. I can't believe it.—And the garden's a mess. We really ought to fix it up.

DONNA   I thought she hired someone.

DAVID   The guy's useless. I mean look at it.

ANDREW   We could do some work on it.

SASHA   Wouldn't bother. Anyway, where would you start?

> *Pause.*

ANDREW   We did alright, though. We brought him here, just like he wanted. This is where he wanted to die, not in that hospital. It was the last thing he said, do you remember, before he couldn't speak anymore. The nurses and doctors all said he wouldn't survive the trip, but we knew he would. Mom held his hand the whole way up, she kept stroking his forehead and saying he was going to be alright.

SASHA   Do you have to keep talking about it?… Just don't talk about it when Mom's around. You know how she gets. The slightest thing.

DAVID   So we're not supposed to talk about him?

SASHA   Not the end time. You have to get that awful stuff out of your mind, you have to push it away, remember the good things about him. If you can.

> *ANDREW lies down again.*

DAVID   Well. I oughta get that bookcase.

> *Enter FAYE, holding a box of chocolates.*

Hello Auntie Faye.

FAYE   Hello Andrew.

DAVID   It's David.

FAYE   Oh stop joking. Little whippersnapper, you're always joking with me. Would you like a chocolate?

DAVID   Oh… thanks.

SASHA   What's the vintage on those chocolates?

FAYE   Just bought em the other day.

SASHA   *(sotto)* That could mean ten years ago.

FAYE　I wouldn't mind a coffee.

> *DAVID prepares a coffee.*

Where's your father, boys?

> *Beat.*

SASHA　He's not here. He died, Aunt Faye.

FAYE　When did he die?

SASHA　Long time ago.

FAYE　Oh…. Where's Lou?

SASHA　Lou died.

FAYE　Did he? Was he here?

SASHA　Yes, he was here. Then he got sick.

FAYE　You boys are all so handsome. We had a nice time in London. Your father got into some awful trouble. He used to ride the tram without paying!

SASHA　Catcha later.

> *SASHA goes.*

DAVID　*(handing her a coffee)* Here you are, Aunt Faye.

FAYE　Oh, a coffee! Isn't that nice? I was just thinking I might like a coffee.

> *Enter ROSE, JACK, LEN and MORRIS, a neighbour. ROSE and LEN are trying to remember the words to a song.*

ROSE　How did it go, do you remember? "Hail, hail, the gang's all here…"

> *LEN joins in.*

LEN & ROSE　"What the heck do we care, what the heck do we care."
(*louder*) "Hail, hail, the gang's all here—why the heck should we care now?"

LEN　Ha ha ha!

ROSE　We kids used to sing that.

LEN　A long time ago, and look at us now.

JACK　Time marches on.

LEN　What's that?

JACK　I said, time marches on.

LEN　Uh huh.

ROSE　Look who stopped over.

DAVID　Hello, Morris.

MORRIS   Hello, hello. Nice day and so on. Came to find my granddaughter. We're going to the movies. There's a fellow nearby and—you won't believe it—he turned an old farmhouse into a movie theatre! It's something else, I'll tell you.

ANDREW   I'm going to lie down.

ROSE   You look so tired. I want you to see a doctor.

ANDREW   Because I'm tired?

ROSE   It's just... your father, he was always so tired at first...

DAVID   Mom, please. First of all, what he had, it's not hereditary, the doctors said so.

MORRIS   What do doctors know anyway? We used to think they knew everything, but it's obvious, take a look around, they don't know a thing. All these new diseases, and the doctors haven't got a clue about any of em. Those little bacteria are a hell of a lot stronger than human beings are, stronger, and a lot smarter, too.

ANDREW   Mom, I'm just tired from the trip. And the kids don't let up. Matthew always climbs into bed with us, and he won't go to sleep until I've read him three books.

ROSE   I just worry. You're my baby. You'll always be my baby.

ANDREW   Well. I'll see you later.

ANDREW goes.

LEN   He looks just like you, Rose. He always did, more or less, but he looks just like you when you were his age.

ROSE   He didn't sleep much in England. Something was bothering him, but he wouldn't say what. None of my boys like to talk about what's bothering them. Just like their father.

MORRIS   When you get right down to it, we're just guinea pigs. When I found out about my prostate, I said to myself, "That's it, that's the end." So to speak. The doctors were talking about surgery and this and that. Then my granddaughter, she started giving me all kinds of books and articles, all kinds of stuff about diet, exercise. David, if it should ever happen to you, and I pray to God it doesn't—

DAVID   Thank you.

MORRIS   I just want to say one thing: cranberries. Blueberries are fine, too, but *cranberries*.

ROSE   The important thing is that you've got your health back.

FAYE   Where's Sidney?

Beat.

ROSE   Would someone get me a coffee? The coffee in England was terrible. So bitter. And they charged for it an arm and a leg.

FAYE   Why isn't Sidney here?

DAVID   Bookcase.

DAVID leaves.

ROSE   Well, here we are. I feel like… I don't know, it's strange to be here without… I missed coming here. It's so nice to get away to the country. But everything's changed so much, in just a few years. Even the town, it's gotten so big, and there are so many people. We stopped to pick up a few things and we had to circle for ten minutes just to find a parking spot. It wasn't until we got closer to the cottage that things started to look the same. That's nice coffee.

JACK   Well, I should be going. I have a meeting in the city first thing in the morning. I was hoping we'd have a chance to talk, Rose. It's a little disappointing…. You look wonderful, but then you always did.

MORRIS   Better than wonderful. She looks like a new woman—I feel twenty years younger just looking at her!

FAYE   I can't find Lou.

ROSE sighs.

LEN   Lou died, Faye.

FAYE   He did? What's wrong with me? I can't remember things.

ROSE   *(rising)* There's something wrong with this chair.

LEN   The back's loose. It needs to be glued.

ROSE   One of the boys can fix it.

FAYE   Where's Sidney? Why isn't Sidney here?

ROSE   And the deck—some of the boards are coming apart.

JACK   Frankly, the whole place is coming apart. I mean it's obvious. I had a look around before. The roof's leaking in the back room; half the eavestroughs have fallen off; there are cracks in the ceiling. *(looks at his watch)* There's a long list. I can't go into it now. Just take a good look around, you'll see what I'm talking about. So you see maybe this new by-law's not such a bad thing. On the one hand, it means that, yes, the cottage is now too close to the water and it's going to cost an extraordinary amount of money to push it back; on the other hand, there's an opportunity here.

ROSE   What do you mean, "opportunity"? Opportunity for what?

JACK   Just listen for a second. Do you realize that your property line extends from the forest to practically half way round the lake, right to Morris's place? That's why no one's been able to build on that whole side. You own it! All you've got to do is clear the forest, and the gardens, knock this place down, and you'd have room for five or six small cottages, which you can rent for three thousand a month—each! And if you and Morris here sell together, why you can double all those figures!

LEN   That's the stupidest thing I've ever heard.

ROSE   I don't understand…. "Knock this place down?"

JACK   Or, if you don't want to do that, just sell it outright. There would be a bidding war like you've never seen. Could go as high as six, seven hundred thousand. Just think what you could do with that money. I could personally put you in touch with several people I know who are looking to buy up here. And this is an ideal spot. Close enough to town but without a lot of traffic nearby. The thing is, you've got to decide soon. Right now it's a seller's market, but you never know, it could turn around in a month.

ROSE   Jack, I don't think you understand—Sidney *built* this house. And the garden, he spent so much time out there…

JACK   And he did a very good job. But the times have caught up with him, or with his work anyway—the town says the cottage is too close to the water, so either you move it or you tear it down and start all over. I say the time has come to move on. The cottage is practically worthless; but the land it's sitting on is worth fifty times what Sid paid for it.

ROSE   How can you say it's "worthless"? We spent forty years up here; every weekend in the spring and fall, and in the summer we were here almost every day.

LEN   This house was written up in the Peterborough *Examiner*.

JACK   (*looks at his watch*) It's up to you, of course. But decide, and soon. You're sitting on a gold mine, and you don't even realize it.

FAYE   They were always building things, Sid and Lou. Bookcases, chairs, tables— people used to say, "The two of you should open a carpentry shop."

ROSE   Sid was always trying to show the boys how to make things.

FAYE   They've forgotten it all. Sid and Lou loved to work with their hands. Not like now. Now it's all made for you, and if it breaks, out it goes in the trash, and you buy a new one to take its place.

LEN   Faye, drink your coffee.

FAYE   Oh, did someone get me a coffee? How nice.

> *Pause.*

MORRIS   Well, and how was London? Did you see any shows?

ROSE   We saw the Andrew Lloyd Webber, but it wasn't up to his usual.

MORRIS   The theatre here did *Fiddler on the Roof.* It was a big production.

ROSE   Oh I love that one. We did that one at the synagogue. You should have seen Sid, he played Tevye, and everyone said, "You should be on the professional stage!"

> *LEN bursts into a rendition of "If I Were a Rich Man," until cut off by JACK.*

JACK   The point is, when Sid bought this place, it was still pretty far from the city. But now Toronto's grown so much that people need to go even farther looking for a summer place—never mind summer, nowadays they build for year-round use. I personally know the widow of a dot-com multimillionaire who's tearing her hair out looking for a place to build a new summer home. She has three kids, and they need a lot of space. Just say the word and she'll write you a cheque for seven hundred and fifty thousand.

LEN   Look, we don't want to hear it.

> *DAVID returns, carrying an old bookcase.*

Careful, David.

ROSE   There it is. It's the very first thing your father made by himself. Look, he carved his name into the back. And the date.

LEN   It's 40 years old—on the button. How about that? Calls for a celebration. How about we all go into town tonight, to that Italian restaurant?

ROSE   Oh yes, let's do that, and I'm buying.

LEN   You're not!

MORRIS   You know, some of the stuff at my place is a hundred years old.

LEN   Yes, but this—Sid *made* this. *(holding an imaginary wine glass)* Blessed art thou, O Lord Our God, Ruler of the Universe, who has given us this wonderful bookcase.

ROSE   Amen! He loved to make things, especially for the grandchildren. Do you think they remember him, the children?

DAVID   Sure they do.

ROSE   Sometimes they point at his picture and I say, "That's your Zaydie," and they say, "I know," but I don't know if they're just saying it.

LEN   I never had Sid's skill. Whenever I tried to make something, it would come out all crooked. The only thing my hands were good for was crunching numbers. That's not something you remember. But a bookcase, just look at it... he left it behind, he left it for us to look at, to talk about. Sid was a strong man, you know. Right to the end. I'll never forget shaking his hand, the last time I went to see him. He—well.

Pause.

JACK   Well, anyway I should—

LEN   "Hail, hail, the gang's all here! What the heck do we care…"

JACK   I should be going.

CAROLINE enters, holding a cell phone.

Those aren't much good up here, I'm afraid.

CAROLINE   Hm? Oh. Hello, Jack. No, you're right. I can't get a signal.

JACK   Try down by the water, that sometimes works.

LEN   Throw it in while you're at it. Used to be, you'd go to the cottage, you didn't *want* someone to call you.

CAROLINE   Now, now, Len, the 21st century's just around the corner.

LEN   I'll be waiting with a mallet.

JACK   Caroline, I'll join you, if you don't mind. I've got a couple of calls to make myself. And then I really have to get going, it's, goodness look at the time. *(goes about shaking hands)* Goodbye, Len. Morris, see you again. Nice talking to you, young man. *(to ROSE)* I kind of hate to leave. But you think about what I said now. You've got to act sooner than later. Now I really have to go. Should be smooth sailing into town.

He goes, following CAROLINE out. DAVID takes note.

LEN   Money grubber. Even as a kid, he was always playing the angles. Five ball in the corner pocket—and your money in his.

ROSE   He's a good agent, that's all. He sees a property and right away he thinks about selling it.

DAVID   Who's selling?

LEN   No one, it's just a lot of talk.

MORRIS   People have been trying to get me to sell forever. A few years ago, I found a note tucked in the door. "If you should ever want to sell, please call me." And there was a name and a number.

ROSE   As though you'd sell something that held so many memories!

MORRIS   You know, I was reading the other day in the paper, one of these big shot developers, a real macher, talking about how these millionaires and movie stars are moving in around here.

ROSE   You'll never believe who bought a place just on the other side of the bridge. What's her name, the movie star, well, she used to be on television, oh, I can see her, she was on that show where people jumped out of the walls—well, they didn't exactly *jump*, but they were behind the wall and they would peek out and say a joke.

MORRIS   Yes, exactly, and she's putting up a mansion and a huge fence. Well, the neighbours of course started complaining, and this big shot, you know what he said? "Who cares? Their time's over."

LEN   Who's time?

MORRIS   *Our* time.

LEN   I never heard such a thing.

> *Silence.*

MORRIS   Once in an orange moon, I think to myself it would be nice to leave a little money to the grandkids.

ROSE   My father always used to say, "if you need money, it'll turn up."

MORRIS   Yes, and he was right. The Lotto's up to seven million tomorrow; you never know!

ROSE   Well, that's the last of the coffee. Should we make a reservation for the restaurant?

DAVID   Why don't we stay in tonight, hm? I'll cook.

ROSE   You sure? You're so busy.

DAVID   I want to.

ROSE   Liz and the kids coming?

DAVID   Maybe next week.

LEN   *(at the window)* The garden still looks good. I don't know what that Skepian's talking about. That path Sid made, with the lights all along it, I wish we had something like that.

DONNA   The zinnias are beautiful, Mom. Should I bring some in?

ROSE   Well, they might have bugs. Just leave them, I think. *(beat)* The garden's so overgrown. It's not the same, nothing's been the same, nothing will ever be the same.

LEN   You don't have to sell.

ROSE   Sometimes I look out there, I think I see Sid... he used to love to sit there, in the arbour... there's so much to be done. He'd be out there right now, if—

> *TRISH suddenly appears in the doorway. ROSE starts.*

TRISH   Sorry. Didn't mean to scare you.... I'm back for the summer. I just wanted to say hello, see how you are.... I was just tidying up, hope you don't mind.

MORRIS   You don't remember my granddaughter? I don't blame you!

ROSE Trish? *(embracing her)* Oh, Trish, Trish… he thought of you as one of his own… he always said, "If I had a daughter…"

TRISH It's alright.

ROSE Now he's gone, he's gone… why? Why did he have to go so soon? *(recovers)* I'm sorry. It's not fair, I shouldn't cry like this in front of you.—Trish, what happened to you? You're all grown up, you're a young woman.

TRISH The other day, a waitress called me "Ma'am."

ROSE You were just a girl when Sid died; it was so cute the way you'd always come over to help out. Now look at you, you look like a boy.

TRISH I'm just wearing my hair up—see?

ROSE Gorgeous. I used to have hair like that when I was your age.

TRISH It's still so pretty.

ROSE Come with me, we'll go sit in the garden. Faye, would you like to come outside? Someone give Faye a hand.

MORRIS *(helping FAYE to her feet)* Upsadaisy.

ROSE *(exiting, to TRISH)* You're in school?

TRISH It's a little complicated…

> Exit ROSE, TRISH, MORRIS and FAYE. LEN and DAVID remain.

LEN My sister has no idea about money; she never did. Sid always took care of the finances.

DAVID She does like to spend money. And then complain about never having any. I'd like to know what happened to what she cleared from the house. Andrew says there's hardly anything left.

LEN It's like a disease with her, only there's no cure. I've thought of a hundred ways to get her some money, but none of them amount to anything. If only we'd gotten our fair share of the inheritance. You must know about that. My father—your grandfather—was one of six kids, and a rich uncle left them a huge pot of money, almost a million dollars. Only by then your grandfather had passed away, and the others didn't want to let your mother and me have his share. We wanted to have a Beth Din—bring in a rabbi, get it all sorted out. Well, the five of them met and, as the story goes, they all but one voted to hold the Beth Din, only it had to be unanimous, so that was that. Apparently, one of them—we don't know the schmuck's name—stood up and yelled, "When it comes to money, I have no religion!" And then he stormed out. That was the last time we spoke to any of them, and that was twenty years ago now. That's all it takes to rip a family apart, even the closest ones. Mind you, I did once get a note from Aunt Gerty, when your grandmother died. She was the nicest of the bunch. She lives in Montreal. I could give her a call, or… I tell you what, maybe Sasha could ask his in-laws.

DAVID   I don't think so.

ANDREW appears in the doorway.

LEN   Why not? Caroline's parents are filthy rich.

DAVID   Filthy's right; they wallow in it. Besides, they don't much like us. After all, Caroline married beneath her station. We're the poor country cousins as far as they're concerned. Her family treated my parents like peasants. At the wedding even—had us in a separate room at the reception.

LEN   I remember. They served us cold cuts and pop.

DAVID   And when Sasha and Caroline separated a few years ago, her family cut him off—wouldn't even talk to him, like he was dirt, like he was nothing, not even human. But the way they treated my parents, that was the galling thing. Especially my father—they couldn't stand him, because he didn't dab the corners of his mouth with a linen napkin. But he had principles, which is more than I can say for those people.

LEN   Alright, David, but they're not monsters. And don't start turning your own parents into saints. After all, your father, for all his good points, and he had a lot, but he treated your mother pretty rotten. Maybe you don't remember; more than a few times she was at our house, in tears, saying how she wanted to leave him. She doesn't talk about that now; seems like she wishes the shiva had never ended.

DAVID   Andrew's here.

LEN   Uh? *(pause)* You know, I think I've got something in my eye. I've been trying to blink it out… anyway, did I mention what happened at the bank?

ANDREW comes in.

DAVID   I thought you went for a nap.

ANDREW   I couldn't sleep.

LEN   You've got your mother worried sick. You've got us all worried. You're a good kid, you're always thinking of others first. But you've got to think of yourself, too.

ANDREW   Sure. Listen, Uncle Len, you've been wonderful with Mom, but you can't go around saying those things.

LEN   I've always had a big mouth.

ANDREW   I mean why were you saying those things?

LEN   You know I never realize what a schmuck I sound like until it's too late. Like saying a prayer for the bookcase. I don't know why I do things like that.

FAYE returns.

FAYE   Where's Sid? I can't find him anywhere.

LEN   Faye, why don't we go sit down on the dock? You could use some fresh air. *(to the boys)* Maybe it'll make her sleepy. Anyway, boys, don't you worry about this business with the cottage. I've fought harder battles than this; I'm a man of the 40s—they didn't call us "the greatest generation" for nothing.

DAVID   Len, you weren't in the war.

LEN   Well I would have been if we hadn't won it so quickly. Anyway, the point is, we were different back then, we grew up with different values. I'm not the sort of man who backs down to anybody. No, sir, you'd have to be a real somebody for me to back down to you.

ANDREW   Thanks, Uncle.

DAVID   We appreciate it.

FAYE   *(angrily)* Len, come on!

LEN   I'm coming, I'm coming…

> *LEN, reprising "If I Were a Rich Man," exits with FAYE.*

ANDREW   I'm so tired. I brought some work up with me, all these books I have to read for the "new curriculum." A friend of mine says the government's out to destroy the school system. I wish they'd hurry up. Anyway, I start to read and fall asleep. Then as soon as my eyes are closed I wake up again. *(beat)* Do you think what Mom said, do you think it's possible?

> *Pause.*

ANDREW   Do you think what Mom said, do you think it's possible?

DAVID   Andrew, it's not hereditary. Stop thinking that. You're over-tired, that's all.

ANDREW   Yeah. You're right. I know you're right.—Still, there's a clinic in town. I might just have them run a test.

DAVID   If it'll make you feel better.—Anyway, I'm going to the guest house. While it's still standing. Gotta finish this script. You wouldn't believe what they pay in television—American television especially. Staggering, really. My agent's put me up for a series. He thinks I've got a pretty good shot at it. About vampire cops. They're cops, who are vampires… or something. Anyway, if it happens, I can put some money towards the cottage. Course I'll have to move to Los Angeles, so I don't know how much use I'll be getting out of it.

ANDREW   To Los Angeles? With Liz and the kids?

DAVID   Well, we gotta figure that out.

> *Outside, someone's been playing a guitar.*

That's Jeremy; he's pretty good. I keep telling myself to learn guitar. *(hesitantly)* I called home earlier. Wish I hadn't. When I spoke with the kids I had a funny sensation. I didn't understand what it was til later: they don't feel like they're mine. I felt so distant from them; like I was talking to someone else's kids. I always thought of myself as a good father. "A good father." When Dad was— when we brought him back here—and we each went in to talk to him… *(long pause)* I sat on the bed. I held his hand, stroked his hand. I knew what I wanted to say, only I wasn't sure I'd find the breath to say it with. You know, I was so afraid to touch him. Even to touch him. Imagine that, nearly forty, and afraid to touch your own father… I managed to calm myself. I leaned over, I said "You've been a good father." And—he said—Dad said—he whispered— "Liar." *(seeing that ANDREW has fallen asleep.)* …Sleeping like a baby.

> *SASHA enters, slightly winded from his run.*

SASHA Hey, we need to talk.

DAVID Yeah. Can it wait, though? I really need to get some work done.

SASHA Sure.

> *DAVID goes. SASHA goes to ANDREW, is about to startle him, as before. Stops. Covers him with a blanket.*

ACT 2

A few days later. The backyard of the cottage, near the guest house.
A sloping hill gives way to the lake. It's late afternoon. JEREMY strums on
a guitar. CAROLINE is applying sun block. SASHA has been for a swim
and is lying down. DAVID stares out at the lake, taking the last drag of
a cigarette, which he stamps underfoot. He has his laptop computer with
him. And a scotch.

CAROLINE   They asked me for my birth certificate at the liquor store yesterday.
Can you believe it? I said, "My God, don't tell me you think I'm anything less
than *eighteen*." And the lady behind the counter, this big beefy woman, said,
"Nope, but we got caught selling to minors, so they're making us card everyone
now." But the way she said it, and the look she gave me. The stupid hick. I'm
telling you the people around here have no manners, none. They dress horribly,
they're out of shape. Not that I should talk. Look at this. (*She pinches her waist.*)
I have *got* to get rid of this. Can you believe I've had four children? (*pats her*
stomach) This is the hard part. (*applies sun block to her legs*) When I was
younger I was into gymnastics. High beam, floor, horse, I did all that, and I was
good too. I went to the provincial finals and won all kinds of medals. I wanted
to go to the nationals, but they were in the week before exams, so my father said
absolutely not. It's too bad. I had all these thoughts of going to the Olympics.
I was really that good. There's no telling what my life might've been like if I'd
followed through. (*lays back, puts cucumbers over her eyes*) No telling at all.
(*pause*) I know I talk a lot. It would just be nice if someone answered back
once in a while. You guys are all the same. You'd sooner talk about some stupid
hockey player and how much he should be paid and blah blah blah. You'll talk
about it for hours. But ask you to open up, express how you feel…

JEREMY plays guitar and sings:

JEREMY   "Think I'll go out to Alberta, weather's good there in the fall/
Got some— (*hits the wrong chord, picks up*) —"Some friends that I can go
working for…"

CAROLINE   Jeremy, for God's sake. Your voice, dear. Really, if you want to sing
you should have taken singing lessons. Your father and I offered to send you but
you had other things on your mind.

JEREMY continues to strum.

You could do with guitar lessons while you're at it.

JEREMY   I just like to goof around.

CAROLINE   Let other kids goof around. You have to apply yourself seriously to
everything you take on in life. I can't stand laziness. You can choose to become
whatever you want, just as long as you're the best at it in the world. There's

no point in being second best. No one remembers second best. No one wants second best. Remember that.

JEREMY *(sings)* "Four strong winds that blow lonely/Seven seas that run high."

CAROLINE Ugh.

> *DONNA wanders in, joins in the song.*

JEREMY & DONNA "All these things that won't change, come what may."

> *They hum, looking for the words…*

CAROLINE It's Woodstock now.

DONNA I always get lost there, too.

JEREMY Is this bothering you, Uncle David? You came up here to work.

DAVID It's fine. It's nice. How do you know all those songs?

JEREMY Found all my dad's old albums.

CAROLINE One more reason to get rid of them all. I mean, *Joni Mitchell*.

JEREMY "They paved paradise, put up a parking lot, oo wha wha…"

CAROLINE Jeremy, Jeremy, that wasn't a request, dear.

> *JEREMY strums.*

DAVID Did you have a good time in London?

JEREMY Great time. I'd like to go back.

SASHA Tell him to get his grades up and he *will* go back.

CAROLINE It's not just his grades. His whole attitude has changed in the last year. I don't know what's gotten into him. He's become so sullen and impolite. And look at the way he dresses; shapeless t-shirts and filthy jeans. I keep telling him that appearance means everything; it tells the world you're confident, that you care, that you're respectful.

JEREMY Why don't I just shoot myself and save you the trouble?

CAROLINE Don't be a child, Jeremy.

> *JEREMY continues to strum.*

DONNA It's so nice to get away. I'm sort of dreading going back to the city. There's so much to do in the house. We're having the basement redone. I have three quotes, each one hugely different from the last. I haven't done any back-to-school shopping; the kids all need new clothes. Plus we finally decided on getting a second car, now that Andrew's going to be working so far out of town. I'm going to take a cooking course. It's through the synagogue. They show you how to prepare all the holiday meals; like, the real way to do it. Passover, Rosh Hashanah. Everything.

SASHA   Do you know much about books? David?

DAVID   Books?

SASHA   Publishing.

DAVID   Publishing books?

SASHA   Yeah, some guy called me the other day, asked if I'd be interested in writing a book on prozac.

DAVID   Oh yeah.

SASHA   You know, are we over-dependent on it, over-proscribing it to our kids, and what exactly is attention deficit disorder.

DAVID   Right, right.

SASHA   Personally I favour a return to shock therapy. What do you think I should charge for it?

DAVID   Shock therapy?

SASHA   The book.

DAVID   Depends on who it's for. Is it a textbook?

SASHA   Dunno.

DAVID   Or is it aimed more at the general, you know, public?

SASHA   Don't know.

> *Pause.*

So you don't know.

DAVID   Well—.

SASHA   It's fine, I know another guy who—it's fine.

DAVID   I could get you some information.

SASHA   Don't worry about it. *(yawning)* Donna, you should talk to Caroline's father about the basement.

DONNA   No, I don't want to impose.

SASHA   He won't mind.

CAROLINE   *(pointedly)* He never does.

> *Pause.*

DONNA   Anyway—

CAROLINE   It's no problem, Donna. In fact he's got a new development going in about ten minutes from you. He can send a couple of his men over; the basement will be done in a week.

DONNA   Really, I couldn't. Your father's done so much for us already.

CAROLINE   It's important to help each other out. We're family.

DONNA   That's so nice of you.

SASHA   *(reading the paper)* Hey, listen to this: "scientists have discovered a giant ant colony that stretches all the way from northern Italy to western Spain."

DAVID   That's a lotta ants.

SASHA   Whole lotta ants.

DONNA   Oh, that reminds, me I made a really nice pesto—different—with walnuts instead of pine nuts—will the kids eat it, or should I throw on some chicken fingers and fries?

DAVID   The thing I don't get is how you went from an ant colony to pesto—could you just walk me through that?

DONNA   I don't know. I just thought of all those ants, and how we had a terrible ant infestation in the backyard. They were coming up through this one little hole, and there must have been hundreds of thousands of them, it was the most disgusting thing I've ever seen, and the kids were crushing them. So I guess crushing ants reminded me of crushing things up. It's funny how you think of things.

CAROLINE   Mine will eat the pesto, it sounds delicious, I don't know about the others. What kind of pasta are you using?

DONNA   Fettuccini.

CAROLINE   Really? Because it's so nice with the little thin ones.

DONNA   Spaghettini?

CAROLINE   No, no. It starts with a "p." And you let the noodles come to room— I don't suppose we can get fresh pasta anywhere? Nevermind—you let it come to room temperature, then toss it with the pesto, not too much, just enough so it's nice and green, you know? And just a light salad. Anyway, do what you think is best.

DAVID   Hold the cucumbers.

> *DONNA goes. JEREMY returns to "Four Strong Winds."*

JEREMY   *(sings)* "All these things that won't change—"

CAROLINE   Oh God, he's back to that.

JEREMY   "—come what may."

CAROLINE   Jeremy, would you stop that awful *moaning?*

> *JEREMY stops playing. Starts to walk away.*

Where are you going?

JEREMY   For a walk.

CAROLINE   Don't go too far. It'll be dark soon.

JEREMY   It's pretty dark now.

> *JEREMY goes.*

CAROLINE   Are you ever going to speak to your son again?… Sasha?… I see, now it's me you're not going to talk to. Fine. *(removes the cucumbers, sits up)* Don't talk to me. Don't talk to anyone. I'm sick of it. Sick of it.

SASHA   *(as CAROLINE leaves)* The thing about these ants is that they work really well together. Like, there's red ants and black ants, and usually they fight to the death, but these ants, somehow, they've learned to work cooperatively, toward a common goal.

DAVID   They must have seen a therapist.

SASHA   Yeah. Listen, when Andrew gets back, the three of us should talk. About the cottage, I mean. Skepian's right, it's falling apart. We've already let half a week slip by. If we sell now—

DAVID   I thought you wanted to talk when Andrew gets back.—I mean, if you want to talk now, that's fine. But uh, you know. The three of us own it, so.

SASHA   Yeah. Sure. We can wait. The thing is, we don't want the town deciding this for us, right? I mean there's nothing we can do about the zoning stuff— the house has to move. That's all there is to it. Now I don't know about you, but I don't have a hundred thousand dollars lying around. Matter of fact, things are a little tight right now. So it seems to me —

DAVID   Look, are we waiting for Andrew or not?

SASHA   You want to wait for Andrew, we'll wait for Andrew.

DAVID   That's all I'm asking. Why is that so difficult?

SASHA   *Look*…. Forget it.

> *SASHA goes.*

DAVID   *Shit.*

> *Tries to get back to work. Can't. Puts the laptop aside. Makes a cell phone call.*

(too loud) Jenna, hi, it's David Levy. Is Ted around?… Thanks…. Ted, David. Good, good. Just wondering if—oh, sorry. *(normal level)* Just wondering if we've heard anything about—uh huh. Uh huh. So we don't know when they're gonna decide. Uh huh.

> *JEREMY and TRISH wander in. She's showing him photos. Their dialogue overlaps with the end of DAVID's phone call.*

Okay, so it's just wait and see. Alright, well I—hello? Hello?

The connection lost, he switches off. He gets to work.

TRISH   This is where we stayed.

JEREMY   Cool.

TRISH   This is us at the fishing village.

JEREMY   Who's this guy?

TRISH   Oh, that's Luke.

JEREMY   "Luke."

TRISH   He's this really cool guy from Vancouver, runs the Peace & Justice Centre. They arranged the whole trip. Here's where we set up the information booth, to show the farmers how to apply for loans from the Millennium Fund.

JEREMY   We should go somewhere else.

DAVID   It's fine. Keep talking. Try to sound like teenagers, though, would you? I'm trying to write a scene where two young lovers trip over the naked, decomposing body of a hooker. That ever happen to you?

CAROLINE   *(off)* Jeremy!

   JEREMY hangs his head.

JEREMY   *(to himself)* Just five *seconds*.

DAVID   Hey, listen. I know a guy around here with a wood chipper. If you want, we could—

CAROLINE   *(off)* Jeremy, inside please. You left your things lying all over the floor, now I'd like you to come and pick them up.

JEREMY   Back in a sec.

   He goes. DAVID continues to work. After a moment.

TRISH   Cool shirt.

DAVID   Hm?

TRISH   I said I like your shirt.

DAVID   Oh. It belonged to my father. It was the only one I could find that fit. He was a trim young fella til he hit, well, thirty. But he never threw a damn thing away. Let me see your pictures.

TRISH   I thought you were working.

DAVID   *(types)* "Oh my God, noooooooooo!"

   He repeatedly presses the letter "o." Puts the laptop down. TRISH hands over the photos. Notices his shirt.

TRISH   Those collars are back now. And, look, I love these little tabs on the sides.

DAVID   That's a hell of a shot.

TRISH   We were on top of this rickety old truck going about a hundred K down a mountain pass.

DAVID   Jesus.

TRISH   Yeah, and it was raining, too, and foggy. Three kids held my legs so I could get the shot.

DAVID   I think it's terrific what you're doing. I always wanted to travel to distant places. Give of myself.

TRISH   Is it too late?

DAVID   Fraid so. I'm in my Disappointed Years. That's where no matter what you do, everybody's disappointed. Apparently I'm due for a turnaround. A friend of mine says that when the dog star circles the hunter... or the fish, or... well, when something circles something else, all will be well.

TRISH   I don't understand. You're like this incredibly successful guy.

DAVID   *(laughs)* Now you sound like a teenager.

TRISH   It's true.

DAVID   No, my dear. I'm a failure. A 40-year-old failure. I've failed at everything really. I'm in a sort of catastrophic retreat. You ever been to Alaska?

TRISH   Nuh uh.

DAVID   I was there one time, took a little boat ride out to the glacier. The ice was blue, I forget why. Something to do with... I forget. Someone on the boat explained to me that the glacier was moving forward and backward at the same time. "Catastrophic retreat." *(hands back the photos)* Thanks for your memories.

TRISH   I have more. Not mine. Look. I found some photos in the shed, in a little box of nails. And this list of things to do in the garden.

DAVID   *(reading)* "One: trim roses. Two: transplant hostas. Three—." *(stops reading)*

TRISH   I love this photo.

DAVID   Look at that. In his sailor's outfit.

TRISH   He worked on a minesweeper, didn't he?

DAVID   In the radio room. They called him Sparks. God, he always loved the sound of water. He sought it. The back yard of our house was right next to the highway. He'd sit out there and listen to the traffic. He said it sounded like waves. And up here, he was always just a few steps from the water. Listen to it. Like the lake is breathing.

Pause. He hands back the photos and list. Lights a cigarette.

TRISH You okay? Maybe I'll go rescue Jeremy, huh?

> *DAVID nods. Voices, off. DAVID puts out the cigarette, sticks it in the pack. Enter ROSE, LEN and JACK.*

JACK You've got to decide, and quickly. Just tell me, yes or no, are you interested in my plan?

ROSE Who's been smoking?

LEN Hello, David. Finished writing?

DAVID Yeah.

JACK I'm waiting for an answer—yes or no.

LEN David, we went to town for lunch. You should have come with. We passed by the theatre; it was packed. People were lined up around the block. I said to Rose, I said, "We ought to go in there and ask them why they never do plays by David Levy." She said, "Oh, he'd be so angry if we did that."

ROSE I didn't say "angry."

JACK One word!

LEN *(yawns)* Sleepy. I need to go for a run. Where's Sash, maybe he'll go with me.

DAVID He went for a swim.

ROSE So late?

DAVID *(under his breath)* Christ.

ROSE *(peering out at the lake)* I worry about him. Him and Caroline, something's wrong, I can tell. Money. It's always money. It's her, though. She spends like it's going out of style. And he works like a dog to keep up. I know he likes to spend, too—just like his mother.

LEN Can you believe she tried to pick up the bill today?

JACK I wouldn't hear of it.

LEN You wouldn't believe this place, David. Twelve dollars for an appetizer! And when it came, like this. *(indicates a small portion)* I said to the waitress, "Excuse me, does this come with a microscope?"

ROSE The look on her *face*.

LEN "Because I can't *find* it." She didn't like me at first. But by the end, I was cracking with the jokes, I was making with the faces—then I said to her, I said, "You have a nice smile, you know that? You ought to bring it out more often." You'll never guess, David, she started to cry, ran into the kitchen.

ROSE We could hear her from our table.

LEN Like I insulted her. All I said was she had a nice smile.

JACK   She does. But she's had a very hard life. I happen to know her a little. Wanted to be an actress; it never worked out for her. Now listen, Rose—

LEN   So—what—she's not used to people being kind to her?

JACK   I don't think that's it.

LEN   I never heard of such a thing. Tell a pretty girl she has a nice smile—she weeps! But that's how it is with me. People are always taking what I say the wrong way. Isn't that right, Rose?

ROSE   Always, since we were little kids.

> *SASHA enters, towelling himself off.*

LEN   Here's Johnny Weismuller already. How was the swim?

SASHA   Good, good.

DAVID   Break the record?

SASHA   Nah, I started cramping up.

ROSE   Oh God, where?

SASHA   Ma, it's nothing, a little cramp.

ROSE   My boys never tell me what's wrong.

SASHA   *(laughing)* I just *did.*

JACK   Don't you people understand that unless you do something—and quickly— your cottage is going to be condemned?

LEN   Everything's under control. I spoke with Aunt Gerty; we had a good talk. She said she never wanted things to end up the way they did.

ROSE   It's a shame, to lose your family. What have you got if you haven't got your family?

LEN   She finally told me who it was voted against us. Morton Fink. As if we didn't know. I always said, "Fink—you're a fink." I said it to his face one time; he nearly punched me.

ROSE   He was a real piece of work, that Morton.

LEN   Once a Fink, always a fink.

JACK   People, people.

LEN   Anyway, Gerty said she'd be happy to loan us some money.

JACK   How much?

LEN   Two, maybe three.

JACK   "Two, maybe three"! You need seventy-five thousand—*at least*! And that's just to push back the main house. The guest house has to come down, too, or did you forget about that? Then there's going to be extensive repairs. I'll tell you something, once you move a house, it's never the same; and *this* house, my God, it'll be a miracle if it's still standing after the move. I mean forgive me for saying this, but you people have no idea what's going on; you have no business sense at all.

ROSE   Tell us, then, Jack.

JACK   I've told you. I don't know if I should scream, or cry, or fall down dead in a faint. You people have the opportunity of a lifetime and you—

> *Len suddenly bursts into an imitation of Walter Huston's character from "The Treasure of the Sierra Madre," dancing and waving his arms back and forth.*

LEN   Ee hee hee! You crazy fools! Yer sittin' on a gold mine, a gold mine I tell ya, and ya don't even know it! Ee hee hee!

JACK   You're an idiot!

LEN   Ee hee hee!

> *JACK starts to go.*

ROSE   Jack, wait. Don't go. Stay for dinner. We'll talk it over with the boys.

LEN   Well, I think I'll go for a swim.

ROSE   Before dinner?

LEN   Ach.

> *LEN goes.*

DAVID   Well. I have to make a phone call. Mr Skepian.

JACK   Good to see you again.

> *DAVID goes. SASHA goes into the house. ROSE and JACK are left alone.*

ROSE   I have a bad feeling. I keep thinking the house is going to fall down, and all of us inside it, just collapse on our heads. I'm so afraid all the time. I can't even say what it is. I can't put a finger on it.

JACK   Well, Sasha would call it dime store Freud, but if you don't mind my saying, I think it might be nothing more than guilt. Inside, you know the best thing to do is move on, but you feel beholden to Sid's memory. But I'm telling you, Sid himself would probably agree that the best thing to do is take the money and run. I always said he was a smart man.

ROSE   I look at his picture and he says, "Rose, don't sell!"... I keep thinking he'll be angry with me. He had a terrible anger. The fights, it was so hard, and the children heard every word. I almost left him.—Things didn't turn out the way he'd hoped. He had to drive an hour to work and an hour back, every day. He hardly ever saw the boys, even on weekends. But he worked so hard, and then he felt like he just never got a break. Being turned out of the house, that was the worst; I pawned my wedding ring just to make the mortgage, but the next month there was nothing. They put our things on the lawn. We went to live with my parents… it was alright at first, but my mother and Sid did *not* get along. She thought I could have done better; she never said it. She thought it. And my father—God rest him—

JACK   The best of men.

ROSE   Oh boy was he ever. I never saw him angry, not once in his life. I was his princess; he'd take me to all the shops on his route—he was a window-washer—they called him The Mayor of Spadina—And he'd take me to Mendel's Shoes, and Mr Mendel was always so happy to see me. One time I wanted heels—oh, I wanted them so badly—and my mother said, "No heels!" When we got to the store, my father said, "Mr Mendel, this girl wants heels!" And when we got home—the look on my mother's face! And my father said, "I can't deny her a thing, Rachela, not a thing." *(through tears)* Daddy, Daddy.

> *JACK goes to her.*

JACK   There now, Rose. There now…. I see him in you, Rose. I see his spirit in you. You're a wonderful woman—you never seem to get any older; you have the spirit of a woman half your age, Rosey…. Good Lord, did you hear that? I called you "Rosey." Ha! Like the way I did. Like we were still a couple of teenagers. Oh God, Rosey, the way you lit up a room.

ROSE   I still can, buster!

JACK   There you go! That's the Rosey I fell in love with!

> *Pause. She breaks from him, gently.*

ROSE   It's cooling down. That wind.

> *She takes out a kerchief, wraps it around her head, ties it beneath her chin. Music is heard.*

JACK   Listen to that. It's coming from across the way. Looks like a wedding.

ROSE   I love Klezmer music.

JACK   They don't play it like that anymore. Now it's all these bleeps and bloops, who needs it? *(He takes her hand.)* Rose. Sweet Rose. The way I'm seeing you right now, it was just like the last time I saw you. You'd wrapped a kerchief around your head, it was so windy by the lake. You held yourself tight. I knew it would be the last time I'd see you. I couldn't understand it. I thought, probably she thinks I'm not good enough for her. I thought, maybe my father scared her off. He was an idiot, that man; he knew nothing, he taught me nothing. One time I came home from school. My teacher had called to say I was slacking off. The old man was waiting for me. "You're lazy," he said, gave me a whack across the back of my neck, called me a good-for-nothing, said I'd never amount to anything, all kinds of things he said, and sent me to my room. I was maybe nine or ten. There wasn't even anyone around to comfort me…. I didn't meet a kind soul in this world til I met you, and that's the God's honest truth. I don't think there's another person in this world like you, so incapable of hate. I can't tell you how many times I wondered about how things might have turned out differently, if only I'd had some sign from you, not even a word, but a sign, as we went on our walk, a sign that you'd wait for me.

ROSE …What walk, Jack?

JACK …Why…

> LEN enters, with FAYE. LEN holds a sweater for her.

LEN Faye, Sid died.

ROSE Oh God.

FAYE He did?

LEN Yes, Faye, a long time ago. Now, will you put this sweater on? It's cold.

ROSE She keeps saying it, over and over. I can't stand it anymore.

FAYE Let's go for a walk. It used to be so nice to take a walk by the river. We'll hop on the tram.

LEN She thinks she's in London.

FAYE What'd you say?

LEN I said, it's too far to walk. We have to drive.

FAYE Now, how much is the fare? What's happened to my head? I can't seem to remember anything. What's wrong with me? I've gotten so old.

LEN You'll outlive the bunch of us, Faye.

FAYE Got married when I was sixteen. Three kids by the time I was twenty, and would have had a fourth but we lost that one. We were always losing them then. Mum lost three—maybe more. The police came to arrest her one time, they accused her of smothering her own children…. Well, maybe it was true. No one ever found out for sure. All I know is, she didn't take the pillow to me, or to Sid. We used to have much bigger families back then. Nowadays it's one child, two at the most, and, oh, how they're spoiled. It's all because of that women's liberation. All of a sudden, women didn't want to stay at home. They wanted to go out and get jobs. Everything got so mixed up; no one knows their place anymore. The other day I saw a man pushing a stroller through the park—in the middle of the day! *(seeing JEREMY approach)* Oh, Sid, there you are!

ROSE It's not Sid you stupid old woman! Stop asking for Sid, do you hear me? Stop it!

> Pause.

FAYE What's she talking about? Are we going to the river or not?

LEN   Sure we are. We'll just wait here for the tram, Faye.

FAYE   Oh, that's alright then.—She oughtn't to yell at me.

> *Enter ANDREW, DAVID (holding a replenished glass of scotch), JEREMY and TRISH.*

LEN   Here they are, the young and the reckless.

ANDREW   Hey, Mom.

> *DONNA enters.*

ROSE   Andrew… David… come here, come here. *(embracing them, tight, almost squishing them)* I love you so much, do you know that?

DAVID   Got a rough idea.

DONNA   Dinner'll be ready soon. Caroline's got it under control.

JACK   Good Lord, we just had lunch not too long ago. I tell you, hanging around with you people is bad for my waistline.

ROSE   Where were you a whole day?

ANDREW   I had a couple of errands to run in town.

DONNA   Trish, that is a fabulous skirt. Did you make it?

TRISH   Mm hm.

DONNA   It's *so* pretty. You could start your own line.

TRISH   I just do it for myself.

ROSE   She's going into fashion design at Humber College.

JACK   Oh? I thought she was going into activism.

TRISH   Ha ha.

JACK   Oh, where's your sense of humour? You gotta laugh once in a while; it's good for the soul. Tell you what. Why don't the bunch of us go into town tomorrow and see the play they're putting on? My treat. A couple of friends of mine saw it, said it was very funny, very "risqué."

DAVID   *(acting a buxom blonde)* "Oh, Mr Abercrombie, there's something I need to get off my chest."

JACK   You don't approve. I suppose you don't like those old fashioned plays. Well, I like a corny joke and a few plot twists. Not like your modern plays, where nothing happens and everyone's depressed—including the audience. And your plays—

DAVID   Which you've never seen.

JACK   I've been told about them. I know people who see them. And I've read about them. Why do you say those things about Israel? About the Jews?

DAVID   What things?

JACK   You write that Israel's to blame for everything that's wrong over there. Don't you understand, young man, you contribute to the bad feelings against the Jews.

DAVID   Rubbish.

JACK   Instead of talking about the bad things, you should write about the achievements.

DAVID   Of—?

JACK   The Jews. Why is it that everywhere we go, we blossom? We become leaders in practically every field—not just in business, or medicine or law, where you'd expect, but in journalism, education, the arts—practically anything you can think of, and out of all proportion to our numbers. Just look at the statistics, and you'll see it's true: the Jews always do better than the rest.

DAVID   You know, if you said that with a German accent, it wouldn't sound so good.

JACK   My point is, the Jewish people are indestructible; our enemies have been trying to kill us off for centuries, but we endure; we adapt, but we always stay true to our core being, which is a deep love for all humanity.

DAVID   Tell that to the Palestinians.

JACK   Well, there he goes again.

ROSE   Really, do we have to talk about this?

JACK   Look, you're a talented fellow. No one's telling you what to write. All I'm saying is, why not use your talent for something less destructive? Why depress people? I'll tell you what: I'll give you a suggestion, and you can take it or leave it. It seems to me that what we really need now is a play about intermarriage. Think about it; it's a big problem. The Jews are marrying themselves right out of existence.

DAVID   I really think "Bridget Loves Bernie" was the last word on the subject.

JACK   Now you're making fun, but I'm telling you—in fact, I was talking to a Rabbi not too long ago, and he said, "Jack, intermarriage is a scourge; a second Holocaust."

DAVID   Good God.

JACK   Well, someone ought to write about it.

DONNA   It sounds pretty interesting, actually, I'd see that.

DAVID   (*mincing*) "Sounds pretty interesting actually, I'd see that." (*holding up a glass of scotch*) To mediocrity! Common sense art for a Common Sense Revolution!—I came up here to get away from this kind of idiocy.

DONNA   Now I'm an idiot?

ROSE   David!

DONNA   I don't appreciate that.

DAVID   I'm not talking about you, I'm talking about him. Don't tell me what "the people" want! Who are you to speak for "the people"? It's "people" like you who keep "the people" from hearing or seeing anything *except* the sort of crap you're advocating.

JACK   I merely said—

DAVID   I mean you go around, you sell, you sell, you buy, you sell, well we're not selling.

ROSE   David, what's wrong with you?

LEN   I think he's on drugs.

DAVID   Look, what exactly are you hanging around here for? We've already told you, we're not interested in your offer.

JACK   I don't know what you're so angry about, young man.

DAVID   And that's another thing—quit trying to put me in my place with that "young man" stuff.

JACK   Oh, you've "lived," have you?

DAVID   I mean it's funny you just happened to be in the neighbourhood the other day. First time in three years my mother's been here, and you just happen to have a For Sale sign in your back pocket.

JACK   Now look. I think you'd better watch what you're saying.

DAVID   I don't watch what I'm saying. Gets me into all sorts of trouble.

DONNA   I think we should stop this.

DAVID   *(overlapping)* Where's the scotch?

ROSE   Haven't you had enough?

DAVID   *(pretending to be staggering drunk)* "Is there an officer, problem?"

JACK   You're very sure of yourself, aren't you?

DAVID   I mean, don't you own enough? Can't you leave *some* to the rest of us?

ROSE   *David.*

DAVID   Never mind, never mind.

JACK   It's alright. It doesn't bother me. I'm used to it. Anyway, he's supposed to say things like that, otherwise his fellow artists will think he's a sell out. You should try running a business some day. Spend a year balancing the books—or even a month, an hour. It's not so easy to do what I do. But that's alright. You think what you want.

ROSE   Please, let's change the subject.

DONNA   I saw a really good show on TV the other day.

DAVID   She said change the subject, not the station.

DONNA   Well, I—

ROSE   Go ahead, don't listen to him.

DONNA   No, it was just, it was on one of the educational channels. I just sort of flicked it on, and—. There were two people, and they were talking about, was there any progress made in the last hundred years? Like, were we moving forward or backward?

LEN   Definitely forward. That's my answer.

DONNA   Well, I guess it depends on how you measure it. I suppose in terms of science and medicine, we're moving forward. But what about poverty, war, hunger. Those things are all still with us, we haven't figured out a way to eradicate them, and it doesn't look like we ever will.

JACK   That doesn't mean that we're not moving forward. It's sad to say, but those things will always be with us.

DONNA   But why? That's what I can't understand. And the thing is, people don't seem to care about it anymore. Oh, once in a while there's a benefit for the homeless or something, but mainly we sort of don't care. Like, why? Are we basically a selfish, uncaring, you know, people? Or did we become that? It really bothers me. And I think, are my kids going to think any differently? The junk they watch on TV, the video games, the movies, it's all—none of it's *about* anything. It's like they're being brainwashed into believing that the One True Good is making profit, and to hell with anyone who gets in your way. It just—it makes me so sad…

ROSE   Donna?

DONNA   I'm sorry. It just makes me so upset. I wish I could do something. I want to do something. I just don't have the time…. Anyway, it's a nice sunset.

JACK   Glorious.

> *Suddenly a loud boom is heard, in the distance. They all react.*

ROSE   What was that?

JACK   I don't know. It sounded like it was coming from across the lake.

LEN   It sounded like a rifle shot.

DONNA   Do you think it's poachers?

JEREMY   No. Look. They're shooting off flares. There—see? Just kids, goofing around. Having fun.

> *Another blast is heard.*

ROSE   Oh, it's horrible.

FAYE   It was like this during the raids. We went to the basement, all of us. We all sat there, huddled together, in the dark. No candles, nothing. Sidney was away at war; we wondered if we'd ever see him again.

ROSE   Let's go into dinner. Come on, children.—David?

DAVID   Be there in a minute.

ROSE   Come, Andrew.

JACK   Look, I have to say it one more time—unless you come up with the money to meet the order, the planning office will take over the property. You've already let one week slip by. Please, think about it. Think!

> *Everyone goes except TRISH and JEREMY. JEREMY strums the guitar.*

TRISH   It's so nice out here.—Your mom doesn't much like me, does she?

JEREMY   She thinks we're in love.

> *TRISH laughs. JEREMY keeps picking away at the strings, absentmindedly.*

I don't want to go to university. My dad's not talking to me. I thought I'd come here and figure it out. Something about this place. But I'm not figuring it out. I'm even more confused than before. This used to be a kind of home.

TRISH   Jeremy, the whole world is our home. The world is an amazing place, filled with amazing people and incredible places. You need to break away, Jeremy. You do. If you live your life the way they want you to live it, do you think you'll be happy? Do you think *they're* happy?

> *She stops him playing guitar.*

Your grandfather was a great man—a giant—you know why? Because he had principles. He stood for something, and you knew what it was. He used to tell me great stories about fighting the Brownshirts in London; he and his friends used to go chasing them down the streets, get into fights. Sometimes they got beat up, but the point is they stood up to the fascists.

> *CAROLINE enters, unseen by TRISH and JEREMY. JEREMY continues to strum the guitar.*

Your family pretends to be these great liberals, who care about social justice. But in the end, they only care about themselves. Like your Aunt Donna, saying nobody cares. That's so wrong. How can we live in such a big country, and the people be so small? *(beat)* You see that cottage there? I basically grew up in that place. Every summer and just about every weekend I was there. I know every island in this lake. Now I want to get to know the world like I know this place…. There's going to be this amazing gathering in Seattle, in November. All the big powers are meeting to talk about global this and global that, and then there's going to be all these other people, from all over the world, coming together to have a real discussion, to talk about what really needs to happen, what matters to the rest of us. Come with me.

JEREMY   I'd like to. Only…

TRISH   Only you need permission? You don't, Jeremy. You're an adult. You can do whatever you want…

> *He tries to kiss her.*

Don't do that.

JEREMY   Sorry.

CAROLINE   Jeremy? Dinner.

JEREMY   I'm not hungry.

CAROLINE   That's fine, but you can come sit at the table with the rest of us…. Jeremy.

> *JEREMY heads in, very suddenly.*

TRISH   See you, Jeremy.

> *JEREMY gives her a wave, disappears.*

CAROLINE   Nice night.

TRISH   Yeah. The weather's been nice.

CAROLINE   All set for first year?

TRISH   Pretty much.

CAROLINE   That's nice. So's Jeremy.

TRISH   Yeah. I should get going. Goodnight.

CAROLINE   Night.

> *CAROLINE stands there a moment, looking out at the lake. Music from the wedding can be heard again. She wipes away tears. A third loud boom is heard. The sky lightens momentarily. Blackout.*

ACT 3

The garden. Late August. A winding path from the house leads to an arbour with a built-in bench, room enough for two people to sit. It's early evening. CAROLINE, DAVID and ANDREW, waiting for news on the fate of the cottage. From inside the house come the sounds of klezmer music. Company has been invited.

ANDREW   What's taking them so long? They should be back by now.

CAROLINE   Who knows? Could be anything. Maybe the planning office is going to grant an extension.

DAVID   Doubt it.

Pause.

ANDREW   Got the results back. They can't find anything.

DAVID   This the second test?

ANDREW   Just want to rule out everything. Anyway, there's one more test they can run.

CAROLINE   Are you still not sleeping, dear?

ANDREW   Not a wink.

MORRIS   *(off)* Sounds wonderful! You don't happen to know "Alle Breder"?... Terrific... I haven't heard that in years! *(entering)* Ha ha! You know, this was a lovely idea, this little party. Your mother's tickled. She had tears in her eyes before. Maybe I'll dance on a chair! I feel like doing something, uh, what's that word?

DAVID   Impulsive.

MORRIS   Yes. Then again, my count's gone up, just a bit, just a bissel. I can't understand it. I was always healthy as a horse. My father—*olev ha'shalom*—had a wonderful sense of humour, and he used to say—ha ha ha—that—ha ha ha—that— *(beat)* Now what was I going to say?

CAROLINE   Morris, we were just—

MORRIS   Ah, I remember: he used to say, "We Siegels are descended from the horse that Caligula made senator," and—you see—well, it always seemed funny to us.

CAROLINE   That is funny. It's just, we're having a little conversation.

MORRIS   Mm?—Oh! Oh, I see. Yes. Don't let me bother you. Not to worry. That's just the way I get when I don't sleep. *(sitting down)* I won't say a word. Matter of fact, I'll probably just nod off. Didn't get much sleep last night, all this business with the property. I don't suppose there's been any word.

ANDREW Not in the last five minutes, no.

JEREMY and TRISH wander in.

DAVID You sure you weren't descended from a mule instead of a horse?

MORRIS What's that? I don't think so. You know I've never seen a mule.

DAVID They have very big ears.

CAROLINE Jeremy.

MORRIS That's right. And they always seem so sad.

CAROLINE Jeremy, why don't you show Morris those pictures from London?

MORRIS London? Wonderful. Haven't been there in twenty years. More.

CAROLINE They're in the living room, on the bookcase.

MORRIS *(being led out by JEREMY)* It's very expensive, you know.

ANDREW Well… maybe, maybe it's a sign, if, you know, if it's taking this long. Maybe something's being worked out.

DAVID No doubt.

CAROLINE Here he comes again.

Enter MORRIS, in a panic, followed by JEREMY.

MORRIS Where is it? I had it on me. I know I had it on me when I was out here.

JEREMY He's lost his wallet.

MORRIS I just took a hundred dollars out of the machine.

They all search for the wallet.

I was sitting right here. And I…

TRISH Here it is.

MORRIS Oh, thank God. *(kisses the wallet, then searches it)* Let's see… twenty, forty, sixty… Visa, Mastercard, Shoppers, Second Cup, all here, all here—look, I have three free coffees saved up.

CAROLINE Trish, be a darling, take your grandfather in for a drink.

MORRIS Yes, a drink, I could use one. *(heading off)* It's a terrible thing to lose your wallet. I remember one time, I turned the house upside down. The cab was waiting outside, but what could I do?

CAROLINE Jeremy.

MORRIS It was a terrible dilemma, because the meter was running the whole time…

CAROLINE We need a little privacy.

JEREMY   Oh. Sorry.

CAROLINE   Why don't you go find your cousins?

JEREMY   They're playing video games. I'm gonna take a walk.

CAROLINE   Don't go too far. There was a fox wandering around loose before.

> *JEREMY, behind CAROLINE's back, pretends to dig his claws into her neck, then goes.*

DAVID   Look, let's go into the guest house. We'll never be able to talk out here.

ANDREW   What else is there to say? We know the situation. We'll just have to wait til they get back. Still, I wish they'd call.

CAROLINE   They'll call when they have some news. These things take time. Careful negotiation. You boys wouldn't know that, because it's just not your world. That's not meant as a criticism. But if you boys wanted to go into business, you would have, instead of doing what you do, which is important. It's important what you do. You boys are terrific, you really are. It's such a shame we don't see you. Our kids love playing with each other. You saw how they were when they all got together—well, David, not yours, because they haven't been here, but, well, you know what I mean. Now, I know part of the problem is we live so far apart, but let's face it, it's been a difficult few years these last years. Sasha feels it. He knows he's drifted apart from you boys. He came into my family and I think he felt—well—he felt more at home somehow. He became so friendly with my brothers, he felt a real camaraderie with them. But now—maybe it's your father passing, I don't know—Sasha really wants to know you again. You know—and we've said this many many times—you're always welcome to stay with us, whenever you're in Montreal. David, you've been there a few times lately and haven't called—we know because your mother tells us everything—but you must believe me, please, that we want to see you. You can stay with us. I know hotels are so expensive, and there's no need for you to take another room when you could have an entire basement to yourself. Andrew, the same goes for you and Donna. All we have is each other. We saw that when your father died. It was so moving to see how you boys came together, and supported one another. At the funeral, when you all walked in together, and your mother in the middle, it was so powerful, so moving. I can't say enough about you boys. If we all try, I mean really try, we can be close, we can be close again, like we were in the beginning. You must believe me; that's what I want.

DAVID   No agenda, huh?

> *Silence.*

ANDREW   I'm going inside.

> *He lingers a moment, then goes.*

CAROLINE   You always think there's an agenda…. You know, it's—. (*CAROLINE dabs at her eyes.*) It's very difficult. Maybe you won't believe this, but when I first came into your family, I felt so… I was happy. Your parents were so welcoming. They didn't expect a thing from me. I could see you didn't have much, but when I saw how much love there was in that house, I… Sasha always talks about how hard it was, growing up, and having so little. But he always says, you know, there was something he had that other kids… (*DAVID is looking away.*) I'm trying to talk to you. When did you start disliking me? I really would like to know, I would, because I don't deserve it, I don't, I don't…. You know there's something I can't quite get out of my mind. I think about it every once in a while. At my wedding, when we were all dancing, you kissed me. I mean, everyone was kissing me, giving me congratulations. But the kiss you gave me…

DAVID   I was drunk.

CAROLINE   Was that it?

>   *ROSE and DONNA enter.*

ROSE   Hello, my children, can I sit with you?

CAROLINE   Of course, of course. You know, I cannot get over your hair. I just love what they did with it.

ROSE   For what they charged…

CAROLINE   Please, it was the least we could do.

ROSE   Hello, David.

DAVID   Evening.

ROSE   …Still no word. What could be taking so long?

CAROLINE   It's not an easy thing they're doing. Stop worrying. Did the kids do their play for you?

ROSE   Oh, they did. It was so cute! They even made costumes.

DONNA   They rehearsed for a week at home. Were you surprised?

ROSE   I never knew I had such talented grandchildren. And that thing Jeremy wrote, it's so beautiful. David, you should hear it. (*beat*) The music stopped. Someone ask the musicians if they want something to eat.

DONNA   Sure.

DAVID   I'll go.

>   *DAVID goes.*

ROSE   Something's on his mind. He won't say. They take after their father.—Sasha shouldn't have hired the band. I love the music, but it must have cost an arm and a leg.

DONNA   Ah, just a leg. They gave us a deal. They're the guys who played that wedding last month, remember? Across the lake. Turns out the guy who plays the clarinet, the, the—

ROSE   The clarinetist.

DONNA   —is a cousin of my mom's. I was talking to her—my mom—and I said "Mom, there was this fabulous"—you know—"klezmer band playing at the hotel," and she said, "I'll bet you that's Ron Katzenbaum, he always plays up there."

ROSE   I just wish they'd call.

DONNA   So—wait, I'm not finished. So I called the hotel, I said, "Was that Ron Katzenbaum?" And… sure enough…

ROSE   I can't think straight. My mind's, it's all over the place. I've got goosebumps.

CAROLINE   Let me get you a sweater.

ROSE   Look at my skin. I used to have the softest skin. All winter, everybody would be putting on the lotions and the creams, and I wouldn't have to do nothing. Now look. Corn Flakes.

CAROLINE   You have beautiful skin. You look incredible. You have—you know what it is? You *glow*.

ROSE   I glow?

CAROLINE   You glow! But you *are* cold, and I'm going to get you that sweater.

　　　　CAROLINE exits.

ROSE   Oh, I'm so frightened. I was sitting in the cottage just now and I don't know if by tomorrow they'll let me sit in it again.

DONNA   …Oh, hey, I meant to tell you. I was downtown the other day, and you'll never guess, I went into Harbord Bakery.

ROSE   It's still there? We used to walk over there for bagels practically every morning. Me and Faygie and Lettie and Hilda—we were so tight. We did everything together. Faygie died five, six years ago. She was such a beautiful woman, never lost her looks. We used to tap-tap-tap all the time, between the houses you know? Her bedroom was right opposite mine, like it was a duplex, and when we figured that out, oh that was so much fun, we figured out a code, like—what's it called—

DONNA   Morse?

ROSE   No, not—yes, Morse, that's right. Well, there was just a wall between us, and we'd send each other secret messages. Now she's gone. They're all going. And… well, I'm not going to be here much longer…

DONNA   Yes you are, a long time.

ROSE   Please God.

DONNA   Look what's happened in the last few years. You're a new woman. You work out, you *go* out, you travel. You've got so much ahead of you. Hey, Andrew and I were talking, we're thinking about going to Cuba.

ROSE   Cuba?

DONNA   Next winter. You could come with us.

ROSE   What do I need with Cuba?

ROSE slaps at a bug.

Still so buggy…. It's good you're going away. Things are better?

DONNA   Well, we hardly see each other, we're so busy.

ROSE   You're having sex?

DONNA   Uhh…

ROSE   *(seeing him)* Here's Jeremy.

DONNA   *(looking heavenward; sotto)* Thank you.

ROSE   My first grandson. Come sit with me.

DONNA   I'm gonna see what the kids are up to.

JEREMY   Level Six, I think.

DONNA goes.

ROSE   Nu, my grandson, have you thought some more about school?

JEREMY   Mm hm.

ROSE   It starts in a week, "mm hm."

JEREMY   I just don't care about it.

ROSE   Pish pish. You've got so much going for you. You could do whatever you want. America, you can go to another time. It's not going anywhere. Jeremy, what's on your mind?—Are you speaking to your father? *(He shakes his head.)* What's gonna be with you. It's not right, a son doesn't talk to his father. He cares so much about you. He wants you to do well.

JEREMY   Only because it'll make him look bad if I don't.

ROSE   That's not true.

JEREMY   It is, though. He just wants me to—

ROSE   "He"? If my father ever heard me call my mother "she," oh, he'd get so mad. "'She'? 'She'? Who's 'she'?"

JEREMY   My *father*—all he wants is to be able to brag about us at the club. It doesn't matter if what we're doing is important to us. Like, I don't want to go to school. "Jeremy, you've got to get an education. You'll never get anywhere without an education." My parents want to control everything I do, the way I look, the way I think.

ROSE   Now—

JEREMY   They don't even want me to see Trish; all we're doing is hanging out. They think we're going to fall in love or something, when all we're doing is talking. I don't know anyone like her, she's so smart, she has great ideas, she's been all over the world. She says we have to stop thinking about money all the time.

ROSE   She can say that because she *doesn't* have to think about money. Who do you think pays for her trips all over the world? Her grandfather.

JEREMY   All I meant…

ROSE   You're just a boy, Jeremy. Please God when you're a man, with a wife and children and a house and a good job, we'll have this conversation again. You don't know what's coming. You're so young, so young. I can't understand why you children are so angry at your parents. I loved my parents, we all did back then. They didn't let us do whatever we wanted, they were strict, but they were our parents, so we listened. Now I see that's changing, and I can't understand why. I can't understand nothing—anything.

> *Beat.*

I didn't want to come back here. But now that I'm here, I don't want to leave. He was always so relaxed up here, not like in the city, and every summer I was reminded of the man I fell in love with. He's angry now. He's angry we're letting it fall to pieces. Just like when I sold the house in Toronto—he was angry about that, too, I could tell, the way he looked at me from his picture. My hand was shaking when I signed the contract, I had to hold it steady. I could hardly breathe. But they made me, my boys, they forced me into it, they said the house was too big, they said I couldn't take care of it, and I didn't want to, I didn't want to— *(takes out a tissue to wipe her eyes; a letter falls from her pocket to the ground)* —my own children, my own children, they made me leave my house.— What am I saying? Don't listen to me, Jeremy. I don't know what I'm saying. I don't mean it.

JEREMY   But it's true. Everything you're saying is the truth.

ROSE   It's not! It's just terrible things that get into your head, in the middle of the night, and it all seems to make sense, but when you speak them, they sound like lies, and that's what they are.

JEREMY   It's not lies. You give them everything, and they never give you anything back. And the way my father talks about Zaydie, it's disgusting. And my mother, she pretends to be so nice, but she's cruel, she's mean, she's—

ROSE   *(takes him by the shoulders)* Be quiet, be quiet, be quiet! You don't know what you're saying! You don't know why people are the way they are. You don't know anything. You're just a boy!—Oh no, no, Jeremy, please, please, I'm sorry. I'm sorry, Jeremy. Don't listen to me today, I'm so upset, I don't know where to turn.

> *JEREMY runs out.*

Jeremy! Please don't!

> *She follows him off. DAVID comes in, scotch in hand, picks up the envelope, reads the letter. The klezmer band begins to kick it up in the next room. Sound of dancing, stomping, hand clapping, cheering. ROSE returns. DAVID looks up from the letter.*

DAVID   Sorry. I think this is yours.

ROSE   What is it?

DAVID   A note. From Skepian.

ROSE   —Oh, it must have fell out of my pocket...

> *He hands it back to her.*

DAVID   Fallen, Mom.

ROSE   My son, the writer. I guess he still fancies me...

DAVID   You think?

ROSE   He says some nice things...

DAVID   He's a salesman. I mean... it's not you he wants, Mom, it's the property.

> *Pause.*

I mean—ah shit.

> *Something crashes in the house. The music stops. There is laughter. DONNA runs in, laughing hysterically.*

ROSE   What's going on in there?

DONNA   It's—ha ha ha!—Andrew, he—ha ha ha!—He was trying to dance on a chair and—a ha ha ha!—It *broke!* He's—he's—

ROSE   Is he alright?

DONNA   Yeah, he's fine—landed right on his ass—ha ha ha!—The look on his face! A ha ha ha ha ha!

ANDREW comes in, moving gingerly. DONNA bursts out laughing again.

ANDREW   Hilarious.

DONNA   I'm sorry. Ha ha ha!

The music starts again—a slow piece. FAYE enters.

FAYE   It's nicer out here. Not so loud.

DONNA   *(to ANDREW)* You okay?

ANDREW   Yeah, just great.

DONNA   Come on. Let's dance. We hardly ever do this. We used to go out all the time.

ANDREW   If you insist.

She helps pull him up; he slips; they both tumble to the floor, then burst into hysterical laughter.

FAYE   Crazy kids.

DONNA   *(still laughing)* Come on.

DAVID   Suddenly he was 70 years old.

ANDREW   I feel it.

DAVID   How you doing, Faye? Can I get you something?

FAYE   Hm?

DAVID   You like the music?

FAYE   Hm?

DAVID   Come on, Faye.

Takes her by the hand.

FAYE   Hee hee hee! Oh, my! It's been so long since anyone asked me to dance.

DAVID   Well, we figured you were taken.

FAYE   Oh, go on with you! Crazy kid!

JEREMY enters during—

We used to go the dance every Saturday, me and Sid. He just liked to stand there, pretending he was Humphrey Bogart, leaning against a pillar, one hand in his pocket, the other holding a cigarette. *(looking at JEREMY)* Isn't he handsome? Who's that?

DAVID   That's Jeremy.

FAYE   Oh. What's your name?

DAVID   Luigi. Luigi Mortadella. I'm a count. And a-one and a-two…

ROSE   Jeremy.

>   *She embraces him, kisses him on the forehead.*

If only you knew how much I love you children, if only you knew.

JEREMY   It's alright. I understand.

>   *They dance.*

ROSE   You don't, though. But it's alright. It's alright. You kids are so good to me. It's so nice when you come for a visit. The condo is so quiet. I can't get used to it. And that awful buzzer when I let people in. Whatever happened to a doorbell? But you'll come, you'll always come, you'll find a nice girl, you'll bring her to me, we'll walk to the mall for a coffee. Only you have to go to school, you hear? And shave off that mustache! It looks terrible.

JEREMY   I don't care how I look.

>   *CAROLINE enters, with a sweater.*

CAROLINE   Here you go, Mom.

ROSE   Brr, thank you, it's so chilly all of a sudden.

CAROLINE   Let me help you. *(helps ROSE with the sweater)* David, there's a phone call for you. Los Angeles.

DAVID   Thanks.

>   *DAVID helps FAYE to her seat, then goes.*

ROSE   I'm sweating.

>   *FAYE laughs to herself.*

What's she laughing at?

FAYE   *(as though talking to someone)* Go on with you!

>   *MORRIS enters.*

MORRIS   Rose… Rose!… I just heard!… Isn't it wonderful?

CAROLINE   Morris…

MORRIS   *(sings along with the music)* Hee hee! That's one of my favourites. Boy, they don't write em like that anymore. Let's dance, Rose… a little celebration… come on, come on… I can't believe it…

ROSE   What are you talking about, Morris?

MORRIS   I'm talking about starting a new life! Yes, the old one is over, and to hell with it. I'm still, well, not young, but I've got years in me yet. But didn't you hear? I just had a call from my lawyer. The sale's gone through. I got ten thousand over the asking price! Isn't it wonderful?

ROSE   But—I didn't know you were selling.

MORRIS   It's time for other people to move in, Rose. Let's face it: our time *is* over.

ROSE   But—

MORRIS   So, you see—

> *JACK and SASHA enter. LEN is with them, downcast, holding a shopping bag.*

FAYE   There you are. And no coat? It's cool out.

LEN   It's not so bad.

JACK   Greetings all.

ROSE   What's going on? Someone tell me.

JACK   Thanks for the warm welcome.

ROSE   Would someone tell me what happened?

SASHA   In a minute, Ma. We're just waiting for David.

CAROLINE   He's on the phone.

SASHA   I told him to come out.

ROSE   Jeremy, run, get your uncle.

> *As they wait:*

FAYE   What have you got there?

LEN   Picked up some bagels… not very good bagels… buns with holes in the middle, but they'll do… haven't eaten a thing all day… herring… from a jar, but…

ROSE   Len?

LEN   Starving. Cream cheese, two kinds. This one has chives in it.

ROSE   What happened?

LEN   Well, it's… the thing is, they really…

ROSE   Well?

LEN   These aren't bagels.… No one outside Montreal knows how to make a decent bagel anymore…

ROSE   Someone tell me… I can't stand it…

> *DAVID enters.*

Here's David. Len, tell me. Sasha—.

JACK   The property's been sold.

ROSE   But…

JACK   We couldn't get an extension.

ROSE   But *sold*, I don't—

DAVID   Wait a second.

JACK   Just listen.

DAVID   No. I want to know how—

JACK   I'm trying to explain.

DAVID   I'm not talking to you! Listen! It isn't *possible*. It isn't *possible to sell* because we own together, my brothers and I *own* it—do you understand? You *can't* buy this house, you can't buy this lot, you can't—

JACK   I didn't.—Alright? You need to know something. I didn't buy it.

DAVID   Then—?

SASHA   I did.—I bought it. I mean—I'm going to buy it. From you. From the two of you.

> *DAVID and ANDREW look at one another.*

LEN   You see, they—they figured it out. They figured a way.

JACK   There's a clause in the will—it's called a shotgun clause. It allows for one of you to buy the other ones out, to make an offer to the other ones, and then the others ones can accept it, or better it. But you can't refuse it. It's right there in black and white.

ANDREW   I never heard of it. I never even read the will.

JACK   No. Well. The thing is, you have a set number of days to respond; you have fifteen days, if you want, to better the offer. The offer is—

DAVID   Just a second.

JACK   You should know that—

DAVID   I'm not talking to you. *(to SASHA)* Is this for real?

SASHA   It's the only way. The planning office wouldn't grant an extension; they just didn't want to hear it. We had to go in there with a back-up plan or we'd be screwed. Caroline's parents offered to put up the money.

DAVID   To buy us out?

SASHA   It's a good price.

JACK   It's an excellent price. You're getting full value, I can tell you.

DAVID   I don't— *(to JACK)* —Would you be quiet, it's got nothing to do with you.

LEN   I wouldn't say that.

DAVID *(to SASHA)* You're buying—you're buying us out—

LEN He's not keeping it. He's going to turn right around and sell it to Skepian. Five ball in the corner pocket.

> *Beat.*

DAVID Is that true?

SASHA Guys, listen—

DAVID You are.

JACK You have to admit—it's a brilliant scheme. Although, "scheme," that makes it sound a little sinister, doesn't it? And it's not! It's not at all! In time, you'll see that. I hope you will. Because the fact is, you were going to lose this place; it would have been put up for sale, and then who knows what price you'd have gotten? But now, thanks to Caroline's parents, you're going to reap quite a reward. Then, yes, I'm going to take it off Sasha's hands. You boys aren't in the development business; you don't want to be. You have your lives, you all need money—who doesn't—and now you'll have it. I'm even willing—listen, let's not have hard feelings—this is about business, nothing more, nothing less—but at the same time, just to show how I feel about you people, I'm going to give you the first option on the cottages.

DAVID Cottages.

JACK There's room for fifteen, maybe more, once we clear the forest. Tennis, a practice green, all kinds of—yes, a resort, it's just what's needed now. All these weekend families—summer people—a week or two away from the city. But at the same time, if you want, I'd be happy to set aside one of the cottages for your year-round use—I'm going to winterize them, too—did I mention that? I've got all kinds of ideas. *(looks out the window)* I can't believe it. I've had my eyes on this place for a long time. *(unable to restrain himself)* Ha ha! Good God, I can't believe it! Tell me it isn't happening, that it's only a dream, or I've gone mad, something, anything. Not this, though, it isn't possible. Is it? Is it mine? It is. Christ Jesus, it's mine. If my old man could see me now—lazy, that's what he said—took me out of school, I still remember the day, I'd just gotten home: "You're going to have to work"—I didn't get to finish high school. My last day, I remember looking down at my feet as I walked home, I knew I'd never take that walk again, I wanted to remember every step; the next thing I knew, I was on a train, heading west. Now look at me! I'm Jack Skepian! God*dammit!* They had nothing, my father and his father, they were ignorant, they didn't read, they drank themselves stupid every night, and me, I swore to myself, on that train ride, I said goddammit I'm not going to be kept down. I'm not going to give in to bitterness, or anger, I'll work, I'll work a hundred times harder than the next man. *(goes to the doorway)* Hey! Strike up the band or something! Play it loud, too! Wake up the dead!

> *The music plays.*

Ha ha! Right on cue!

> *ROSE has sunk down on a chair and is weeping.*

Rosey, listen to me. Fifty years, Rosey. How different things could have been. What a mess we make of our lives, and we don't even know we're doing it til it's too late.

DAVID   Leave her alone.

JACK   Of course, I was only—

DAVID   Just go, would you? Would you just go? Would you go?

> *JACK straightens himself; takes a moment, then goes.*

JACK   *(off)* Ha ha! Now that's what I call dancing! Come on everyone!

SASHA   Guys, we'll talk in the morning, huh?

> *No one answers. SASHA goes; the others drift out as ANDREW leads ROSE into the house. DAVID stays behind.*

ANDREW   It's alright, Mom. Mom, it's for the best. It really is. You'll see. There was nothing else to do…. Mom, will you come and stay with us? Come and live with us for a while, as long as you want. We don't want you to be alone, Mom. You can come, you can stay with us. Next summer, we can travel. France, maybe, or Italy. You've always wanted to go there. There's so much ahead of you, Mom. Mom, we love you. Mom… Mom…

> *TRISH wanders by.*

TRISH   I heard. It's awful.

DAVID   Yeah…. I hate this country.

> *He goes. She watches. JEREMY moves to her. She goes.*

ACT 4

Last day of September. The living room. Nearly empty. A few boxes are scattered about, still being filled with loose ends. Suitcases wait to be picked up by the door. A couple of pieces of furniture—the bookcase, a chair or two—have also gone unclaimed.

JEREMY is putting trinkets into a box. SASHA is picking up loose ends, going through a few boxes that have yet to be sorted. LEN hovers. JACK stands waiting. He has brought two bottles of champagne and some glasses. DONNA is looking through a garbage bag stuffed full of clothes, separating items into piles to keep and to give away.

SASHA   Ever seen so much junk?

SASHA goes to pick up the bookcase.

LEN   I think David wants that.

SASHA   Up to him.

JACK   Amazing how big it looks with everything taken out.

A truck engine is heard from outside.

SASHA   Is that the truck from Goodwill? *(goes to the door)* Hey! Hey!

DONNA   They ran out of room.

SASHA   What?

DONNA   On the truck. Anyway, there's not much left. We can take the rest in the van and drop it off on the way home.

JACK   How about a farewell toast? I meant to bring some from Toronto; the liquor store in town doesn't carry quite the same inventory. Still.

Pops a cork. Pours. No takers.

No?... Well, seems a waste. But, if you're not going to drink, then neither am I.

SASHA   Bad luck not to toast. *(takes a sip)* Mm. Disgusting.

JACK   That's expensive stuff.

SASHA   Just needs to chill. I'll put it in the fridge.

JACK   Uh... the power's off.

SASHA   Oh.

LEN   It's cold enough in here, just leave it out.

JACK   It is cold, isn't it. I have to say, I've always loved this time of year.

DAVID enters during this speech, carrying a box filled with books. He finds a place to sit, and begins looking through the books.

The leaves are changing colours; you can feel the change in the air. It's the real new year. Harvest time. That's why Jewish New Year makes so much sense—it's the only new year that goes by the natural calendar. I mean it really *feels* like we're starting a *new year.*

LEN   Or ending one.

JACK   Well of course. Of course. This year, by the way, I'm starting a new tradition. I'm holding a Rosh Hoshanah dinner for homeless Jewish men.

DAVID   Former clients?

> *Beat.*

SASHA   I'm gonna take another look around. We should think about heading out soon. Kids still down at the dock?

DONNA   They're taking turns with the paddle boat.

> *SASHA exits, making a call on his cell phone.*

LEN   Find something, David?

DAVID   Just some books, in the crawl space.

LEN   I'll take this to the car. *(goes)*

JACK   *(checks his watch)* Well, I ought to get going. I've got a bit of a drive ahead of me.

DAVID   The Chosen. *(tosses it aside, picks up another)*

DONNA   *(holding up a coat)* Jeremy, you should have this jacket.

JEREMY   Nice.

DONNA   It's back in style now. Your grandfather was quite the clotheshorse.

DAVID   *(another book) Why Do They Hate The Jews? (beat) Volume Four.*

> *TRISH enters, wearing a coat.*

TRISH   You're still here.

DONNA   It took us the whole weekend.

TRISH   I heard a truck leaving, I thought—anyway, I just wanted to say goodbye. Jeremy, you haven't seen my hiking shoes, have you?

JEREMY   Hm?

TRISH   I think I left them out back. Could you help me look?

JEREMY   In a sec.

DAVID   *(another title) The Practical Handyman. (looking through it)* One of Dad's old books. He used to sell em from a van. Anything to make a buck.

JACK   *(yawns)* Scuse me. Well, I really ought to hit the road. There's a piece of property I'm going to look at. But that's how it is with me, I work on one project, and the second it's ready to go, I'm on to something else, even bigger. Whenever I look at my hands, and they're not doing something, I think, "Do something!"

TRISH   Well, we'll be gone soon, so you can get on with your important work, clearing the land, putting up cheap housing.

JACK   I don't know about the cheap part, but I'll drink to the rest of it. *(offers her a glass)* It's warm, but still bubbly. What do you say?

TRISH   No thanks.

JACK   I suppose you think the grapes were stomped on by ten-year-old orphans making a dollar a week for their labours.—Well, you've got your principles. I can respect a person with principles. It's cynics I don't much care for.

DAVID   *(reading)* "How To Make a Bookshelf."

> *DONNA is holding up a sailor's hat.*

DONNA   Would you *look* at this hat?

DAVID   Here, toss it over.

> *She does. DAVID puts it on.*

DONNA   Perfect.

> *DAVID goes back to looking through the books. DONNA takes a bag of clothes outside.*

JACK   *(to TRISH)* So, you're off to Seattle, gonna give those finance ministers what for?

TRISH   That's right.

JACK   Did you pack your bullhorn? "Turn off your air conditioners!"

TRISH   You need new material, Mr Skepian.

JACK   You're right. Maybe David could write me a few jokes.

DAVID   You'd still have to work on your *(beat)* timing.

> *JACK laughs.*

TRISH   Well. Goodbye.

DAVID   Take care of yourself.

JACK   Onward, Christian Soldier!—You know, I meant what I said just now, about having a lot of respect for you. You should hear some of the things this girl has to say. I was at her grandfather's the other day, and boy did she give me an earful. It's a lot of nonsense, but it comes from the heart.

From the distance comes the sound of a large truck approaching.

We may see the world differently at the moment, but life goes on, anyway.

TRISH   Well, you learn something useless every day.

JACK steps outside.

Jeremy? I have to go soon.

JEREMY   Okay, well. Goodbye.

TRISH   Goodbye?

JEREMY   Well, it's not like I'm ever gonna see you again.

TRISH   Don't say that.

JEREMY   When would I see you?

TRISH   I don't know, I—it's just weird to think that.

Beat.

JEREMY   You going to school?

TRISH   What? No, I'm, no, I'm gonna wait a year. You?

JEREMY   I kinda had to go. It's good, though. I've got a pretty cool prof. He's all about The World Bank. First day, he was like, "Okay, what do you all want to do with your lives?" People started raising their hands, you know? Like, "I want a house. A family. A car. A swimming pool." And he just kept nodding his head, and then he said, "You people are all so middle class. Don't any of you want to *change the world?*" Then there was like this silence. It was pretty cool. I'm gonna take these things out to the car.

As he goes, TRISH following—

TRISH   There's still room on the bus, you know. I mean, if you're interested…

JACK has stepped back in.

JACK   Tell me, did that TV series work out for you?

DAVID   No. I was, however, the runner-up.

JACK   Well, that's a shame. Keep plugging away.

DAVID   *(bitterly)* "I'm alright, Jack."

JACK   Young man, can I give you a word of advice? Don't take things so personally. You're far too sensitive. The world doesn't owe you a damn thing. It's you who owes the world something. Your anger isn't going to do you any good. It'll eat you alive if you're not careful. Your father struggled with it. I could see it in him, the couple of times I met him.

    ANDREW enters.

ANDREW   Mr Skepian, would you mind keeping your trucks off the property til we leave?

DAVID   See what I mean about timing?

JACK   Yes, yes, you're right. I'll tell them myself.—Oh—fellas, listen, I need to speak to your mother before I go. A private matter; would you let her know?

ANDREW   Sure thing.

    JACK goes.

Have you seen Aunty Faye? David?

DAVID   No.

ANDREW   Do you think you could take her in your car? I mean, we could take her in the van… but, there's all this stuff. A truckload already went to Goodwill and there's still so much *stuff. (beat)* Maybe we can fit her in. It's just, the home's not too far from you. You'd just have to hand her to one of the nurses. Or not.

DAVID   Fine.

ANDREW   If you don't want to do it—

DAVID   *(sharply)* I just said I would.

ANDREW   Look—.

    SASHA enters.

SASHA   There isn't an empty box around, is there? Caroline wants to take a couple of hostas uhh—

DAVID   Hostages?

    SASHA shoots him a look. He finds a box with a few trinkets, empties them into another box.

Get what you wanted?

SASHA   What?

DAVID   Nothing.

SASHA   What did you say?

    Pause.

It was the only way out.

DAVID   For whom?

SASHA   All of us. You can't see it right now. Don't make Skepian out to be a bad guy. He offered to let you take one of the cottages; you turned him down.

DAVID   Who said anything about Skepian being the bad guy?

SASHA   *(overlapping)* Okay. You want to have it out? Cause I'm tired of your pissant little comments. *(growing angry)* There's only one person in this room who figured a way out of this mess—and it wasn't you.

ANDREW   Guys.

SASHA   *(in DAVID's face, following him around)* If we'd left it to you, we'd have come away with *nothing*. But, no, you want to hold on to things. *Things. (He knocks over the bookcase.)* That's all they are, and this *place*, it's *nothing*. Well, alright, you got a nice little payday.

DAVID   You got a nicer one.

SASHA   I'll slap your fucking face. *(waits; then:)* Now have you got something to say to me? Have you? Have you got something to say?

>   *SASHA stares DAVID down; DAVID walks away. SASHA scoops up the box, goes. DAVID goes to the bookcase.*

ANDREW   You alright?

DAVID   Fine.

ANDREW   Guess we should load the rest of this. Are you taking the bookcase?… David?—You want me to see if I can fit it in the van? I can strap Donna to the roof or—Oh. Did I mention we're gonna do Rosh Hoshanah dinner at our place this year? Mom—she—you know—I don't think she's up to having it at the condo. Donna and I got to talking about it and—

DAVID   Sounds good.

ANDREW   Yeah. Now that Mom's getting older, I guess we need to start taking turns with these things. *(sits)* I got the test results back. Negative. They don't know what it is. They said I was just over-tired. Anyway, it's a bit of a relief. I was thinking… well, you know. You get all irrational at times like this… I mean—when you think—you think something's wrong with you—you imagine the worst. And even though they tell you there's no way your father could have passed anything down to you, still, you think…

DAVID   Goddammit.

ANDREW   David?

DAVID   Goddammit, goddammit…

>   *ANDREW puts a hand on DAVID's shoulder.*

Don't worry about it. I'll be fine. Oh yeah. We'll be fine. It's okay. Dad didn't pass anything down to us. Nothing in the blood. *(points to his head)* Just here. *(to his heart)* Just here.

>   *DAVID pours and downs a glass of champagne.*

I need a place to stay. Can I stay with you?

ANDREW   Of course.

DAVID   Just for a little while. Just til things get sorted out…

ANDREW   Yes, yes, as long as you like.

DAVID   Alright, thanks.

>   *Enter ROSE, LEN and CAROLINE.*

LEN   Well, let's get going. Traffic's going to be awful, just awful. We should have had lunch, but—tell you what, we'll stop at the burger place. We should—for old's time sake, huh? My treat!

ROSE   Is it time to go already? *(looks around the room)* This room looks so big with everything gone. I haven't seen it like this since the day we moved in. This place, this place. So much happened here. The kids spent their summers here. David, do you remember the time you crawled out of your crib, and we had no idea where you were?

DAVID   No.

ROSE   We were sick with worry. Oh, David, David, let me hug you. Have you been crying?

DAVID   No.

ROSE   It's alright. My boys, they never cry. But you can cry, it's alright, today of all days, so much is ending.

ANDREW   Beginning, Mom, beginning.

LEN   That's right! There's no reason to be upset anymore. Just think, before the sale, we were all upset and worried—because nothing was settled. That's the worst. But now the sale's gone through—life goes on. Am I right?

>   *Pause.*

Anyway, there's no reason to be sad anymore. Look, boys, even your mother cheered up a little, didn't you, Rose?

ROSE   I'll be fine. Everything will be fine.

>   *She is helped into her coat.*

I feel like that weight's been lifted off my chest. I still don't know what it was.

ANDREW   Mom, we're gonna have Rosh Hoshanah at our place this year.

ROSE   Are you? I was hoping one of you would do it.

ANDREW   We'll take care of everything.

ROSE   You won't! I'm going to do all the cooking.

ANDREW   You don't have to.

ROSE   As long as I've got two hands, I'll cook. We'll have brisket, chicken soup, cabbage rolls, maybe I'll do a duck.

ANDREW   We don't need that much, Mom. People don't eat that much anymore.

LEN   Don't listen to him, Rose. You just go ahead and make what you make.

ROSE   I'll stay with you tonight, Andrew. Do you mind?

ANDREW   Course not.

ROSE   The condo's so quiet, I can't get used to it.

CAROLINE   One of these years, we have *got* to have the seder in Montreal. Will you promise me you'll come?

ROSE   Oh, that would be wonderful. Caroline. I'm so glad you and Sasha worked things out. I know you two love each other. Listen, Sasha's father and me, we had our rough times, too. But we got through them.

CAROLINE   Mom, did I tell you? You're looking so well these days.

ROSE   You mean it?

CAROLINE   You know I do.

> *All go, except for ROSE.*

ROSE   *(barely audible)* ...I'm sorry, I'm sorry...

> *JACK enters.*

JACK   All alone, I see. *(beat)* Will you have a glass of champagne with me?

ROSE   Maybe a little. But *just* a little. It goes right to my head.

JACK   Well, that's what it's supposed to do. *(as he pours)* Well, let me get to the point. Rose... *(pause)* I don't know how you're going to feel about this... it's a crazy idea... I'm sort of embarrassed to propose it, after everything that's happened.... What the hell...

ROSE   L'chaim. *(They drink.)* Go on, Jack.

JACK   Well, I wanted to talk to you about the garden.

ROSE   ...The garden?

JACK   Yes, Rose. It's a real work of art. I was looking at it earlier. I was talking to my architect. I said—and this is the God's honest truth—I said, "Can we not incorporate this garden into the plans?" He knew exactly what I was talking about. Can I show you? Would you mind? I know you want to be on your way, but let me show you... *(takes out some drawings, spreads them over the bookcase)* Now, here's the property. You see, this is forest at the moment. Of course that's all going to be cleared. Now, the cottages will be here and here... tennis courts... playground... the main office and store will be here... this, right here, where I'm pointing—Rose?

ROSE   Yes, I'm listening.

JACK   Yes. Well, this is where the house is now… and you see how the garden would become part of the grounds, a sort of focal point—that's what my architect called it, anyway. We'd have to do some work on it, of course, it's a bit of a mess, frankly—but essentially we'd keep it the same. A sort of… what… a sort of monument to what used to be here… to Sid, if you will.—We could even—tell you what, this just came to me, we could even put a plaque there, explaining the history of the grounds. Now what do you think about that?

ROSE   A plaque sounds very nice.

JACK   Yes. Then you think it's a good idea. Naturally I want your blessing.

ROSE   That's very nice of you, Jack.

JACK   No, no, listen, it's the least I could do. And—what am I thinking?—Well, clearly I'm *not* thinking, but everything's happening so fast—of course we'll put *your* name on the plaque, as well.

ROSE   I don't think so, Jack.

JACK   Are you sure?

> *Pause.*

I understand. Yes, of course…. Well. It was so good to see you again, Rose, after all this time. You're a lovely person, but then you always were.

> *He prepares to leave.*

You know, I don't think I'm going to need my coat, after all. It's cool, but very pleasant. It's funny, I remember some years where by now we'd already have an inch of snow on the ground. Now look at it, beautiful and sunny. The leaves will have turned. Should be spectacular. *(looks at his watch)* Ought to make it back before dark.

ROSE   Safe drive.

JACK   And you. Are you alright, Rose?

ROSE   I have my family. They're my monument. How could I not be alright?

JACK   Goodbye, Rose.

ROSE   Goodbye, Jack.

> *They embrace. They kiss, once, on the lips.*

JACK   Goodbye. Sweet lady.

> *JACK goes. ANDREW, LEN and JEREMY enter.*

ANDREW   We're ready to go, Mom.

LEN   The moment of truth. Here we are. We're about to leave this place for the last time. Amazing. Amazing.

> *SASHA, CAROLINE, DONNA and DAVID enter.*

Nearly everyone's here. I can't believe it. Where did the time go, Rose?

ROSE   It went, it went.

LEN   Someone needs to say something.

ROSE   You do it, Len.

SASHA   Uh oh.

LEN   Well. *(sings)* "Hail, hail, the gang's all here! What the heck do we care? What the heck do we care?"

> *Other begin to join in until everyone is singing.*

ALL   "Hail, hail, the gang's all here! Why the heck should we care now?"

LEN   One more time!

ALL   "Hail, hail, the gang's all here! What the heck do we care? What the heck do we care? Hail, hail, the gang's all here! Why the heck should we care now?"

> *After a moment.*

SASHA   Alright, let's get this show on the road.

ROSE   One more look…. They're going to keep the garden.

LEN   Is that right?

CAROLINE   Sash?

SASHA   Yeah. Alright, everyone. Safe drive. Bye, Mom.

ROSE   Goodbye, darling. Drive safe, you hear? And call me when you get home.

SASHA   Yeah. Uncle Len, we'll see you for Rosh Hashanah?

LEN   You bet.

SASHA   So long guys. Take it easy. Jeremy, let's go. Let's go.

JEREMY   Goodbye, everyone.

LEN   So long.

SASHA   Jeremy, did you tell Uncle David about the essay you wrote?

JEREMY   Dad.

CAROLINE   Oh, tell him. He wrote an essay on one of your plays, and got an A.

ROSE   Come here, Jeremy. Let me give you a kiss. Be good. And study hard, do you hear me?

SASHA   He will. Come on, kid. *(heading out with JEREMY)* We'll listen to the game on the way home.

LEN   Are you ready, Rose?

ROSE   In a minute, in a minute.

LEN   Why don't you boys get your things ready? We'll see you outside.

> *ANDREW and DAVID go.*
>
> *ROSE and LEN are left together. They have been waiting for this; they throw their arms around one another, hold each other tight, and sob quietly, not wanting to be overheard.*

ROSE   It's all gone, Len. He's gone, and now this place, and I can't say goodbye, I don't want to say goodbye.

ANDREW   *(off)* Let's go!

ROSE   One last look… he used to sit there…

ANDREW   *(off)* Mom, come on!

ROSE   I feel like my whole life's gone by, and I haven't lived it.

LEN   Don't say that, Rose… you can't think that way… come on… you'll see… everything will be fine when we get home… you'll see… you'll see…

> *They go off together. The stage is empty. FAYE enters.*

FAYE   Where is everyone?… Lou?… Must be in the shop…. Cold…. Look at my hands…. How'd my hands get so old?… I could do with a coffee.

> *DAVID enters.*

DAVID   Faye. We should get going.

FAYE   Oh, there you are. Which one are you again?

DAVID   David.

FAYE   That's right. Where's your father?

> *Pause.*

DAVID   In the garden.

FAYE   Oh, he loves his garden. What's he doing?

DAVID   Just sitting there.

FAYE   Let's go see him.

DAVID   No, he doesn't want to be disturbed. He just wants to be left alone now.

FAYE   He likes being alone. Always did. Except one time. It was in England. Mum and Dad ran a pub, we lived up top of it, so they didn't think nothing of leaving us on our own upstairs. One time, Sid was having a nap, and they left him. He woke up, there was no one home, it was dark, no one thought to leave a light on. He was only five or six; he climbed out of bed, started walking, calling for Mum, calling for Dad, for me, somebody, and no one answered. Finally Mum heard him. He wasn't crying, just scared. He said, he thought he'd been left alone, he thought everyone had gone and forgotten about him. But we didn't forget him. We knew he was there.

DAVID   That's right. That's right. *(pause)* Come on, Faye.

FAYE   Where are we going?

DAVID   Home.

> *He helps her out. The door closes.*
>
> *The end.*

AFTER THE ORCHARD—DELETED SCENES

The following two scenes were cut from the play after the second draft. Some of the dialogue was retained (in slightly different form), but the character of Kate was not.

—JS

[From ACT 2.]

DAVID Look, are we waiting for Andrew or not?

SASHA You want to wait for Andrew, we'll wait for Andrew.

Enter KATE.

Hello.

KATE Hi.

DAVID Oh… Kate. Hi.

KATE Just dropping by that book.

DAVID Right. Sasha, this is Kate. Kate, my brother.

SASHA Well. Think I'll go for a swim. Gonna see if I can beat my old record. Seven minutes, eighteen seconds to the other side and back. Nice to meet you.

KATE And you.

He goes.

Sorry. I couldn't wait anymore. I felt like an idiot sitting in the car. Like a spy.

Pause.

I hate this sneaking around.

DAVID You look beautiful.

KATE Please. I'm a mess. My stomach's churning like a whirlpool. I don't know what it is.

DAVID Come here. Sit with me.

KATE Your family…. Anyway, I can't stay. Another packed house tonight. The entire run's sold out.

DAVID Hurray.

KATE The show's awful. I feel like such a fake up there. I look out into a sea of white hair. White hair and glasses, row upon row of white hair and glasses. And I'm standing up there and I'm saying lines that have no connection to anything—awful, stupid lines, and I'm standing in a bra and panties and giant bunny ears, and I'm saying lines like *(in a British accent)* "I wonder what's keeping Walter?"; saying these awful stupid lines to a sea of white hair and glasses, and I hear laughter, wave after wave of laughter, and I get sick, I get sick to my stomach. *(pause)* I'm thirty-five years old. I keep trying to tell myself it's not over, casting agents will see me in this play and see that I'm good and things will turn around, and by this time next year I'll be making my acceptance speeches, only for real. But no one comes; "it's a little too far," they say; "something came up." And you begin to understand that the reason you're standing in a bra and panties and bunny ears in an old barn before row upon row of white hair and glasses is that that's exactly what you deserve, because, after all, you're not very good. And no matter how many times you sit and watch your rivals and think, "I'm better than her," the fact is that you're the only one who thinks it. And though you're being paid, you're doing nothing more than glorified community theatre; you'll never rise above that level.

DAVID   I know how you feel.

KATE   It's not the same for you. You're respected.

>   *DAVID laughs derisively.*

It's true. You know it's true.—When the run is over, I'll be back in the city, teaching drama to seven-year-olds; catering; commercial auditions. I was asked to audition for a reading. *(beat)* I can't do it anymore. I have to make some decisions. Finally. Things have to change.

>   *Pause.*

DAVID   My agent called this morning. A new TV show just fired half its staff writers. The producer called about my availability. I might have to go down this weekend for an interview.

KATE   Down...?

DAVID   To L.A.

KATE   And if you get the job?

DAVID   I'll move there. Make a pile of money. How hard could it be to write "Freeze! Put the gun down!" Easy. "Awright, you scumbag—where'd you dump the body?" Piece of cake. "It's ovuh between us Charlie—you're takin' the fall."

KATE   You might be better at it than you think.

DAVID   Yeah. That's the problem. I might end up staying. Anyway, it's not gonna happen.

KATE   Don't say that.

DAVID   What should I say?

>   *Pause.*

Will you come back tonight? I really need to see you.

KATE   I'm not comfortable with your family being here. I feel like—.

DAVID   Like what?

KATE   Never mind. It's stupid.—Look, I have to tell you something. Henry called.

DAVID   Oh?

KATE   He's coming down tomorrow. Wants to take me to dinner.

> *DAVID takes out a cigarette, lights it.*

DAVID   And why not?

KATE   Don't be angry. I can't wait for you anymore, David. It's been almost five years, do you know that? On and off, for five years, and we keep finding each other. Sometimes you find someone, and you long to be with that person; you ache for that person. But finally if he's not available to you, you have to move on.

> *Pause.*

DAVID   I called home earlier. Wish I hadn't. When I spoke with the kids I had a funny sensation, and I didn't understand what it was til later: they don't feel like they're mine. I felt so distant from them; like I was talking to someone else's kids.

KATE   You're a good father. You love your children. I've seen it.

DAVID   *(beat)* "A good father." When my father was—when we brought him back here—the three of us went into talk to him. Together. It was something we had to do, to tell him, to say to him… *(long pause)* Andrew was sitting on the bed, holding his hand, stroking his hand. He said, "You've been a good father." And—he said—Dad said—he whispered—"Liar."

KATE   David. I love you so much. What can I do?—Oh God, your family's coming. I have to go.

DAVID   Yeah.

> *She starts to head off.*

Please. Come back tonight.

KATE   I'll try.

> *She goes. He takes a drag off the cigarette; stomps out the end, puts it back in the pack. Enter ROSE, LEN and JACK.*

JACK   You've got to decide, and quickly. Just tell me, yes or no, are you interested in my plan?

ROSE   Who's been smoking?

LEN   Hello, David. Finished writing?

DAVID   Yeah.

ROSE   David, what is it?

DAVID   *(wiping his eyes)* Allergies.

ROSE   I don't know why you won't take something for them.

DAVID   I'll be fine.

· · ·

[From ACT 4.]

ANDREW   I got the test results back. Negative. They don't know what it is. They said I was just over-tired. Anyway, it's a bit of a relief. I was thinking… well, you know. You get all irrational at times like this… I mean—when you think—you think something's wrong with you—you imagine the worst. And even though they tell you there's no way your father could have passed anything down to you, still, you think—

DAVID   Well, you're fine.

ANDREW   Yeah. I guess.

> *Pause. They stand there. KATE enters, buoyant.*

KATE   Hi.

ANDREW   Oh.

KATE   Kate. You're Andrew. We met once before.

ANDREW   Right. *(sensing KATE and DAVID want to be alone)* I'll just throw a few more things in the van.

DAVID   Why don't you tell Mom that Jack wants to see her?

> *ANDREW goes.*

What are you smiling about?

KATE   You won't believe what happened. I mean it's incredible. Is that champagne? I have to have some. Just one sip, I have a matinee. *(takes a sip)* Mm. Oh. That's awful, but it's wonderful. Oh, David. *(She throws her arms around him, kisses him.)* A producer came to see the show last night—he has a cottage around here; anyway he came backstage, he— *(through tears)* Oh my God, it's so incredible. *(recovering)* He loved the show, he said it was the funniest thing he's seen in years, and he wants to bring it to Toronto—a thousand-seat house—he wants to transfer the show, just the way it is—with the cast. Can you believe it? David, do you know what this means? I mean— I'll believe it when I sign on the dotted line and everything, but—everyone I know says he's the most wonderful man, and he was so warm to us, just so kind and—ha!—He was wearing the most awful clothes, so when he came backstage we all thought this must be someone's Uncle Charlie or something but—then he said who he was and we all just about died! In fact, Henry's done a show with him before, and he said it was the most wonderful fantastic experience of his life. Oh, David, David, finally—finally things are turning around. You know? I really think they are, and darling, darling— *(stroking his face)* I want us to be together, I want to be with you, I just love you so much, I wanted so much to share it with you last night, there was a chair next to me at the bar, it was empty, and I just imagined you sitting there, with your arm around my shoulders, whispering in my ear, oh God, listen to me, I'm so—I'm so—after all these years, and I was just about ready to give up. He's going to take the show just as it is, we're going to start in October—one of his other shows fell through. It's just a dream, it really is. Kiss me. Kiss me. I don't care if someone walks in.

> *They kiss. Pause.*

That was cold. That was so cold. Can't you be happy for me?

DAVID Why? Because now you get to be in a bullshit play in a thousand-seat house?

KATE Don't do that.

DAVID So you can get to feel like a fraud on a larger stage? Alright, I'm happy for you. When it's over you can bronze your bunny ears.

KATE Don't do that. I know why you're doing this.—If you're going back to your wife, just tell me.

DAVID I'm not going back.

KATE Have you left her?

DAVID I left her a long time ago. I just didn't get around to telling her.

KATE Are you going to tell her?

DAVID Probably not.

KATE Are you're going to stay?

DAVID Probably.

KATE Sometimes I want to shake you, I want to shake, shake, shake you.—Please, talk to me. Just make a decision.

DAVID I can't. I can't.

KATE David…

DAVID I can't. I think about my own parents, how long they stayed together, and why; maybe they didn't even know why. Maybe they just hung on, because the alternative was even worse.—My family's coming. You'd better go.

KATE When I get back to the city…

DAVID Don't wait for me, alright? Please don't.

She goes. DAVID drinks a glass of champagne; then another. Enter ROSE, LEN, ANDREW and CAROLINE.

LEN   Well, let's get going. Traffic's going to be awful, just awful. We should have had lunch, but—tell you what, we'll stop at the burger place. We should—for old's time sake, huh? My treat!

ROSE   Is it time to go already? *(looks around the room)* Is someone taking the bookcase?

DAVID   I'm taking it.

Jason Sherman has written extensively for the stage, radio and television. His other plays include *Remnants (A Fable)*; *It's All True*; *Patience*; *Reading Hebron*; *The Retreat*; *The League of Nathans*; and *Three in the Back, Two in the Head*, which won the Governor General's Award for Drama. He served as executive story editor and writer on the TV series "ReGenesis," earning Gemini and Canadian Screenwriting Award nominations. For CBC Radio he wrote "National Affairs," "Irving Invectus" and "Graf," for which he received the Canadian Screenwriting Award for radio drama. He is currently working on several television and film projects.